T0248769

Mobile Multimedia: Technological Aspects

Mobile Multimedia: Technological Aspects

Edited by **Anna Sanders**

CLANRYE INTERNATIONAL

New Jersey

Published by Clanrye International,
55 Van Reypen Street,
Jersey City, NJ 07306, USA
www.clanryeinternational.com

Mobile Multimedia: Technological Aspects
Edited by Anna Sanders

International Standard Book Number: 978-1-63240-350-6 (Hardback)

Contents

Preface

The technological aspects of mobile multimedia are described in this elaborative book. Multimedia mobiles such as smart phones and tablets are fast becoming popular among all ages as their day-to-day computing devices. Users have started to expect multimedia applications and services to run smooth and high-quality at par with desktop experience. The biggest challenge in providing multimedia to mobile devices using the Internet is to ensure a quality experience that meets the expectations of the users within reasonable costs and supporting heterogeneous platforms and wireless network conditions. The purpose of this book is to provide a comprehensive overview of the current and future technologies used for providing high-quality mobile multimedia applications, with emphasis on user experience as the first priority. It discusses the challenges in mobile video delivery as one of the most bandwidth-intensive media which demands pleasant rate of streaming and a user-centric strategy to ensure quality experience. It deals with this challenge by introducing significant concepts for future mobile multimedia coding and the network technologies to deliver quality services. It also brings together user and technology viewpoints by demonstrating how user experience can be evaluated using case studies on urban community interfaces and Internet telephones.

This book is the end result of constructive efforts and intensive research done by experts in this field. The aim of this book is to enlighten the readers with recent information in this area of research. The information provided in this profound book would serve as a valuable reference to students and researchers in this field.

At the end, I would like to thank all the authors for devoting their precious time and providing their valuable contribution to this book. I would also like to express my gratitude to my fellow colleagues who encouraged me throughout the process.

Editor

Part 1

Mobile Video – Quality of Experience

QoE for Mobile Streaming

Vlado Menkovski and Antonio Liotta
Eindhoven University of Technology
The Netherlands

1. Introduction

After its debut in personal computers and home entertainment devices, streaming video has found its place in the mobile environment as well. However, the characteristics of the mobile devices present a different set of challenges for delivering satisfactory video services. They are typically smaller in size designed to be handheld or carried on person in some manner. They have reduced screen size and somewhat limited computational power due to restrictions in size and power consumption. These technical challenges necessitate the adaptation of the content to the particular device so that successful reproduction is possible and desired quality is met. When the mobile device is exposed to unadjusted content in spatial resolution and frame-rate, unnecessary penalties in computational load are incurred mostly due to processing of the downscaling. This in turn leads to higher power consumption and can lower the quality if the device fails to execute the task on time. In general the issue of over and under-provisioning is present in any video streaming service. However, in mobile streaming it is particularly evident due to specific limitations of the mobile devices and the larger variety in the design of the user interface and the mode of interaction.

Another key feature of the mobile devices is that they rely on wireless access to connect to the outside world to gather information and use services. The types of wireless networks used are varied, consisting of a multitude of technologies that have different characteristics. This variability results in different bandwidth capability, round trip time and reliability of the link. Wireless connections are also more prone to errors because of exposure to various sources of noise and diminished reliability due to limitations in coverage. All these factors affect the networked services, but particularly multimedia services such as video streaming that rely on high throughput and high reliability of the link for successful playback (Wu et al., 2001).

Furthermore, due to the specific mechanics of consumption of the content in handheld devices the perception of quality is different than in desktop or large screen devices. This creates the need for separate exploration of the process of optimizing the tradeoff between the used resources and delivered quality from traditional video delivery systems.

To satisfy the ambition to deliver high quality of the service to its customers, providers need foremost an accurate estimation of the perceived quality. In order to be accurate in this estimation, they have to account for the unique characteristics of the mobile devices. These characteristics range from the way that the device is held, and used, to its screen size and computational power as well as the user expectations.

Quality of Experience (QoE) is a metric that quantifies this multifaceted, multidimensional factors that account for the perceived quality. QoE appears in the literature by different definitions, but generally it is agreed that QoE measures the quality experienced while using a service (Jain, 2004). Accurate estimation of QoE for video streaming on mobile services allows for control over the delivered quality and an implementation of user centric management of these services. User centric management focuses on managing the services according to the user or customer needs. In other words it offers constant quality to the user rather than constant amount of spent resources from the provider, which increases the value of the service to the customers (V. Menkovski et al., 2010).

This chapter begins with a discussion on the factors that affect the QoE in video streaming with particular interest on streaming for mobile devices. Next the chapter continues on to the objective and subjective methods for QoE estimation. This is followed by an elaboration on the impact that different video streaming technologies have on QoE. That section covers technologies for multimedia encoding such as video compression, transcoding, scalable video coding and multi description coding. Then a section on technologies for network transmission and reproduction of video and multimedia content follows. Finally we conclude with a summary of the current state of QoE and its possible future directions.

2. Factors that affect QoE in multimedia streaming

Video quality is affected by a multitude of factors in every stage of its existence from the creation of the content to transmission and finally reproduction. There is a vast amount of research on quality of the recording equipment, lightning conditions and other factors that contribute to quality at the content creation. However, these topics are out of scope of this chapter. Our interest here is to discuss how the quality is affected by the process of encoding, transport and presentation of the multimedia. Multimedia QoE is a complex metric that depends on many parameters. In the literature however QoE is modeled restricted to more specific aspects of a service. The authors of (Tran & Mellouk, 2010) implement a QoE model for network services by defining key performance indicators of service availability, accessibility, continuality, responsiveness, and delay. Other efforts focus on freezes in the playback (Huynh-Thu & Ghanbari, 2010) and their relationship with the spatial quality.

Adaptive services can vary the quality of the content as availability of resources changes. However, this variation of quality has negative effects on the QoE. The authors of (Zink et al., 2003) conclude that the rate and the amplitude of the variation are proportional to the degradation of the QoE. Audio and video synchronization also has a significant effect on the QoE. The investigation of media synchronization in (R. Steinmetz, 1996) concludes that the effect on quality depends on the type of content. In another investigation of audio and video correlation and lip synchronization (Mued, et al., 2003) concludes that the effects are different if the multimedia is of passive or active communication.

However, arguably the most important QoE factor in multimedia streaming is the video quality (S. Winkler & Mohandas, 2008). Significant amount of degradation of video quality comes from the encoding or the compression process. The main goal of the encoding process is to reduce the size of the original video. Uncompressed video requires very large storage space and is not suitable for transmission over restricted network channels. Lossy encoding is necessary to accommodate the restrictions in data throughput in the transmission channel, storage and processing capabilities of the terminal devices. This loss of fidelity can come from the encoder itself or as a part of a pre-encoding process to downgrade the spatial and temporal resolution of the video. In this manner the loss of quality from this initial step can come from downscaling of spatial resolution, frame-rate or bit-rate. Similar degradation is present in the audio, when sampling rate, sampling frequency and bit-rate are downscaled.

The spatial resolution of the digital video is one of the key factors for the size of the video after encoding. The recording equipment usually has much higher resolution that what can be practically used in video streaming applications. Particularly for mobile devices the resolution needs to be adjusted to the limitations of the screen resolution, computational power or network throughput. Lowering the spatial resolution creates the effect of blockiness. Blockiness is a visual impairment effect, particularly visible around the edges. It makes the edges jagged and pixelized.

Another way to restrict the size is to decrease the color depth, which makes the amount of data per pixel smaller. However, the images with smaller color palette seem less natural. With the advent of screen technology and the increase in user expectation this technique is rarely used nowadays.

On the other hand, a more commonly used technique, in addition to the spatial resolution decrease, is temporal resolution decrease or decrease in frame-rate. Frame-rate is usually kept to less than 30 frames per second due to the characteristics of the human visual systems. However framerate acceptability depends on the type of content (Apteker et al., 1995). Certain types of content that have low mobility and small spatial resolution, frame-rates as low as 10 frames per second can be acceptable. This is particularly useful for very low bit-rate channels in mobile environments where lower frame-rates help achieve the required low throughput.

The digital video encoding process produces a video stream with a specific bit-rate. The bit-rate is directly linked to the quality of the video stream and most encoders accept bit-rate setting as input. It can be either set as a soft (indication) or as a hard (constraint) limit on the encoder in constant bit-rate encoding. In variable bit-rate the indicator is usually a quality setting and the resulting stream is with constant quality rather than having a constant bit-rate. Based on this setting and the complexity of the video, the encoder compresses the video with certain average bit-rate. The bit-rate is also a very important factor for the content delivery system because the costs incurred for data the transport and storage are directly associated with it. Furthermore, specific parts of the transmission have limitations on the throughput that they can handle. Similar limitations exist in the terminal devices.

Therefore the amount of bits required to encode the video, or bits per second of video (i.e. bit-rate), depends on the type of encoding algorithm, the complexity of the video and the desired quality. Typical MPEG-like algorithms will introduce increasingly larger amounts of blockiness and blurriness as the bit-rate is reduced. In other words the video data will be more coarsely quantized in the frequency domain, which will lead to blockiness in the decoded video. The encoder attempts to limit the blockiness effect on low spatial frequencies of the video, which are less perceptible to the viewers. However, very constrained compressions result in highly visible artifacts. Another type of artifact resulting from the encoding is blurriness. This one arises from inadequate temporal fidelity of the encoded video.

The audio is of course as important as the video in the overall QoE of multimedia content, and many cases even more important. Even so, due to the fact that it is significantly easier to compress audio (as it needs less resources), most delivery systems use higher-quality compression level on the audio and focus on optimizing the video compression.

Finally, significant amount of artifacts and impairments come from the transmission errors, delays and jitter in the data reception (Kanumuri, et al., 2006)(Reibman & V. Vaishampayan, 2003). Typical symptoms are visual artifacts due to errors, freezes in reproduction and startup delays. These have significant effect on the QoE and depend on the undying transmission technology, as discussed in the following sections.

3. Estimating the video quality

Since video quality has such a significant effect on the overall QoE of multimedia streaming services, this section is dedicated to a review of a range of methods for video quality assessment. Video quality estimation has been of significant importance since the early days of digital video, so many methods have been devised. These are generally grouped into 'objective' and 'subjective' methods. The objective methods focus on objectively measurable impairments present in the video. This is done by comparing the impaired video to the original unimpaired video, in a full reference approach. Furthermore, the reduced reference (RR) and no-reference methods (NR) use partial information or no information on the original video to estimate the quality. These methods are more flexible, because they do not need to have copies of the original material, but suffer from reduced accuracy. On the other hand, a subjective methods aim at quantifying quality based on direct response by the person. These are more accurate, as they better take into account the human perception factor. However, they are more costly and cumbersome.

3.1 Objective video quality methods

Video quality estimation benefits extensively from the exhaustive work done in the image quality domain. Many image quality assessment (IQA) methods are used for estimation of video quality by evaluating the quality of individual pictures and, then, averaging over time.

The method that cannot be omitted when an overview of objective video quality methods is made is the peak signal to noise ratio (PSNR) (equation 1). PSNR estimates the difference between the original image and the distorted one by calculating the mean squared error (MSE) between the two signals and giving the ratio between the maximum of the signal and the MSE. Regardless of its significant drawbacks (mainly its low accuracy) (Avcıbaş, et al., 2002), PSNR is still very present in video quality analysis. It is easy to compute and provides a first impression on the quality achieved.

$$MSE = \frac{1}{mn} \sum_{i=0}^{m-1} \sum_{j=0}^{n-1} [I_{orig}(i,j) - I_{imp}(i,j)]^2$$

$$PSNR = 10 \log_{10} \left(\frac{MAX_I^2}{MSE} \right)^2$$

(1)

A more advanced IQA approach that tries to circumvent the drawbacks of PSRN is the structure similarity index method (SSIM) (Z. Wang, et al., 2004). SSIM focuses on the structural distortions in the image, not purely on the bit-errors, to calculate a more accurate quality value.

These approaches however do not consider the specific temporal effects of video. The video quality metric (VQM) model of Prinson and Wolf (Pinson & Wolf, 2004) is a linear combination of loss of spatial information, orientation shift, color impairments and moving edge impairments to calculate an overall video quality index. Because this model weighs in motion components, in addition to structural components, it covers a larger portion of the QoE factors in video.

A conceptually similar approach is DVQ (digital video quality), developed by Watson, et al. (Watson et al., 2001). In addition to the structural temporal distortions, DVQ incorporates factors such as light adaptation, luminance and chrominance distortions and contrast masking. These factors are motivated by the human visual system (HVS) models.

Another HVS-inspired method is PVQM (perceptual video quality metric) (Hekstra et al., 2002). This method computes the video quality index as a linear combination of three indicators: edginess of the luminance, normalized color error and temporal de-correlation.

To address the importance of the motion degradation for quality estimation, Seshadrinathan and Bovik developed the MOtion-based Video Integrity Evaluation (MOVIE) VQA index (Seshadrinathan & Bovik, 2009). This index calculates the impairments not only in space and time, but also in space-time. This algorithm as well as the other full-reference VQA makes a tradeoff between accuracy and computational resources. Even though MOVIE is an objective method that correlates well with subjective feedback from viewers, its high cost in computational power and memory limits its implementation in real-time systems.

A more suitable alternative for real-time quality estimation in content delivery systems are the RR and NR methods. The methods or models are usually much more specific than the FR methods and only deal with specific types of impairments and are not very accurate for general use.

Gunawan and Ghanbari have developed a RR method (Gunawan & Ghanbari, 2008) that uses local harmonic strength features from the original video to calculate the amount of impairments or quality of the affected video. Harmonic gains and loss correlate well with two very common types of impairment present in MPEG encoded video, i.e. blockiness and blurriness. This RR method has low overhead of the harmonic data of 160 to 400 bits per second, which is a negligible amount compared to the size of the video.

NR methods are even more flexible than RR because they are applicable to any video environment, even ones that do not have any information on the original source of the video. Naturally their accuracy and generality is highly constrained. NR models are frequently used to calculate the impact of transport errors on the delivered video. In (Reibman & V. Vaishampayan, 2003) authors present a model for estimating MSE caused by packet loss, by examining the video bit-stream. A single packet loss does not affect only the pixels of the video frame that lost information in that packet but, due to the temporal compression mechanisms of MPEG videos, these errors are propagated by the motion vectors in the subsequent frames. The location of the packet is of significant importance, because different types of frames carry information of different nature. A similar approach for MPEG2 video is presented in (Kanumuri et al., 2006). This method uses different machine learning (ML) algorithms to predict the visibility of the lost packet on the presented video. The additional complexity that these NR methods face is that they are not aware of the decoder's approach to conceal the error. A typical concealment approach is zero-motion concealment, in which a lost macroblock is concealed by a macroblock in the same location from a previous frame. However, the visibility of this concealment depends on the content at this position, size of the screen and many other factors that are generally related to the overall QoE.

Another group of methods exist that also do not use any information about the original video, but falls in the group of Hybrid Subjective and Objective methods. These methods first start with feature extraction from the specific system that they are evaluating. These features are objectively measurable in the particular system. Then this feature space is explored and labeled with a subjective study that provides subjective feedback on the human perception of quality. This step can be done in a full reference manner by presenting to the participants both the unimpaired and impaired video or, in a non-reference method, by only showing them the impaired video.

Finally, with statistical methods or ML techniques a model is built, which maps the objective features and the subjective labels that is later used in an online NR objective fashion for assessment of quality. An example of this approach is given in (Venkataraman et al., 2009) where the authors create a k-dimensional feature space for a specific application. In this work an example is given for 3 features of a video streaming system, bit-rate, delay and loss, which form a 3-dimensional data-space. Based on the subjective data, this space is divided into regions and the regions are assigned QoE values. When an objective measurement is later made, the datapoint falls into one of the regions and is classified with the specific QoE.

The authors of this chapter also developed methods of this type using ML algorithms. In (V. Menkovski et al., 2010) and (V. Menkovski et al., 2009) decision tree models are built from existing subjective datasets that are further used to estimate the QoE, based on the measurements on the objective features.

We have also explored online learning methods (V. Menkovski et al., 2010) for dynamic environments where the QoE accuracy of the models is short lived.

3.2 Subjective video quality methods

Subjective methods are directly estimating the multimedia quality from the targeted audience, the human viewer. They are the most accurate methodology and are therefore used as a reference for the rest of the methods (S. Winkler & Mohandas, 2008). There are different ways to carry out subjective studies. The most commonly used and standardized approach is done by rating (Recommendation ITU-R BT. 500-11, 2002). The recommended setup for a subjective study is that the viewing conditions are strictly controlled, 15 or more non-expert participants are selected and prepared. The grading scale is defined as Mean Opinion Score (MOS) and it has five values: 1 Bad, 2 Poor, 3 Fair, 4 Good, 5 Excellent. Similarly for impairments: Very annoying, Annoying, Slightly annoying, Perceptible and Imperceptible. There is also a comparisons scale for Differential MOS (DMOS) going from "Much worse" to "Much better" with an additional value in the middle "The same".

The actual rating can be done with Absolute category rating for the MOS or by a variety of double stimulus and single stimulus methods. Example of a subjective study is (De Simone et al., 2009.), which deals with impairments from H.264 compression and transmission over noisy channels. A typical evaluation of many objective methods with a subjective study was done in (Seshadrinathan et al., 2010), where the authors used DMOS.

However, these methods all rely on rating that is inheritably biased due to the variance in the internal representation of the rating scale by the subjects (Krantz, 1968)(Krantz, 1972)(Krantz et al., 1971)(Shepard, 1978)(Shepard, 1981). This bias and variance is propagated to the test output and results in the inefficiency of this type of subjective studies. This is not surprising, in fact psychophysicists have argued for a long time that the human perceptual system is more accurate at grasping 'differences' rather than giving absolute rating values (Watson, 2000).

In a later analysis (Winkler, 2009) of the properties of subjective rating, Winkler discusses the MOS variability and standard deviation in a set of subjective databases. The analysis shows that the standard deviation of MOS for the midrange is between 15-20% of the scale and decreases at the edges.

The further analysis of the subjective scales (Brooks & Hestnes, 2010) presents some interesting perspectives. A striking one is that the MOS scale is an ordinal qualitative scale and should not be used as a quantitative scale. Therefore analysis of MOS in decimal values would be invalid as well as its variability calculated to less than one fifth of the scale. In other words, numbers associated with the 5 labels do not represent actual distance between them. To avoid these issues with the scales, the authors propose a label-free scale or labels only at the end of the scale. This approach, however convenient for the analysis of the results, opens the question as to how people would map their internal representation of 'Good' and 'Bad' on this scale.

Another type of scale is the Just Noticeable Difference (JND) scale. In (Watson, 2000) Watson proposes this scale for Video Quality. The benefit of the proposed JND method is that there is no rating involved, which circumvents the drawbacks of the previous methods. JND relies on executing comparison tests on two samples consecutively, while the examined parameter intensity increases or decreases in one of the samples. As soon as the user notices the difference, the method defines this distance as 1 JND on the subjective scale. An example of this approach would be to scale the difference in quality of a video, due to different encoding bit-rate. Users in the test tend to notice the difference with a certain probability, as result of the imperfections of the HVS and the cognitive processes. Therefore the method finds the most likely JND scale of the parameter by maximizing the likelihood of all of the responses to the tests, executing the test set multiple times with different people. JND avoids the variability and bias of the rating scales, because the method relies on the capability of the participants to discriminate between two levels of quality, which comes quite easy to the viewers. When the videos are shown next to each other, most viewers will discriminate between them with high accuracy. However, if the videos are viewed independently they might find them both with the same subjectively quality. As a consequence, direct comparisons like this tend to sort the stimuli intensity rather than scale them well. Furthermore, the examiner needs to be able to very finely tune the tested parameter, in our example produce videos with given bit-rate. Therefore, this method cannot scale a directly predetermined set of parameter values.

Benefiting from the accuracy of the pair-wise comparison, usually referred to as two-alternative-forced-choice (2AFC), is also the MLDS method. MLDS stands for Maximum Likelihood Difference Scaling, and is also a method that scales the differences in quality, as in JND. However, this method presents the viewer with two pairs of stimuli, rather than one pair. The participant is then asked to discriminate between the two ranges of quality given by the two pairs. Because the discrimination is done on the ranges, the difference scale presents an actual scale of differences in quality. Maloney and Yang present the MLDS method on subjective analysis of image quality in (Maloney & Yang, 2003). Later in (Charrier et al., 2010) MLDS is used for measuring the performance of different IQA.

Because of its superior performance the authors of this chapter have also used MLDS for subjective estimation of quality in video (Menkovski, et al., 2011a). MLDS as well as the other difference scaling methods does not deliver absolute values of quality as the MOS scale does (as 'good' or 'fair'), but it only gives relative difference in the quality. This relative difference in quality, on the other hand, represents the utility of the tested parameter on the visual quality. As this is commonly the case in estimating QoE, the tester needs to optimize the service so that the delivered quality is justified by the spent resources. In these cases the benefits of MLDS in accuracy cannot be challenged by the direct results of rating.

The main drawback in the use of MLDS is that it requires much more testing than pair-wise comparisons for JND or rating tests. This drawback is minimal when the comparison is on images that require short time, but it becomes more significant on videos. To address this problem we have worked on an adaptive MLDS approach in (Menkovski et al., 2011b). In this approach the pairs for the MLDS tests are not selected randomly, but through a guided approach based on the previous responses in a iterative manner.

4. Multimedia encoding technologies and their effect on the QoE

Video encoding is an active area of research and development, with a large number of video encoding algorithms produced so far. These algorithms vary in compression efficiency and performance. However, currently the established player is based on the H.264 standard that came out of the collaboration between the ISO MPEG and the ITU-T video coding expert groups (Ostermann et al., 2004). This type of coding techniques divides the image in macro blocks. Each macro block consists of three components, i.e. the Y – luminance and the two chrominance components, Cr and Cb. The luminance component is kept at a higher spatial resolution than the chrominance components due to the fact that the HVS is more sensitive to luminance.

The macro blocks are then coded into Intra mode or Inter mode. In the Intra mode, all the blocks of the given frame are fully coded into an I-frame. The I-frame as such does not depend on any previous or subsequent frames. In the Inter mode, P-frames or B-frames are coded, where only differences from previous or subsequent frames are coded. Additionally, motion of the macro blocks is estimated with motion vectors in order to minimize the need to encode data. Main reasons for degradation of the quality and in turn the QoE are restrictions on the bit-rate, which cause the blockiness effect. The more efficient the encoder is the better quality it will produce on lower bit-rates.

In comparison to other coding algorithm (Wiegand et al., 2003), H.264 shows superior performance over the whole range of bit-rate constraints. This performance gains are paid by increased complexity compared to the other codecs. Additionally this highly compressed bit-stream is more sensitive to errors. A subjective study by Pinson et al. (Pinson, Wolf, & Cermak, 2010) shows that H.264 suffers from higher degradation of quality than MPEG2 on the same amount of errors in the transmission channel.

4.1 Transcoding

The purpose of transcoding, or re-encoding, is to convert a previously encoded media signal (video and/or audio) into another one with different format. This is a commonly used procedure in mobile streaming due to the need to adapt the content to different types of devices. Media transcoding is most efficient when the source stream is of the highest possible quality. Ideally, the input signal is directly the original one as captured from the recorder. The parameters of the re-encoding process, such as frame size, frame rate and bit rate can also be adapted to the various available resources. In this way, the clients connected through a broadband connection can be served with the best possible quality, while clients on lower speed connections can still have access to a lower quality version of the video.

Since the encoders are lossy, each conversion adds degradation to the media quality. Compression artifacts are cumulative, so the number of transcoding steps should be kept to a minimum. In most applications the main reason for transcoding is bit-rate reduction. The complete process of re-encoding would require the use of a pixel-domain approach, in which the original signal is fully decoded, processed as necessary and then re-encoded according to the constraints of the new wanted stream. While this is always possible to do, and sometimes necessary, this process is usually very costly and difficult to be implemented efficiently in a real-time environment.

Two types of transcoding systems can be defined: open-loop and closed-loop (Assuncao & Ghanbari, 1998). Open-loop systems are the simplest ones, and require a very limited elaboration of the input stream because only the encoded DCT (Discreet Cosine Transform) coefficients are modified. The roughest technique consists of discarding all the coefficients below a certain threshold level, or above a certain frequency. The number of coefficients removed can be adjusted to obtain the required final bit-rate. However, the open-loop systems introduce a major source of distortion called drift, which lead to a visual blurring. This is due to incoherence between the pictures used for prediction by the encoder and the decoder. As a matter of fact, the new P-frames are directly derived from the old P-frames, without considering the inaccuracies introduced by the re-quantization. This way, a continuous drop of quality is accumulated over predicted frames. The closed-loop approach tries to solve this problem by approximating the complete decoder-encoder architecture. The stream is still not fully re-encoded, but a feedback loop containing a frame buffer is used in order to compensate for the transcoding distortion, so that it won't be propagated into the successive frame.

In addition to bit-rate reduction, transcoding is also used for spatial resolution downscaling. Reuse of motion parameters and MacroBlock information can help in reducing encoding complexity and consequently transcoding efficiency. A simple way to implement spatial reduction is to filter the input signal in order to retain only low-frequency coefficients, and then reconstruct new reduced MacroBlocks with the retained ones. Pixel averaging is a typical technique for spatial resolution downsampling in which an n-by-n region of pixels is encoded with a single pixel having a color value of the average of all of the pixels. This technique results in blurriness.

In case of temporal transcoding, some of the frames that were originally present in the video are dropped. The necessary task in this kind of transcoding is the re-estimation of motion vector. Bilinear interpolation techniques can be repeated iteratively to approximate all skipped frames. Other alternatives are: Forward Dominant Vector Selection, Telescopic Vector Composition and Activity-Dominant Vector Selection (Ahmad et al., 2005).

When the video is transmitted through a channel with high error rates, like a wireless network, the transcoding process can be optimized using stronger protection mechanisms in order to compensate these losses and supply the user with a better quality of experience while maintaining the same required rate. By adding more redundancy, the total video size is augmented, so it's necessary to reduce the encoding quality in order to retain the same bit-rate. A trade-off between resiliency and effective bit-rate needs to be estimated in order for the overall delivered quality to be maximized.

4.2 Scalable video coding

Scalable video Coding (SVC) is an extension of the H.264/MPEG-4 Advanced Video Coding standard, which introduces a special layered encoding; this is similar to progressive JPEG, used for image compression and transmission over the Web. A video encoded in SVC format is created composing multiples sub-streams derived from the original video signal. Each sub-stream can be transmitted independently from the others. However, in order to reconstruct the video the client has to start from the base layer and then sequentially use the available improvement layers. This way, starting from a single encoded video stream is possible to achieve a multi bit-rate streaming service. In contrast, other currently used technologies require separate encoding of each individual stream at different bit rate. This operation needs to be done once, if the streams are stored as independent files, or each time the content is required if done on-the-fly. In the first case, for a typical streaming service, between 3 and more than 10 copies of each video are created and stored on the transmitting source, introducing a great redundancy. While the storage costs are becoming less of a factor, this approach greatly increases the initial efforts and the ongoing maintenance complexity of the system. In the second case, we remove the storage requirements, but the encoding process has significantly higher computing cost. SVC tries to reduce those costs while keeping encoding efficiency and an efficient granularity.

Using SVC brings a penalty of increased bit-rate by 10 to 20% compared to the highest bit-rate needed for a single-layer H.264 encoding. However, if we want to achieve the same flexibility with single-layer encoded streams we would need to pay much higher cost in storage. For example, using 6 streams with bit-rates ranging from 0.15 to 3 Mbps would require a total of 6.25 Mbps for the normal encoding (0.15 + 0.3 + 0.5 + 0.8 + 1.5 + 3 Mbps) and only 3.6 Mbps for SVC (-42%).

There are four main classes of scalability in the SVC definition (Schwarz, Marpe, & Thomas Wiegand, 2007):

- temporal: reducing the temporal resolution (number of frames per second)
- spatial: reducing the spatial resolution (number of pixels per spatial region, frame size)

- fidelity: also called Signal to Noise Ratio (SNR) or quality scalability, reducing the fidelity of the video (coarsely quantized pixels)
- a forth class of scalability is obtained by a combination of the other three.

Temporal scalability is the result of the introduction of hierarchical B-frames. In the classical prediction structure, B-frames are derived only from preceding and subsequent I/P frames. In the new scalable model, B-frames are used to predict other B-frames of enhancing layers in a cascade way. For instance, the base layer could be composed of I and P frames, which are used to predict the B frames of the first temporal enhancement layer. In turn, B-frames of the first layer are used to predict B-frames on the second layer (together with key frames of the base layer), and so on. As a result, the total number of B-frames between two key frames (of type I or P) is 2^k -1. Hierarchical B-frames can be organized in different orders. A simple sequence is to iteratively put one B-frame of a higher layer between two predicting frames of the lower layer. A consequence of this kind of hierarchization of B-frames is that the first frame to be predicted and decoded is the central one, while in the classical approach it would usually be the first one of the group.

In the spatial scalability, intra and inter-layer prediction mechanisms are exploited. Each following layer corresponds to one of the supported increasing spatial resolutions. Again, the base layer is used to encode the following enhancement layers in a bottom-up fashion. An intuitive constraint is that the resolution cannot decrease in enhancing layers. An important property of SVC is that each spatial layer is decodable using a single motion compensation loop, keeping a low complexity level. Spatial scalability generally performs better when high-resolution material is used as input.

Quality scalability is based on an improvement of the concept of coarse-grain quality scalable coding, called medium-grain quality scalability. The improving signal contained in each successive enhancing layer is re-quantized using a finer quantization step compared to the previous layer. Motion compensation is done using only key frames composing the base layer. Both spatial and quality scalability are sources of loss of encoding efficiency compared to a single-layer system. Several analyses of SVC performances have been conducted. In (Van der Auwera et al., 2008), traffic characteristics of the various scalability modes proposed by SVC are compared with MPEG-4 Part 2.

Even though, SVC is still a little more costly in terms of encoding efficiency or overhead, the gap with H.264/AVC single layer coding is small enough to be considered a good alternative in most cases. Furthermore, rate-distortion comparison shows that SVC outperforms almost all other video encoding technologies currently available(Wien et al., 2007). Another positive property of SVC is its strong error resilience, which results in a graceful degradation in quality when the transmission is impaired by packet losses (Wiegand et al., 2009). Some layers are more important than others for the final perceived quality of the video displayed. Based on this assumption, a stronger protection (redundancy) should be used for these layers to allow for better degradation on quality.

4.3 Multiple description coding

The idea behind Multiple Description Coding is quite similar to Scalable Coding, where a single source is encoded in multiple streams with different quality. The more of these streams are received by the final user, the better the quality of the decoded signal is. Each single stream is called 'description' and can be ideally self decoded. Since the purpose of MDC is to contrast packet losses and sudden link failures by increasing the redundancy, each description should be sent through different paths, even if this reduces routing efficiency. Using multiple paths can however have additional positive impacts in traffic dispersion and load balancing, which is useful to prevent or mitigate congestions. The benefits of MDC come obviously at the price of using more bits to achieve the same quality than using a 'single description' encoding (Y. Wang et al., 2005). The various descriptions are not necessarily required to have the same bit-rate, allowing a certain degree of adaptability to specific transmission channels.

Different ways exist to create MDs (multiple descriptions). The simplest one is to divide somehow the source data into several subsets and compress them separately to produce different descriptions. Interpolation is then used to decode any received combination of descriptions. A classic example is to separate odd and even samples, for example alternate frames, obtaining two subsets at half the rate of the original signal. Three decoders can then be used by the receiver: two for each separate description and one in case both the streams are properly received. Generally N descriptions would then require $2^{(N-1)}$ decoders to be decoded. A different approach is to use successive refinements to reduce the total number of decoders. In this case, one decoder is used when a single stream is received, a different one is used to decode two descriptions and so on. Another possibility is to repeat some part of data in every description created. Not all information has the same usefulness, so the most important parts are replicated more than the others. This approach is called Unequal Error Protection.

5. Multimedia streaming technologies and their effect on QoE

In multimedia streaming the content is continuously received over a transmission channel as it is reproduced to the viewer. This technique offers viewing of live content with reduced delay and offline content without the need to store the entire content locally before viewing. The cost for these benefits is that there is a possibility for additional degradation in quality coming from the transmission process. The degradation comes from delays or untimely reception of the content or from errors in the transmission.

There are different methods for video streaming. These methods implement protocols that deal with the issues of transmission of multimedia content in different manner. Today's streaming solutions either take place over the Internet or other private or proprietary networks that implement the IP protocol stack. In these environments the streaming protocol is either implemented over a UDP or a TCP protocol. In both cases the streaming content is segmented in data packets and transmitted over the network. The UDP protocol does not provide any guarantees about the delivery nor does any transmission control. Protocols that work over UDP need to have their own transmission control and error recovery mechanisms. Protocols that utilize TCP benefit from its error correction mechanisms, however these mechanisms can add unacceptable delays for streaming multimedia.

A commonly used protocol for multimedia streaming over UDP is the Real-time Transport Protocol (RTP). The protocol works in conjunction with the RTCP (Real-time control protocol) and the RTSP (Real-time streaming protocol). The RTP is responsible for the transport of the audio visual content. RTCP provides statistics monitors the transmission for the purpose of Quality of Service estimation and management. RTSP provides an application-level control over the playback of the content and works over a TCP channel (Schulzrinne, 1996)(Schulzrinne, 1998)(Huitema, 2003).

The underlying UDP transmission in RTP provides for simple and efficient transport of the content. The protocol presents minimal overhead in the transmission and can operate even in a unidirectional transmission channel for the RTP only implementation. This type of transmission is usually desirable when the application requires low latency or has very limited buffering requirements. The cost of this simplicity is that UDP does not offer any guarantees for delivery, which leaves the RTP susceptible to errors and data loss, if no higher level protection mechanisms are implemented.

Degradation in quality due to transmission errors and data loss in IP networks is a problematic that has been significantly examined in the literature (Kanumuri et al., 2006)(Mu et al., 2009). Transmission of RTP packets over TCP is also standardized, but is not used very commonly. The mechanisms of TCP provide guarantees for delivery of the data, however these mechanisms are implemented through time-outs and retransmissions that can add significant delay to the overall delivery. Particularly, in error-prone channels TCP transmission leads to excessive delays and connection failures. These problems result in playback freezes, skipping of content segments or interruptions. These types of impairments are severe and could possibly be alleviated by error concealment mechanisms of the player, if the control over error correction is left to the application layer. In offline video playback these problems can be reduced to some extent with large buffers. The drawback of this approach is that the playback startup is delayed in the beginning, proportionally to the amount of data in the buffer.

With the proliferation of video on the Web the progressive download method has gained significant popularity. Part of the popularity of progressive download comes from its compatibility with HTTP technologies that underpin the Web. The method is a multimedia content transmission over TCP and HTTP. The difference with traditional download is that the content is being displayed to the viewer while being downloaded. This method relies on the TCP guarantees for data delivery and on significant buffer size to deal with the delays coming from the TCP transmission. Since progressive download does not adapt and is not designed for particular transmission channel characteristics, usually a significant portion of the content needs to be downloaded before successful playback can be executed. The amount of data that needs to be buffered is crucial to the delivered QoE for this method. The degradation in QoE in progressive download comes mainly from the amount and frequency of freezes in the playback and their duration as well as the delay in the video reproduction startup. The effect of freezes on quality is evaluated in (Huynh-Thu & Ghanbari, 2010).

As we have previously stated the popularity of progressive download comes from its compatibility with Web server technology. Another streaming method that builds on this compatibility but tries to address some of the issues of progressive download is adaptive streaming or stream switching. This adaptive streaming paradigm is recently gaining a lot of interest in web based services. Its success is due to many factors. First of all, it can be simply built on top of existing and widespread open technologies like HTTP. Dedicated and optimized servers exist for adaptive streaming, however it can be completely implemented using normal web servers already deployed. One of the main advantages of using plain HTTP is that it is usually permitted even in the most restricted environments, passing through firewalls and proxy servers. Another advantage derives from the cacheability of web contents. Since videos are seen as normal web content, intermediate caches placed between the original server and end user will allow for a significant reduction of network load, bringing contents closer to the consumer.

In progressive streaming, multiple versions of a single video may be available to users, diversified according to bit-rate, and as consequence, quality level. At the beginning of streaming session, the user is required to select the most suitable version that meets its requirements and available resources. In case of considerable variation in bandwidth, the viewer may experience frequent freezes due to buffer under-runs. Moreover, in progressive streaming usually the client tries to greedily get and cache in the buffer as much content as possible, regardless of the current position in the video playback. This attitude can waste substantial network resources, because many videos are not watched all the way to the end.

To overcome those issues, while still retaining the simplicity of progressive streaming, the HTTP Adaptive Streaming approach has been proposed, and is currently deployed by several media content providers. The idea is to encode and store multiple versions of each single video at different bitrates, and let the client choose instant by instant the best suitable version to download. To do so, every stream is fragmented in chunks of fixed length, typically in the range between 1 and 10 seconds. The reference frame at the beginning of each chunk is synchronized, so that switching between different streams does not create glitches. The client keeps a limited buffer and does not try to get more chunks than necessary to fill it. The available bandwidth can be estimated by the download time required for previous chunks. When changes in network conditions are detected, a different version of the video can be selected for the next chunk. As discussed in the previous sections, frequent changes in video quality should be avoided because they degrade the QoE.

Since HTTP is a pull-based protocol, each client is required to autonomously manage its streaming session by actively requesting each chunk. This means that servers are relieved from keeping track of the status of each client. Moreover, each client can potentially implement its own adaptive algorithm. The list of available streams and chunks must be known by the client. To do so, a manifest file is published by the server, and this is first file that a client requests and later parses before starting its streaming session.

One of the most important Content Delivery Network service available today is Akamai. The performances of its adaptive streaming implementation were analyzed in (De Cicco & Mascolo, 2010). Each video appears to be encoded in five different bit-rate versions. The client communicates with the server passing variables and commands through POST messages. The frame rate is never modified, so the adaptation mechanism relies only on the quality level of the video. The control algorithm is executed on average each two seconds. Nevertheless, when a sudden increase of the available bandwidth occurs, the time required by the transition to fully match the new bandwidth is roughly 150 seconds. This large actuation delay can also be noticed in case of drop of the bandwidth, leading to short interruptions in video playback.

A study of client-side intelligence for adaptive streaming was conducted in (Jarnikov & Özçelebi, 2011). A system using reward and penalty parameters is used in order to personalize the streaming strategy. Experiments showed that considering the past two minutes of network conditions is enough to have a sufficient feedback for the adaptation algorithm. Increasing this period leads to a more conservative strategy that tends to keep a lower quality level. Comparisons with Apple's implementation shows that the proposed solution can deliver video at quality level at least as good as the Apple solution, and usually better exploit the available bandwidth at the cost of more changes of quality levels. It is also pointed out that the Apple implementation sometimes wastes bandwidth, requesting more than once the same temporal chunk at various quality levels.

A system that uses bit-stream switching and a customized congestion control for adaptive streaming over RTP/UDP is proposed in (Schierl & Wiegand, 2004). The pre-buffering time is fixed at 1 second, and the maximum signaling overhead due to feedback mechanisms is kept below 5% of the total data sent. Experimental results shows that bit-stream switching, combined with temporal scalability (drops of frames), provide the best performances, compared to only temporal scalability.

6. Conclusions

The QoE methods carry quite a big significance for any multimedia streaming service. They provide for efficient service management by balancing resource consumption with delivered quality. Nevertheless, estimation of the QoE is no small task. QoE is a multifaceted and complex metric that aims to quantify the experienced quality. A multitude of factors affect it, some of which may not be directly measurable in specific systems. This chapter presents a discussion on the factors that affect QoE in multimedia services, with emphasis on mobile streaming. It also presents a survey of the methods for estimating the QoE, or more particularly the video quality, from both a subjective and an objective nature. Focusing more on multimedia streaming the chapter continues with a discussion on how different technologies for encoding and streaming video content influence the delivered quality.

In conclusion of this discussion it becomes evident that while there are many QoE models, most of them are significantly constrained to specific aspects. As such they only work well for their attended purpose (Mu & Mauthe, 2009). A more general model that would capture most of the factors that attribute to the experience is still missing. In light of this we need to consider QoE as an evolving domain where the models and methods progress with the advent of new technologies. The lack of generality of the models is mainly because there is still a need for better understanding of the many aspects of QoE and how they influence each other. Significant development in the objectively measurable factors is already underway for some time, with a fruitful community for video and audio quality estimation as well as transport factors that affect quality. However, there is a need to improve our understanding of the psychological aspects of QoE as well. Just an example of the importance of the psychological factors is shown by the results a recent study (Kortum & M. Sullivan, 2010), which shows how the desirability of the content plays crucially important role on the subjective perception of quality.

7. References

Ahmad, I., Wei, X., Sun, Y., & Zhang, Y. Q. (2005). Video transcoding: an overview of various techniques and research issues. *Multimedia, IEEE Transactions on*, 7(5), 793–804.

Apteker, R. T., Fisher, J. A., Kisimov, V. S., & Neishlos, H. (1995). Video acceptability and frame rate. *IEEE Multimedia*, 2(3), 32-40. doi:10.1109/93.410510

Assuncao, P. A. A., & Ghanbari, M. (1998). A frequency-domain video transcoder for dynamic bit-rate reduction of MPEG-2 bit streams. *Circuits and Systems for Video Technology, IEEE Transactions on, 8*(8), 953–967.

Van der Auwera, G., David, P. T., Reisslein, M., & Karam, L. J. (2008). Traffic and quality characterization of the H. 264/AVC scalable video coding extension. *Advances in Multimedia, 2008*(2), 1–27.

Avcıbaş, İ., Sankur, B., & Sayood, K. (2002). Statistical evaluation of image quality measures. *Journal of Electronic Imaging, 11*, 206.

Brooks, P., & Hestnes, B. (2010). User measures of quality of experience: why being objective and quantitative is important. *Network, IEEE, 24*(2), 8–13.

Charrier, C., Knoblauch, K., Moorthy, A. K., Bovik, A. C., & Maloney, L. T. (2010). Comparison of image quality assessment algorithms on compressed images. *SPIE conference on Image quality and System Performance (to appear, 2010).*

De Cicco, L., & Mascolo, S. (2010). An experimental investigation of the Akamai adaptive video streaming. *HCI in Work and Learning, Life and Leisure*, 447–464.

Gunawan, I. P., & Ghanbari, M. (2008). Efficient reduced-reference video quality meter. *Broadcasting, IEEE Transactions on, 54*(3), 669–679.

Hekstra, A. P., Beerends, J. G., Ledermann, D., De Caluwe, F. E., Kohler, S., Koenen, R. H., & Rihs, S. (2002). PVQM-A perceptual video quality measure. *Signal processing: Image communication, 17*(10), 781–798.

Huitema, C. (2003). Real time control protocol (RTCP) attribute in session description protocol (SDP).

Huynh-Thu, Q., & Ghanbari, M. (2010). Modelling of spatio-temporal interaction for video quality assessment. *Signal Processing: Image Communication, 25*(7), 535–546.

Jain, R. (2004). Quality of experience. *IEEE Multimedia, 11*(1), 96–95.

Jarnikov, D., & Özçelebi, T. I. (2011). Client intelligence for adaptive streaming solutions. *Signal Processing: Image Communication.*

Kanumuri, S., Cosman, P. C., Reibman, A. R., & Vaishampayan, V. A. (2006). Modeling packet-loss visibility in MPEG-2 video. *Multimedia, IEEE Transactions on, 8*(2), 341–355.

Kortum, P., & Sullivan, M. (2010). The effect of content desirability on subjective video quality ratings. *Human factors: the journal of the human factors and ergonomics society, 52*(1), 105.

Krantz, D. H. (1968). A theory of context effects based on cross-context matching* 1. *Journal of Mathematical Psychology, 5*(1), 1–48.

Krantz, D. H. (1972). A theory of magnitude estimation and cross-modality matching* 1. *Journal of Mathematical Psychology, 9*(2), 168–199.

Krantz, D. H., Luce, R. D., Suppes, P., & Tversky, A. (1971). Foundations of measurement, vol. 1: Additive and polynomial representations. *New York: Academic.*

Maloney, L. T., & Yang, J. N. (2003). Maximum likelihood difference scaling. *Journal of Vision, 3*(8).

Menkovski, V., Exarchakos, G., & Liotta, A. (2010). Online QoE prediction. *Quality of Multimedia Experience (QoMEX), 2010 Second International Workshop on* (pp. 118-123). Presented at the Quality of Multimedia Experience (QoMEX), 2010 Second International Workshop on. doi:10.1109/QOMEX.2010.5517692

Menkovski, V., Exarchakos, G., Liotta, A., & Sanchez, A. C. (2010). Estimations and Remedies for Quality of Experience in Multimedia Streaming. *Advances in Human-Oriented and Personalized Mechanisms, Technologies and Services (CENTRIC), 2010*

Third International Conference on (pp. 11-15). Presented at the Advances in Human-Oriented and Personalized Mechanisms, Technologies and Services (CENTRIC), 2010 Third International Conference on. doi:10.1109/CENTRIC.2010.14

Menkovski, V., Exarchakos, G., Liotta, A., & Sánchez, A. C. (2010). Measuring Quality of Experience on a Commercial Mobile TV Platform. *Advances in Multimedia (MMEDIA), 2010 Second International Conferences on* (pp. 33-38). Presented at the Advances in Multimedia (MMEDIA), 2010 Second International Conferences on. doi:10.1109/MMEDIA.2010.12

Menkovski, V., Oredope, A., Liotta, A., & Sánchez, A. C. (2009). Predicting quality of experience in multimedia streaming. *Proceedings of the 7th International Conference on Advances in Mobile Computing and Multimedia* (pp. 52–59).

Menkovski, Vlado, Exarchakos, Georgios, & Liotta, Antonio. (2011a). The value of relative quality in video delivery. *Journal of Mobile Multimedia, 7*(3).

Menkovski, Vlado, Exarchakos, Georgios, & Liotta, Antonio. (2011b). Adaptive testing for video quality assessment. Presented at the Quality of Experience of multimedia content sharing, Lisbon, Portugal.

Mu, M., & Mauthe, A. (2009). An interview with video quality experts. *ACM SIGMM Records Issue 4, December 2009.*

Mu, M., Gostner, R., Mauthe, A., Tyson, G., & Garcia, F. (2009). Visibility of Individual Packet Loss on H. 264 Encoded Video Stream–A User Study on the Impact of Packet Loss on Perceived Video Quality. *Annual Multimedia Computing and Networking, San Jose, USA.*

Mued, L., Lines, B., Furnell, S., & Reynolds, P. (2003). The effects of audio and video correlation and lip synchronization. *Campus-Wide Information Systems, 20*(4), 159-166. doi:10.1108/10650740310491333

Ostermann, J., Bormans, J., List, P., Marpe, D., Narroschke, M., Pereira, F., Stockhammer, T., et al. (2004). Video coding with H.264/AVC: tools, performance, and complexity. *IEEE Circuits and Systems Magazine, 4*(1), 7- 28. doi:10.1109/MCAS.2004.1286980

Pinson, M. H., & Wolf, S. (2004). A new standardized method for objectively measuring video quality. *IEEE Transactions on Broadcasting, 50*(3), 312- 322. doi:10.1109/TBC.2004.834028

Pinson, M. H., Wolf, S., & Cermak, G. (2010). HDTV subjective quality of H. 264 vs. MPEG-2, with and without packet loss. *Broadcasting, IEEE Transactions on, 56*(1), 86–91.

Recommendation, ITU-R BT. 500-11 (2002).,"Methodology for the Subjective Assessment of the Quality of Television Pictures," Recommendation ITU-R BT. 500-11. *ITU Telecom. Standardization Sector of ITU.*

Reibman, A. R., & Vaishampayan, V. (2003). Quality monitoring for compressed video subjected to packet loss. *Multimedia and Expo, 2003. ICME'03. Proceedings. 2003 International Conference on* (Vol. 1, p. I–17).

Schierl, T., & Wiegand, T. (2004). H. 264/avc rate adaptation for internet streaming. *Packet Video Workshop.*

Schulzrinne, H. (1996). RTP: A transport protocol for real-time applications.

Schulzrinne, H. (1998). Real time streaming protocol (RTSP).

Seshadrinathan, K., & Bovik, A. C. (2009). Motion-based perceptual quality assessment of video. *Proc. SPIE-Human Vision and Electronic Imaging.*

Seshadrinathan, K., Soundararajan, R., Bovik, A. C., & Cormack, L. K. (2010). Study of subjective and objective quality assessment of video. *Image Processing, IEEE Transactions on, 19*(6), 1427–1441.

Shepard, R. N. (1981). Psychological relations and psychophysical scales: On the status of. *Journal of Mathematical Psychology, 24*(1), 21–57.

Shepard, R. N. (1978). On the status of'direct'psychophysical measurement. *Minnesota studies in the philosophy of science, 9*, 441–490.

De Simone, F., Naccari, M., Tagliasacchi, M., Dufaux, F., Tubaro, S., & Ebrahimi, T. (n.d.). Subjective assessment of H. 264/AVC video sequences transmitted over a noisy channel. *Quality of Multimedia Experience, 2009. QoMEx 2009. International Workshop on* (pp. 204–209).

Steinmetz, R. (1996). Human perception of jitter and media synchronization. *Selected Areas in Communications, IEEE Journal on, 14*(1), 61–72.

Tran, H. A., & Mellouk, A. (2010). QoE Model Driven for Network Services. In E. Osipov, A. Kassler, T. M. Bohnert, & X. Masip-Bruin (Eds.), *Wired/Wireless Internet Communications* (Vol. 6074, pp. 264-277). Berlin, Heidelberg: Springer Berlin Heidelberg. Retrieved from http://www.springerlink.com/content/7159q510q378m234/

Venkataraman, M., Chatterjee, M., & Chattopadhyay, S. (2009). Evaluating quality of experience for streaming video in real time. *Global Telecommunications Conference, 2009. GLOBECOM 2009. IEEE* (pp. 1–6).

Wang, Y., Reibman, A. R., & Lin, S. (2005). Multiple description coding for video delivery. *Proceedings of the IEEE, 93*(1), 57–70.

Wang, Z., Lu, L., & Bovik, A. C. (2004). Video quality assessment based on structural distortion measurement. *Signal processing: Image communication, 19*(2), 121–132.

Watson, A. B. (2000). Proposal: Measurement of a JND scale for video quality. *IEEE G-2.1. 6 Subcommittee on Video Compression Measurements.*

Watson, Andrew B., Hu, J., & McGowan, J. F. (2001). Digital video quality metric based on human vision. *Journal of Electronic Imaging, 10*(1), 20. doi:10.1117/1.1329896

Wiegand, T., Noblet, L., & Rovati, F. (2009). Scalable video coding for IPTV services. *Broadcasting, IEEE Transactions on, 55*(2), 527–538.

Wiegand, T., Schwarz, H., Joch, A., Kossentini, F., & Sullivan, G. J. (2003). Rate-constrained coder control and comparison of video coding standards. *Circuits and Systems for Video Technology, IEEE Transactions on, 13*(7), 688–703.

Wien, M., Schwarz, H., & Oelbaum, T. (2007). Performance analysis of SVC. *Circuits and Systems for Video Technology, IEEE Transactions on, 17*(9), 1194–1203.

Winkler, S., & Mohandas, P. (2008). The evolution of video quality measurement: from PSNR to hybrid metrics. *Broadcasting, IEEE Transactions on, 54*(3), 660–668.

Winkler, Stefan. (2009). On the properties of subjective ratings in video quality experiments. *IN PROC. INTERNATIONAL WORKSHOP ON QUALITY OF MULTIMEDIA EXPERIENCE (QOMEX.* Retrieved from http://citeseer.ist.psu.edu/viewdoc/summary?doi=10.1.1.160.3958

Wu, D., Hou, Y. T., Zhu, W., Zhang, Y. Q., & Peha, J. M. (2001). Streaming video over the Internet: approaches and directions. *Circuits and Systems for Video Technology, IEEE Transactions on, 11*(3), 282–300.

Zink, M., Künzel, O., Schmitt, J., & Steinmetz, Ralf. (2003). Subjective Impression of Variations in Layer Encoded Videos. *IN: INTERNATIONAL WORKSHOP ON QUALITY OF SERVICE,* 137--154.

2

Understanding User Experience of Mobile Video: Framework, Measurement, and Optimization

Wei Song, Dian Tjondronegoro and Michael Docherty
Queensland University of Technology
Australia

1. Introduction

Since users have become the focus of product/service design in last decade, the term User eXperience (UX) has been frequently used in the field of Human-Computer-Interaction (HCI). Research on UX facilitates a better understanding of the various aspects of the user's interaction with the product or service. Mobile video, as a new and promising service and research field, has attracted great attention. Due to the significance of UX in the success of mobile video (Jordan, 2002), many researchers have centered on this area, examining users' expectations, motivations, requirements, and usage context. As a result, many influencing factors have been explored (Buchinger, Kriglstein, Brandt & Hlavacs, 2011; Buchinger, Kriglstein & Hlavacs, 2009). However, a general framework for specific mobile video service is lacking for structuring such a great number of factors.

To measure user experience of multimedia services such as mobile video, quality of experience (QoE) has recently become a prominent concept. In contrast to the traditionally used concept quality of service (QoS), QoE not only involves objectively measuring the delivered service but also takes into account user's needs and desires when using the service, emphasizing the user's overall acceptability on the service. Many QoE metrics are able to estimate the user perceived quality or acceptability of mobile video, but may be not enough accurate for the overall UX prediction due to the complexity of UX. Only a few frameworks of QoE have addressed more aspects of UX for mobile multimedia applications but need be transformed into practical measures. The challenge of optimizing UX remains adaptations to the resource constrains (e.g., network conditions, mobile device capabilities, and heterogeneous usage contexts) as well as meeting complicated user requirements (e.g., usage purposes and personal preferences).

In this chapter, we investigate the existing important UX frameworks, compare their similarities and discuss some important features that fit in the mobile video service. Based on the previous research, we propose a simple UX framework for mobile video application by mapping a variety of influencing factors of UX upon a typical mobile video delivery system. Each component and its factors are explored with comprehensive literature reviews. The proposed framework may benefit in user-centred design of mobile video through taking a complete consideration of UX influences and in improvement of mobile video service quality by adjusting the values of certain factors to produce a positive user experience. It may also facilitate relative research in the way of locating important issues to study, clarifying research scopes, and setting up proper study procedures.

We then review a great deal of research on UX measurement, including QoE metrics and QoE frameworks of mobile multimedia. Finally, we discuss how to achieve an optimal quality of user experience by focusing on the issues of various aspects of UX of mobile video. In the conclusion, we suggest some open issues for future study.

2. User experience in mobile video

Though the term user experience (UX) has been frequently used in multimedia services, as of now, there is no common definition for UX. According to a survey on UX (Law, Roto, Hassenzahl, Vermeeren & Kort, 2009), Hassenzahl and Tractinsky's definition is the most preferred by both academics and industry. They define UX as *"a consequence of a user's internal state, the characteristics of the designed system and the context (or the environment) within which the interaction occurs"*(2006, p. 95). A more formal definition for UX is issued in ISO 9240-210 (2010). It states that UX is an individual person's perceptions and responses; is related to usage; and includes consequences from both current use and anticipated use of a product, system or service (Law et al., 2009).

It is a continuous process in understanding what is user experience and/or what are its building blocks (components) (Alben, 1996; Hassenzahl & Tractinsky, 2006; McCarthy & Wright, 2004; Roto, 2006a). To clarify the UX in the particular mobile video service, we firstly get through the overall understanding of UX; then analyze the important features of UX, so that we can identify the essential issues in the mobile video field.

2.1 Comparison of general UX frameworks

It is very hard to distinguish a UX definition from a UX framework, because the definition of UX is usually given in the form of describing various aspects involved in the interaction process of generating UX (Alben, 1996; Hassenzahl & Tractinsky, 2006). The UX framework can be presented as either the building blocks of UX (Hassenzahl & Tractinsky, 2006; Roto, 2006a) or the interaction processing structures of UX (McCarthy & Wright, 2004; Norman, 2004). The interaction process involves the people's senses, behaviors and reflections, which are more abstract and more difficult to measure than the building blocks. To compare the UX frameworks, we transpose the interaction processing frameworks into building blocks based on the relations between the producing process of UX and the involved objects. Table 1 shows the comparison results of a group of seven important UX frameworks or definitions in terms of their related building blocks.

The definition of experience given by Alben (1996) indicates seven attributes of experience in user-product interaction (shown in Table 1). The way to feel a product in one's hands refers to the attributes of overall appearance of the product, the user's first perception of it, and the user's physical resources – hands (even if it is too narrow to just talk about the hands). Understanding how the product works and using it involves the attributes of the product's functionality and usability. How well the product to serve people's purpose and to fit into the entire using context involves users' needs and the usage context.

Components	Attributes	Alben (1996)	Forlizzi & Ford (2000)	Arhippainen & Tähti (2003)	Norman (2004) & Orist et al. (2010)	Mc-Carthy & Wright (2004)	Hassenzahl & Tractinsky (2006)	Roto (2006b)
User	Emotion		√	√	√	√	√	√
	Needs	√		√	√	√	√	√
	Prior experiences		√	√	√	√		√
	Perceptions	√	√		√	√		√
	Expectations			√			√	√
	Motivation			√			√	√
	Profile (age, sex, preference, skill/knowledge)		√	√			√	
	Physical resources	√		√				√
Product/ System/ Service	Product appearance or system complexity	√	√	√	√	√	√	√
	Functionality	√	√	√	√	√	√	√
	Usability	√	√	√	√	√	√	√
	Aesthetic quality		√	√	√	√		
	Interactivity		√	√	√	√		
Context	Context of use or physical context	√	√	√		√	√	√
	Social context		√	√	√	√	√	√
	Culture context		√	√				
	Temporal and task context						√	√

Table 1. Comparison of UX frameworks

Forlizzi and Ford (2000) deem that experience is influenced by the components of user-product interaction, including the user's emotions, prior experiences, values and cognitive models and product's features, usability, and aesthetic qualities; and the interaction surroundings, such as a context of use and social, culture and organizational behavior patterns. The user's values and cognitive models are relevant to prior experience or knowledge and personality, and the aesthetic quality of the product is associated with the user's pleasure of using the product. Forlizzi and Ford also highlight the interactivity of the product, meaning that cognition dimension of experience enables the product to offer the user a learning experience.

Similarly, Arhippainen and Tähti (2003) also think that user experience forms in the interaction between user and product in a particular context of use and social and cultural environment, but they separate social, culture and context of use into independent components. They list a good amount of attributes for each component; however, some of these attributes were not recognized in their testing with two mobile application prototypes. This indicates that the attributes affecting user experience are variable in different cases.

Regarding the temporal dimension of UX, Donald Norman (2004) states three levels (visceral, behavioral and reflective level) of interaction. At the visceral level, people have the first impression (i.e., perception) of a product through its appearance and their feelings, e.g., like or dislike, occur spontaneously. At the behavioral level, when people start to use a product, their experience is about how well the product's functions fulfill their needs, and how easily the product can be used. Therefore, this level involves product's functions, usability, and user needs. At the reflective level consciousness takes part in the process; whereby people understand and interpret things, and remember past experiences and may use their current experiences for future actions. The reflection level is relative to the product's interactivity and aesthetic quality, and may also engage the user's prior experience and social context when it affects the user's understandings of the product and its usage for social purposes. Recently, Norman's structure is extended by increasing a pre-experience level prior to the visceral level to indicate people's pre-experiences with similar product/services (Obrist et al., 2010). Prior experience is more important at this level.

Wright and McCarthy's framework (2004) analyses experience with technology, which has four intertwined threads of experience and six sense-making processes. The four threads: "sensual, emotional, spatio-temporal and compositional" represent the visceral character of experience, value judgment ascribed to emotions, place and time effects, and coherent experience, respectively. The sense-making processes are anticipating (expectation associated with prior experience), connecting (immediate and pre-conceptual sense), interpreting (working out what is going on), reflecting (evaluation in the interaction and reflection with feelings), appropriating (making an experience one's own) and recounting (storytelling with others or oneself about the experience). Compared to Norman's framework, this framework emphasizes the effects of physical context and the connections of previous sense with the product.

Hassenzahl and Tractinsky's definition (2006, p. 95) clearly lists attributes for each UX component. The user's internal state includes predispositions, expectations, needs, motivation, mood, etc.; the system has the characteristics of complexity, purpose, usability and functionality; and the context involves physical environment, organisational/social setting, and task context (e.g., meaningfulness of the activity or voluntariness of use). Roto (2006a) has followed the definition and developed UX building blocks which consists of three main components: user, context, and system. Here, "System" is suggested to replace "product" in order to include all involved infrastructures (such as products, objects, and services) in the interaction. Furthermore, based on her study on UX for mobile web browsing, she divides contextual attributes into four categories: physical, social, temporal and task contexts. The physical context refers to physically sensed circumstances and geographical location; social context refers to other people's influence on the user and the user's social contribution goals; temporal context refers to the time available for task execution; and task context refers to the role of the current usage task (which is mobile browsing in her case) related to other tasks (Roto, 2006b).

Concluding the similarity of the above UX frameworks, we can distribute their attributes into three components: user, product/system/service, and context, shown in Table 1. In each component, it can be observed that some attributes are highlighted, such as user's emotions, perceptions and needs, functionality and usability of product or system, and context of use. However, there are a couple of attributes (indicated in blue color in Table 1) are either ambiguous or less mentioned.

Firstly, temporal context and task context are only specified by Roto (2006a). Secondly, while people's visceral or sensual experience has been addressed (McCarthy & Wright, 2004; Norman, 2004), the relevant physical resources and characteristics are not mentioned. In many situations, these should be considered as important. For instance, Roto mentioned that in the mobile context the user may only have one hand for the device (2006a). Also, characteristics of human eyes and ears can affect the user's perception on videos and audios. Thirdly, user's motivations and expectations are also seldom mentioned. A user may be motivated to use a product/service by his/her expectation to achieve a goal, current need, social influences, or physical context limitations; whereas, motivations can not cover user's expectations and needs. The motivation refers to why a user uses an object (i.e., product/service/system); the expectation refers to what the user expects to gain from using the object; and the need refers to how well the requirements are fulfilled by using the object. Fourthly, user profile may contribute to a more personalized product/service. People at different ages or with different genders and preferences often experience the same thing in distinct ways. Compared to prior experience that refers to the previous experience of using a similar product/service, the user's knowledge or skill background covers more wide areas that indirectly associate with the current usage. For example, a person who has a computer science background usually has a deeper understanding to a brand new digital device than others without the background.

It can also be noticed, in Table 1, that when a specific domain is concerned, more detailed attributes are provided. For instance, using the case of mobile web browsing as the example, the temporal context and the task context are proposed (Roto, 2006a); while in the case of evaluating UX with adaptive mobile application prototypes, the user's personal characteristics (e.g., motivations, personalities, prior experience) are obvious (Arhippainen, 2003). These situations indicate that it is necessary to get a deeper insight into all aspects of UX in order to achieve a good user experience of mobile video applications.

2.2 UX Framework for mobile video

User experience of mobile video is generated when users manipulate it by selecting video content to watch, perceiving service and video quality and evaluating them. There are a large number of factors affecting UX of mobile video. Many players on the technology side directly associate with video coding, network transmission, and device and system performance. On the non-technology side, the users' characteristics, service provisioning modes and use contexts are diverse.

Based on the previous research, an overall UX framework for mobile video emerges by allocating all kinds of the influencing factors to a typical mobile video delivery framework, as shown in Figure 1. This structure summarizes and simplifies previous work (Buchinger et al., 2011; Buchinger, Kriglstein, et al., 2009; Jumisko-Pyykkö & Häkkinen, 2005; Knoche, McCarthy & Sasse, 2005; Orgad, 2006), where a huge number of factors influencing UX of mobile video are not well organized; and it also extends previous frameworks (Forlizzi & Ford, 2000; Hassenzahl & Tractinsky, 2006; McCarthy & Wright, 2004; Norman, 2004) to the specific domain of mobile video. In accordance with the generally accepted UX components (shown in Table 1), the proposed structure organizes the influencing factors of UX into three components: USER, SYSTEM and CONTEXT, and maps their impacts upon four elements of the mobile video delivery framework, namely mobile user, mobile device, mobile network, and mobile video service.

The following sections will introduce the factors of each component and the relevant research, some of which provide better understanding of UX of mobile video and others make progress in optimizing UX by utilizing the impacts of the factors on UX.

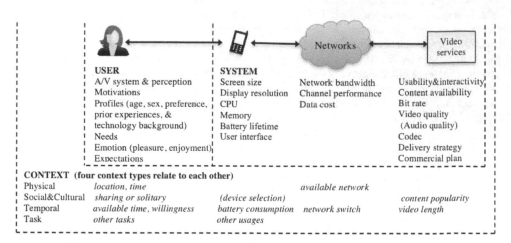

Fig. 1. User experience framework of mobile vide

2.2.1 User

For the mobile user, the factors are human audio-visual system and perception, motivations, user profiles, needs, expectations, and emotions. Mobile video is mainly a visual product, and user's perception of video quality is firstly the result of Human Visual System (HVS) perceiving the video. As a result, the human eyes' features, as physical characteristics, can be utilized to improve user's visual perception. For example, in a resource limited condition (e.g., limited network bandwidth), video coding based on Region-of-Interest (ROI) can increase user perceived video quality by maintaining or enhancing the quality of ROIs, which are detected salient areas in terms of the human eyes' selective sensitivity and visual attention (Buchinger, Nezveda, Robitza, Hummelbrunner & Hlavacs, 2009; Engelke & Zepernick, 2009; Lu et al., 2005). Human auditory system helps the visual system work well, particularly in a situation that the user can not concentrate on the screen of mobile device, e.g., walking, or in a case that the user is viewing a sound-important content such as news and music videos (Jumisko-Pyykkö, Ilvonen & Väänänen-Vainio-Mattila, 2005; Song, Tjondronegoro & Docherty, 2011).

The user profiles consist of several aspects: age, sex, preference for video content type, prior experiences in viewing videos and mobile videos, and technology background (especially in information and computer technology). Although a lot of research has observed the behavior differences of using mobile video (TV) between groups classified by age, gender and technology (Eronen, 2001; Jumisko-Pyykkö, Weitzel & Strohmeier, 2008; Orgad, 2006; Södergård, 2003), the comprehensions in how the differences influence UX is inadequate. For example, are young people (males) easier to satisfy in terms of quality of mobile video service than older people (females)? How does prior experience in viewing videos impact upon current viewing? A few studies have addressed the positive correlation between user's preference (also called interest) for video content and overall user experience (Jumisko-Pyykkö et al., 2005; Song, Tjondronegoro, Wang & Docherty, 2010). Recent studies have found that people's desired quality of mobile video varies with their preferences for video content, viewing experiences of mobile videos, technical backgrounds, and even their genders. There may also be an interactive impact across these aspects of user profiles (Song, Tjondronegoro & Docherty, 2010; Song et al., 2011). For instance, frequent male viewers of mobile video may request a higher quality than occasional viewers. (Song et al., 2011).

Buchinger, Kriglstein and Hlavacs (2009) have summarized a dozen motivations of watching mobile TV. Simplifying those, the major motivations of viewing mobile videos are: consuming time, being entertained, staying up to date (e.g., with news or popular events), sharing with others or isolating oneself from the surrounding.

These user factors do not only work independently. It is very likely that user profiles and motivations are closely bound up with user needs. When mobile video viewing is for killing time on a bus, people may need short videos with fair quality, while when for an entertainment use at home, they might need a good quality video. Expectations have been found to relate to previous experience. E.g., people who often watch high quality video expect a higher quality of mobile videos than those who do not (Song et al., 2011).

Another factor - emotion has been noticed in many UX frameworks. Hassenzahl and Tractinsky (2006) summarized two ways of dealing with emotions in UX: stressing the importance of emotions as consequences of using a product, and using emotions as important evaluative judgments. For example, satisfaction and entertainment were investigated as emotional consequences of task-directed mobile video use (Jumisko-Pyykkö & Hannuksela, 2008), and pleasantness has been found to create affective responses on judgments (e.g., willing to watch in long-term) (Song, Tjondronegoro & Docherty, 2010). Emotions sometimes also mean user's internal state of feelings and moods (e.g., love, sad, happy). However, this kind of personal emotion is secret and its effect on UX has hardly been reported in the mobile video interaction. Therefore, the emotion, in this proposed framework, refers to user's viewing mood, that is, the enjoyment (or pleasantness) of viewing. Song et al. studies (2010; 2011) have shown that the enjoyable or pleasing emotion is not only an important index of positive UX but also a determining factor of user needs for video quality, where users tend to request a much higher quality when their criteria are based on the pleasantness.

2.2.2 System

The component "SYSTEM" is related to the overall performance of the infrastructure of mobile video delivery, and therefore covers three objects from the sender to receiver: video services, networks and mobile devices. For a mobile device, a bigger screen is preferred but reduces its portability (Knoche & McCarthy, 2004; Knoche & Sasse, 2008). A screen with high display resolution can support high quality video playing but cause big consumptions of CPU resource, buffering memory and battery life, which may negatively affect user's usage behavior (Chipchase, Yanqing & Jung, 2006; Kaasinen, Kulju, Kivinen & Oksman, 2009; Knoche & Sasse, 2008). Apart from these factors, user interface of a media player is also an important influence. A good user interface comes from good design of the media player (e.g., interactivity, flexibility and easy to use), but also from effectively utilizing some advance functionalities of the mobile device, e.g., touch screen and gesture recognition (Huber, Steimle & Mühlhäuser, 2010; MacLean, 2008).

Factors in networks are mainly bandwidth, channel features such as jitter, delay and packet loss, and data cost. Narrow bandwidth and poor channel performance will result in a negative UX due to the distortions of video quality caused by the transmission (Bradeanu, Munteanu, Rincu & Geanta, 2006; Ketyko, De Moor, Joseph, Martens & De Marez, 2010; Tasaka, Yoshimi & Hirashima, 2008). The data cost means not only the spent money on using the network, but also how much of a total available data amount has been used. For example, if a user has a free network or he/she has paid for a huge amount of data flow, the user may watch videos quite often and would like to watch high quality videos. In another scenario, when a user knows the data flow is limited (or shared with other people), even though the network is free, the user may be concerned with the data consumption and not use too much. Therefore, user's affordable cost (money or data amount) for video data consumption affects their watching behaviors.

On the video service side, usability and interactivity are two important factors because they are directly associated with the customer's use. Even if the usability and interactivity are reflected in the user interface of a mobile video player, such as content navigation (Buchinger, Kriglstein, et al., 2009), search (Hussain et al., 2008), and easy to play (Carlsson & Walden, 2007), they must be underpinned by the functionality of the video service. The term "functionality" is too narrow to express the connection between video service and the user. Also it is overlapped by the usability and interactivity in mobile video service. Therefore, we choose the term "usability and interactivity" to represent the influence of the service function on UX. Its importance can be shown in at least two aspects. On the one hand, the information for content navigation and searching must be provided by the video service; on the other hand, the user's interaction requirements, e.g., content selection, quality selection, and rating, must be responded to by the service.

Another factor, content availability refers to what and how much video content the video service can provide to users. Abundant and interesting content can meet more users' requirements (Song & Tjondronegoro, 2010). Bit rate of a video affects the user's data cost and the user's perceived video quality. Given a bit rate constraint, the video can be encoded with different parameters by different video coding codecs; and the variations eventually lead to divergent user-perceived video qualities (Ahmad, 2006b; Cranley, Murphy & Perry, 2004; Kun, Richard & Shih-Ping, 2001; Song, Tjondronegoro & Azad, 2010). Audio quality, including the volume, sampling rate, bit rate of the audio, often takes effects with the usage ambient (e.g., noisy or quiet) and the content type (e.g., music videos) together (Jumisko-Pyykkö, Häkkinen & Nyman, 2007). Delivery strategy is about how the video service is delivered to the user. Under different delivery strategies, a user may watch a video in real-time and can access to an arbitrary time point; the user may have to watch a video after it is fully downloaded into the terminal device; or the user may wait for a shorter or longer buffering time before watch. Commercial plan refers to the providing manner of a video service, such as subscription, online free, or pay for individual video. It is suggested that for the success of mobile TV, the right pricing approach should be to give users a choice of various payment options anyway (Trefzger, 2005).

2.2.3 Context

Based on the study on UX of mobile web browsing, Roto (2006a) has classified context into four types: physical, social, temporal and task context. Due to the similarity of the mobile context, we also classify CONTEXT into the four types, but replace the social context with social & cultural context. We relate the roles of the four contexts to the four elements of mobile video delivery system (i.e., users, mobile devices, networks, and video services) based on how their impacts are reflected through these elements.

First of all, the physical context is about where and when a user is using the mobile video. Except from light and noise that will have a direct impact on the user's watching and listening, in mobile environment, changes of the physical context often lead to changes of available networks or network conditions, which may cause a significant variation of UX. For example, shifting from a high-speed Wi-Fi network at home to a low-speed 3G network outside, a user may be unhappy with a longer waiting time to load a video. In addition, during network traffic time, one may have difficulty to watch smooth videos. Secondly, the social context refers to how a user is influenced by others and whether the user joins the influences to others. Its impacts are presented in sharing or solitary use of mobile video, selections of video content, and voting popularity. When solitary viewing or video sharing happens, people are using mobile video to manage relationships with others in shared or public settings. They are trying to either cut off the outside setting or enjoy others' attendance (O'Hara, et al., 2007). In addition, social recommendations highly influence what people watch and how they feel; sometimes, also influence people's options for mobile devices and mobile communication companies. The influences of the culture context itself are not explicit, but contribute to users' viewing habits such as preferred video content and viewing situations (Song & Tjondronegoro, 2010). For example, the study in Belgium (Vangenck, Jacobs, Lievens, Vanhengel & Pierson, 2008) found people tended to use mobile TV at home, while the study in Japan (Miyauchi, Sugahara & Oda, 2008) stated that the main consumption of mobile TV was 'on the go'. In Australia, music video is the most popular content type for mobile video (Song & Tjondronegoro, 2010), which conflicts with the result of "news" in other countries' studies (Chipchase et al., 2006; Mäki, 2005; Södergård, 2003). Since it is hard to draw a clear line between the impacts of social and those of culture, it is better to put them together. Thirdly, the temporal context refers to that given the context restrictions how long the dedicated viewing process will last (i.e., the period that a user immerses into the viewing). The restrictions can be the user's available time (e.g., 5 minutes waiting for a bus), and the user's willingness to watch for a long or short time. Also, the user sometimes has to stop viewing due to a low battery warning; or the user's viewing process can be paused by network switches. The viewing period is also restricted by the duration of a video as well. If the available video is only 2 minutes long, the dedicated viewing will not last over 2 minutes. Fourthly, user's viewing task often runs parallel to other tasks or it is motivated by a higher-level task. For instance, a user's viewing with friends has a higher-level purpose of sharing experience and a parallel task of spending time with friends. While, when the user watches videos on a bus, the higher-level task is to kill time and the parallel task is to take the bus. User's viewing can also be interrupted by other usages of mobile device such as a coming call. A study has found that interrupted viewing such as viewing on a bus will result in a relative lower user perception of a good quality video than relaxed viewing (Song, Tjondronegoro & Docherty, 2010).

In spite of being separated, there are correlations between the four context types. For example, the video sharing behavior often happens in a physical crowd context with a specific task context; different cultures determine the most frequent viewing locations and times (Buchinger, Kriglstein, et al., 2009); a short-time and interrupted viewing often takes place on a bus, accompanying with a higher-level task of taking the bus to the destination (Knoche & McCarthy, 2004).

In the above, we have proposed a UX framework for mobile video and explained each factor in it. It may bring an overall idea of how the UX of mobile video is influenced. Understanding the UX serves a higher-level goal that is to find out a way to optimize the UX under a series of resource constraints of mobile context. Prior to achieve this purpose, there is a central question need to be answered - how to measure the UX? Without measurement of the UX, we are not able to evaluate the holistic system performance in satisfying users and meeting their needs.

3. Measuring Quality of Experience

The term Quality of Experience (QoE), sometimes also known as quality of user experience, has been frequently used to represent the measurement of user experience with a service, especially in web browsing, communication, and TV/video delivery. QoE came after another well-established concept Quality of Service (QoS). QoS is a measure of technological performance, such as network capacity (e.g., throughput, error rate, latency, etc.) and device capabilities and product features (e.g., battery lifetime, video bitrate, frame rate, etc.), but does not deal with user's overall experience. QoE therefore is proposed to involve human dimensions into the measurement of multimedia service performance, together with the objective technical aspects together.

In ITU-T Recommendation of QoE for IPTV service (2007), QoE is defined as overall acceptability of a service/application perceived by a end user; it is influenced by various effects of system (device, network, services infrastructure, etc.), user needs and expectations, and usage context. Wu et al. (2009) proposed a refined definition for QoE based on the study in Distributed Interactive Multimedia Environments (DIME). They defined QoE as *"a multi-dimensional construct of perceptions and behaviors of a user, which represents his/her emotional, cognitive, and behavioral responses, both subjective and objective, while using a system"*. Both the definitions indicate a close relationship between QoE and UX as well as the way to measure QoE. That is, QoE can be evaluated based on the end-users' responses, and it should reflect multi-dimensional effects.

To measure QoE, a great number of QoE metrics for perceived video quality have been developed and used for quality management in mobile video service. However, these metrics are limited in taking into consideration only some influencing factors of user experience. From the overall perspective, a few comprehensive QoE frameworks have been proposed, but it is still extremely challenging to apply these frameworks into a practical use.

3.1 QoE metrics

In terms of the QoE definitions (ITU-T Study Group 12, 2007; Wu et al., 2009), it accentuates how the end-user accepts and perceives the received quality of mobile video. Subjective tests are commonly used to evaluate the perceived video quality. In the tests, the subjects are asked to rate the quality of the presented video sequences that are impaired by controlled conditions, such as (simulated) network and device conditions. The subjective quality assessment is regarded as the most reliable way to assess video quality and the most fundamental methodology for evaluating QoE (Tominaga, hayashi, Okamoto & Takahashi, 2010).

The commonly used subjective testing methodologies are proposed by the ITU-T and ITU-R, including the Absolute Category Rating (ACR), the Degraded Category Rating (DCR) (also called DSIS), the Single Stimulus Continuous Quality Evaluation (SSCQE) and the Double-Stimulus Continuous Quality Scale (DSCQS) (ITU-T P.910 Recommendation,ITU-R Recommendation BT. 500-11:, 2004; 1999). The average ratings obtained from the above assessment methods are called the Mean Opinion Score (MOS), which is in a form of 5/11point scales. A study on performance comparison of these methods for mobile video applications (Tominaga et al., 2010) demonstrates that the ACR and DSIS (or DCR) methods with 5 scales perform better than the others.

Notwithstanding that the scaled assessments are widely used, they are subject to overburden participants, who especially struggle to determine a proper score for the quality of a video (Sasse & Knoche, 2006). Furthermore, they can not sufficiently answer the question: which quality level is acceptable to end users (Schatz, Egger & Platzer, 2011). Binary measure is therefore suggested to use when assessing the acceptability of mobile TV (videos) (Agboma & liotta, 2007; 2008; Knoche et al., 2005; McCarthy, Sasse & Miras, 2004). The idea of acceptability is to identify the lowest acceptable quality level or threshold. A psychological method used to determine threshold is known as the Method of Limits created by Gustav Theodor Fechner (cited in Agboma & liotta, 2007). It is often done through asking participants to simply decide whether or not they accept the quality of a displaying video in successive, discrete steps either in ascending or descending series.

As regard to the relation between the acceptability and the MOS, a little research has been done. One study has proposed a set of mapping formula from MOS scores to acceptability values (de Koning, Veldhoven, Knoche & Kooij, 2007). However, another study did not find a reliable mapping relationship (Jumisko-Pyykkö, Vadakital, et al., 2008). A recent study took this issue into the field of mobile broadband data services and conducted a series of lab and field experiments. It turned out that a consistent mapping between the binary acceptance and the ordinal MOS ratings exists across different applications, such as web browsing and file downloads (Schatz et al., 2011).

Since subjective quality assessment is inconvenient, time-consuming and expensive, objective video quality metrics are then developed to predict the perceived video quality automatically. The objective video quality metrics are commonly considered as the computing models of QoE or objective QoE (oQoE) in (Zinner, Hohlfeld, Abboud & Hossfeld, 2010). The performance of objective QoE metric can be evaluated by comparing the prediction results with the scores obtained from the subjective quality assessments.

According to the availability of the original video sequence, the objective video quality metrics can be classified into full-reference (FR), blind or no-reference (NR) and reduced-reference (RR) metrics (Wang, Sheikh & Bovik, 2004). The FR metric needs a distortion-free reference video and performs the quality assessment by comparing the distortion video with the reference. The NR metric assesses the quality of a distorted video without any reference and assumes the video distortions, e.g., blur and blockiness. The RR metric evaluates a test video based on a series of features extracted previously from the reference videos.

The most widely used FR metrics are mean squared error (MSE) and peak signal-to-noise ratio (PSNR). However, PSNR or MSE is thought unable to represent the exact perceptual quality because it is based on pixel-to-pixel difference calculations, thereby neglecting the effects of viewing conditions and characteristics of the HVS (Masry & Hemami, 2002; Zhenghua & Wu, 2000). To date, many more effective metrics have been developed, such as structural similarity (SSIM) (Wang, Bovik, Sheikh & Simoncelli, 2004), multiscale SSIM (MS-SSIM) (Wang, Simoncelli & Bovik, 2003), video quality metric (VQM) (Pinson & Wolf, 2004), visual information fidelity (VIF) (Sheikh & Bovik, 2006) and motion-based video integrity evaluation (MOVIE) (Seshadrinathan & Bovik, 2010). The performances of these objective video quality metrics has been evaluated by Seshadrinathan et al. (Seshadrinathan, Soundararajan, Bovik & Cormack, 2010) and Chikkerur et al. (Chikkerur, Sundaram, Reisslein & Karam, 2011). The results show that the MS-SSIM, the VQM and the MOVIE metrics outperform than other metrics. However, these metrics seem not to work well for videos playing on mobile devices. According to Eichhorn and Ni (2009), SSIM and VQM perform bad in estimating the scalable video quality on mobile screens. FR metrics are hardly used in many practical video services where the reference video sequences are often inaccessible.

No-reference (NR) metrics estimate QoE though mainly measuring image distortions: blockiness (Leontaris & Reibman, 2005; Saad, Bovik & Charrier, 2010; Zhou, Bovik & Evan, 2000), blur (Marziliano, Dufaux, Winkler & Ebrahimi, 2002; Sadaka, Karam, Ferzli & Abousleman, 2008; Yun-Chung, Jung-Ming, Bailey, Sei-Wang & Shyang-Lih, 2004), and noise (Ghazal, Amer & Ghrayeb, 2007). An overview of existing NR image and video quality estimation studies have been given by Hemai and Reibman (Hemami & Reibman, 2010). These artifactual effects are mostly generated during the process of encoding, decoding and transmission. For example, the blockiness is caused by a block-based video coding such as MPEG-4 and H.264/AVC codec; the blur can be resulted from the spatial scaling and decoding; and the noise may be added due to transmission errors.

Reduced-Reference (RR) metrics are usually developed based on the technical influencing factors of perceptual video quality, such as video coding parameters, video content features and network transmission parameters, which can be known in advance or detected. Therefore, RR metrics have been used in practical QoE predictions or QoE managements. The RR metrics can be further divided into two classes: encoding-parameter-based class and network-parameter-based class.

A well-known encoding-parameter-based model has been given in Recommendation ITU-T G.1070 (2007). In this model, the computing coefficients are determined by codec type, video display format, key frame interval and video display size. Based on this model, a better parametric model is developed, which is able to estimate perceptual MOS values for different codecs (MPEG-4 and H.264/AVC), bitrates and display formats, and video content (distinguished by movement intensity) (Joskowicz & Ardao, 2010). To estimate video quality in mobile video streaming scenarios, two reference-free models have been provided by Ries, Nemethova and Rupp (2008). The first method estimates the video quality using average bitrate and four motion characteristics of the video, while the second model is a content-dependent and low-complexity metric with two objective parameters bitrate and frame rate. However, in the second model, the parameters' coefficients vary with the applied content types such as news, soccer, cartoon, panorama, and the rest, therefore, content classification needs to be performed before using the model.

Many implemented QoE models have considered the important effect of network transmission, which quality can be estimated by QoS measurement. Fielder, Hossfeld and

Tran-Gia (2010) have found that there is a generic exponential relationship between user-perceived QoE and network-caused QoS. Other effects such as video content types and video coding parameters have also been considered together with the network effect. For example, Tasaka, et al. (2008) estimated QoE from the measured application–level QoS. The generated QoE metrics are for three content types: sports, animation, and music, and in the form of nonlinear equations with the indicators of error concealment ratio and MU (which refers to the information unit for transfer between the application layers) loss ratio. Whereas, Bradeanu et al. (2006) used both video coding profiles (based on the encoding bitrate) and network conditions such as transmission error and buffering occurrence to model QoE. While most network-focused QoE metrics were developed under simulated network environment, Ketyko et al. (2010) have focused on measuring the QoE of mobile video streaming under an actual 3G network and real usage context. They conducted subjective assessments under six different usage contexts, including indoor and outdoor at home, at work and on train/bus. Based on the collected data, they modeled a general QoE as a linear function of video packet loss rate, video packet jitter, audio packet jitter, and RSSI (received signal strength indication). This study also found that spatial quality (which is formed by the content, the sound quality, the fit to feeling, and the picture quality) and emotional satisfaction were the most related aspects of the general QoE.

The above QoE metrics are all built using Mean Opinion Score (MOS) as the index. In terms of Schatz et al.'s study (2011), acceptability is a relevant and useful concept for QoE assessment. Agboma and Liotta (2008) have proposed a QoE management methodology with the purpose of maximizing QoE under a constraint network, where binary QoE were employed to predict if a video quality could be acceptable by users. The QoE models were built using statistical discriminant analysis with two parameters video bitrate and frame rate for three different terminals: mobile phone, PDA and laptop. And six content types: news, sports, animation, music, comedy and movie were included in their studies (Agboma & Liotta, 2010). Likewise, another study also focused on acceptable QoE model, but used Machine Learning (ML) classification algorithms to produce more accurate and adaptive QoE predictions, where the spatial and temporal complexity of video content joined the prediction (Menkovski, Oredope, Liotta & Sánchez, 2009).

To sum up, most existing QoE metrics mainly focus on the impacts of network conditions and video encoding on user experience without sufficiently considering other aspects, such as user's personal needs, mobile devices, and context. More comprehensive understandings of QoE are presented in some QoE frameworks.

3.2 QoE frameworks in mobile multimedia

There are a few QoE frameworks in mobile multimedia, which often involve Quality of Service (QoS) into the construction due to the significance of QoS in reflecting the object aspects of multimedia quality.

A taxonomy of QoS and QoE aspects in multimodal human computer interaction have been proposed by Moller et al. (2009). It consists of three layers: 1) QoS influencing factors, which include the characteristics of user, system and context of use, exerting a impact on perceived quality, 2) QoS interaction performance aspects, describing the user and system performance and behavior, and 3) QoE aspects, relating to users' quality perception and judgment. Extending Moeller et al.'s work, Geerts et al. (2010) have presented a QoE framework based on multidisciplinary research to give more detailed insight into different user aspects. The framework combines the technical aspects and the user aspects with use process (i.e., interaction process with a product on a regular basis), and divides context into three levels: the top level is the socio-cultural context, followed by situational context and interactional context. The authors of the above frameworks have also suggested some metrics and methods to measure the aspects, e.g., using psycho-physiological measurement tools and questionnaires to measure user's motions and system usability. However, current measurements focus on either technical aspects or human's emotions and values aspects, but are unable to provide an integrate consideration.

Nokia has suggested two approaches to measure QoE of mobile services: service level approach and network management system approach (Nokia, 2004). Service level approach relies on statistical measurement using a group of QoE KPIs (Key Performance Indicators). Network management system approach maps network QoS performance, which are measured by QoS KPIs, onto user perceptible QoE performance. And the best option would be use both approaches in a complementary way.

Also based on the relation of QoE and QoS parameters, a specific framework for distributed interactive multimedia environments (DIMEs), given by Wu et al. (2009), includes both cognitive perceptions and behavioral consequences of users. The cognitive perceptions consist of flow (enjoyment and concentration), telepresence and technology acceptance (perceived usefulness and perceived ease of use); and the corresponding behavioral consequences contain performance grains, exploratory behaviors, and technology adoption.

A conceptual framework of QoE, proposed by De Moor et al. (2010), attempts to provide multidimensional evaluation of QoE in a mobile, real-life environment, so as to bridge the gap between technical parameters and human experience factors. In the framework, the core component mobile agent, installing on the end-user device, is able to monitor QoS, context and experience by detecting technical parameters (e.g., terminal screen size, battery level, network conditions, content quality, etc.) and contextual entities (e.g., location, mobility, sensors, and other running applications), and gathering feedbacks with questionnaires and other forms. The authors have conducted experiments to evaluate QoE of mobile video streaming in situ. However, so far, they have not offered a conclusion how to use those detected entries evaluate the overall QoE.

The abovementioned frameworks are comprehensive and theoretical; however, more challenging issues, e.g., the mapping relations between various aspects and the real user experience, have to be further considered in real mobile applications. Although these frameworks have been presented in different ways, they all indicate that QoE measurement is a synthetic result of a set of involved factors. Therefore, to improve QoE, in other words, to optimize UX, the effective way is to appropriately deal with all sorts of UX factors.

4. Optimizing user experience of mobile video

For mobile video service, there are many constraints that make user experience optimization become a tough task, such as unstable wireless networks, heterogeneous mobile devices, diverse usage contexts, and complex user needs and preferences. The way to handle the huge variation of resource limitations and at the same time to meet diverse user requirements is generally called adaptation (Chang & Vetro, 2005). In line with the UX framework of mobile video (Figure 1), there are many different adaption strategies that work on different UX factors to optimize UX. We classify them into three categories based on their main focuses: video coding adaptations, video transmission adaptations, and other adaptations. These adaptation strategies can be combined to achieve a better performance.

The video coding adaptations aim to reduce video encoding bitrate at a minimum cost of user-perceived video quality. They directly act on the factors on the side of video services, e.g., objective video quality, bitrate and codec efficiency, video content features, and target on the user factor - visual perception. This kind of adaptation can also benefit other factors of "SYSTEM". For example, low encoding bitrate can easily adapt to the bandwidth limitation and reduce CPU, memory and battery consumptions of the mobile device. There are many relevant studies in this area.

Using a video codec with well performance means efficient video compression and sufficient video quality guarantee. Compared to the video coding standards of MPEG-2, MPEG-4 Simple Profile, H.261 and H.263, H.264/MPEG-4 Part 10 AVC (Wiegand, Sullivan, Bjontegaard & Luthra, 2003) has a higher compression ratio and has gained a landslide victory in subjective perceived quality evaluation (Winkler & Faller, 2005). The performance of H.264/AVC codecs has been improving as new algorithms are developed continually (Guixu, Shibao & Jianling, 2008; Kim & Suh, 2009; Kim, Heo & Ho, 2010). In addition, two extended H.264/AVC-based video coding schemes - H.264/SVC (Scalable Video Coding) and H.264/MDC (Multiple Description Coding) - are becoming available for mobile use (Reguant, Prats, de Pozuelo, Margalef & Ubiergo, 2008), which may bring more benefits in resource saving and good video presentation.

Content-based (content-aware) video adaptation schemes utilize the dependency of user-perceived quality on video content to reduce unnecessary bitrate allocation to the contents, for which a high bitrate does not contribute to a high perceptual video quality. For example, in Chang et al.'s adaptive streaming system (2005), based on the result of semantic video analysis, important segments are displayed as high quality, and non-important segments are replaced by static key frames plus audio or textual captions. Claypool and Tripathi (2004; 2002) have designed a content-aware scaling mechanism based on the subjective phenomena that the temporal continuity is more important for the fast-motion shot, while the image quality is more important for the low-motion shot when reducing bandwidth. This content aware system could improve the perceptual quality of video by as much as 50%. By means of characteristics of content spatial and temporal complexity, Cranley, Perry and Murphy (2006) have developed an optimal adaptation trajectory (OAT) to maximize user-perceived quality by dynamically adjusting encoding configurations.

Considering the impacts of the features of human visual system (HVS) and visual attention, ROI(Region-of-Interest)-based video adaptation can bring better perceptual quality and user experience in a restricted resource condition of mobile video, such as low bitrate and small display size. In Engelke and Zepernick's study (2009), the result from image quality assessment showed that subjects were more sensitive to the image quality distortion in the ROI area than that in the background. According to Muntean et al. (2008), by blurring the background and decreasing its saturation but increasing that of the foreground, better visibility could be achieved on mobile devices; and marginal background changes could reduce the video bitrate. Other studies (Knoche, Papaleo, Sasse & Vanelli-Coralli, 2007;

Song, Tjondronegoro, Wang, et al., 2010) revealed that properly zooming the ROI or enhancing the quality of ROI based on the shot type of video content could efficiently improve the overall UX on a mobile device in a low bitrate condition. The above studies indicate two ways to utilize ROI for the adaptation. One is to allocate more of the limited encoding bits to the important areas than the background (Sun, Ahmad & Zhang, 2006). Many different bit allocation schemes for ROI-based video coding have been presented in (Ahmad, 2006a; Ahmad & Lee, 2008; Liu, Li & Soh, 2008; Lu et al., 2005; Shi, Yue & Yin, 2008; Sun et al., 2006; Yang, Zhang, Ma & Zhao, 2009). The other way is to crop and display the ROI area only on the small screen of a mobile device in order to zoom in the small objects, which has been examined for sports videos (Knoche et al., 2007; Seo & Kim, 2006; Shenghong, Yufu & Shenglong, 2010).

The video transmission adaptations mainly focus on the network transmission factors, which are especially important for mobile networks. A numerous of approaches exist, such as channel adaptive video streaming for reducing latency and package error (Girod, Kalman, Liang & Zhang, 2002), rate-control scheme for achieving good temporal-spatial quality trade-offs (2003), and dynamic congestion scheduling through multi-hop networks (Zhang, 2005). Network-focused approaches can perform better in maximizing the user-perceived quality when involving other factors related to the video content and the video coding parameters. For example, knowing that frame rate is more important for action movie whilst bitrate is for news video in terms of the end-user's perception, an acceptable QoE-aware strategy (Agboma & Liotta, 2008) manages the video quality degradation through decreasing bitrate for action movie and frame rate for news to achieve efficient network utilization. Another QoE-driven scheme (Khan, Sun, Jammeh & Ifeachor, 2010) adapts the video sender bitrate and frame rate based on the video content type and the network package loss ratio. In addition, ROI-based coding can also be combined with network transmission control to improve user-perceived quality. Jerbi, Wang and Shirani (2005) have adopted a non-linear transformation to duplicated ROI macroblocks before encoding, and an inverse non-linear transformation after decoding, in which way a high transmission robustness can be achieved in an error-prone channel. Another approach is to encode the ROI region separately from the background and transmit it with a higher priority to ensure the most important information will not be lost via the error-prone channel (Chen, Song, Yang & Zhang, 2007; Lambert et al., 2006).

Moreover, the video transmission adaptations also depend on the delivery strategy adopted by the video server. Principally, efficient transmission protocols are needed to deliver the big amount of video data. Real-time transport/streaming protocols such as RTP and RTSP used to be the common protocols for video streaming, which allows a client to remotely control (e.g., play and pause) a streaming media server and access to the files on the server. Nowadays, adaptive bitrate streaming techniques based on HTTP (Hypertext Transfer Protocol) become more popular to support large distributed HTTP networks such as the Internet. It requires that multiple bitrate-based qualities of a single video source are encoded, segmented and stored in the server; and a player can dynamically and seamlessly switch between these qualities to match the available resources such as network bandwidth and device capability. Apple Inc. has employed HTTP Live Streaming technology for streaming media to Apple products (e.g., iPhone, iPad and Mac) or HTML5-based website (Apple Inc., 2011). Microsoft's Smooth Streaming (IIS, 2011) and Adobe's Flash Player (Adobe Systems, 2011) have also supported the HTTP-based streaming solution. Other strategies are also proved to be helpful in improving user's viewing experience. For instance, to avoid people waiting for too long to get the first glance of a video, a short and very low start (i.e., low bitrate for the first part of a video) is a good way to shorten the beginning buffering time (Buchinger & Hlavacs, 2008). To reduce the delay between mobile TV channel switches, one solution is to play preloaded video clips, such as short commercial clips and useful information guides (Robitza, Buchinger, Hummelbrunner & Hlavacs, 2010).

Though the understandings of other UX factors such as context and user profiles are limited, there are still some adaptation schemes attempted to tackle these factors. For example, an acceptance threshold adaptive strategy determines the lowest acceptable bitrate and the corresponding encoding parameters based on video content type and user information, including prior experience of mobile video, preference for video content, and age group (Song, Tjondronegoro & Docherty, 2010). Different real usage contexts (Ketyko et al., 2010; Song, Tjondronegoro & Docherty, 2010) and different mobile devices (Agboma & Liotta, 2010) have also been considered when establishing QoE models. Using an emotional index (e.g., satisfaction and pleasantness) to control the video delivery may provide more user-friendly service (Ketyko et al., 2010; Song et al., 2011).

Apart from the above adaptation strategies that deal with the resource limits, there are some non-adaptation strategies to improve UX through exercising control on the factors like commercial plan, user interface, and social context. For charged mobile video services such as Mobile TV, the right pricing approach should be to give users a choice of various payment options anyway according to Trefzger (2005). The options can be a fixed monthly fee model, single content payment, time-based payment, or event-based payment (Buchinger, Kriglstein, et al., 2009; Carlsson, Carlsson, Puhakainen & Walden, 2006; Carlsson & Walden, 2007). Free mode financed by ads may also attract users (The Nielsen Company, 2011; Winder, 2001). Regarding the improvement of usability and interactivity, most current studies focus on effective user interface design, such as content navigation (Jumisko-Pyykkö, Weitzel, et al., 2008), searching (Hussain et al., 2008), and new technology utilization of mobile devices (MacLean, 2008). Huber et al. (2010) have evaluated seven interface concepts for mobile video browsing, including GUI-based, touch-gesture based, and physical interaction; and then derived some design guidelines to improve the usability and user perception of mobile video browsers. The guides include supporting spatio-temporal browsing metaphors and discrete temporal navigation, and carefully placing interface elements. Schatz and Egger (2008) have found that social features could enrich the mobile video experience; they have suggested to use more and flexible interaction means (e.g., audio, text, non-verbal - thumbs up/down display, shaking, and squeezing, etc.) for social mobile video service to address the diverse influences on ratings and user attitudes, and to remove barriers in mobile social activity. Furthermore, allowing users to edit, upload and share user-created contents can provide excellent interactive experience for mobile video users (Orgad, 2006).

Given the truth that user experience is the consequence of interaction of all variety of factors in the entire delivery process, comprehensive considerations of the source, the network environment and the end user is expected to bring great benefits in improving the QoE of the service. However, only a little research has aimed to enable holistic QoE measurement and modeling, but is still at a conceptual stage (De Moor et al., 2010). In conclusion, due to great difficulties in thoroughly understanding UX and implementing complicated adaptations, it is still a grant challenge to achieve optimal UX for mobile video services.

5. Conclusion

With the increase in demand for mobile video, user experience (UX) of mobile video has attracted a lot of attention from both video service providers and researchers. This chapter aimed to provide a better understanding of UX of mobile video by describing three issues: framework, measurement and optimization. We firstly reviewed a body of well-known research on UX and generalized their similarities and differences. Drawing from these studies and combining the concluded UX attributes with the influencing factors of mobile video, we then proposed a UX framework for mobile video and further elucidated the factors with rich literature. The framework is simple but encompasses many factors and clears each factor's contribution to the overall UX. It may benefit in user-centred design of mobile video delivery and relative research. Mobile video vendors may develop effective strategies to improve UX by taking into consideration the factors in different components of the framework. Researchers may use the framework to determine research direction and target (e.g., what will be focused, a single part technical improvement or a holistic understanding?), or to design a proper user study scheme (e.g., what aspects will be investigated? what kind of participants and contexts should be involved?).

To measure user experience, Quality of Experience (QoE) is commonly used in multimedia service. We reviewed many existing QoE metrics that provide predictions of the perceptual video quality, and introduced some QoE frameworks that provide comprehensive considerations of QoE. In line with the proposed UX framework of mobile video, we summarized the methods to optimize UX into adaptation strategies (such as video coding adaptations, video transmission adaptations and other adaptations) and non-adaptation strategies.

Concluding the research in UX measurement and optimization, there are some open issues needing further study. Firstly, in user-centered research, empirical and field studies are needed to collect natural and real user data, which can represent a more realistic UX. To reduce the study cost, a living lab testbed, like that proposed by De Moor et al. (2010), may bring many benefits for future research. Secondly, to achieve a good prediction of the quality of UX, accurate QoE models need take more UX aspects into consideration. However, how to determine the key aspects of UX and how to choose proper indicators to represent them is difficult. It is more challenging to find out the correlations between these factors. Thirdly, some influencing factors of UX have not been sufficiently studied, such as user profiles and context. Also, how to utilize or adapt to the impacts of these factors for UX optimization is still a big question. Overall, automatic adaptation strategies can take care of general user's requirements. However, the automatic adaptation may not always be optimal in terms of individual user's QoE. It was argued that automatic adaptation may benefit from manual adjustments by the user in some cases, such as incomplete usage environment information; incomplete content characteristics; interest of the user in a specific content; limit of user's mobile data contract; and the viewing environment of the user (Murillo, Ransburg & Graciá, 2010).

6. References

Adobe Systems (September 2011). HTTP Dynamic Streaming, In: *Adobe*, 2.09.2011. Avaialable from http://www.adobe.com/products/httpdynamicstreaming/

Agboma, F., & liotta, A. (2007). Addressing User Expectations in Mobile Content Delivery *Mobile Information Systems*, Vol.3, No.4, (October 2007), pp. 153-164, ISSN 1574-017x

Agboma, F., & Liotta, A. (2008). QoE-aware QoS Management, *Proceedings of 6th International Conference on Advances in Mobile Computing and Multimedia*, pp. 111-116, Linz, Austria, November 24-26, 2008

Agboma, F., & Liotta, A. (2010). Quality of Experience Management in Mobile Content Delivery Systems. *Telecommunication Systems*, pp. 1-14, ISSN 1018-4864

Ahmad, A. M. A. (2006a). Content and Resources Based Mobile and Wireless Video Transcoding. *Proceedings of WASET'06 World Academy of Science, Engineering and Technology*, pp. 49-54, November, 2006

Ahmad, A. M. A. (2006b). Content-based Video Streaming Approaches and Challenges. In: *Handbook of Research on Mobile Multimedia*, I. K. Ibrahim (Ed.), pp. 357-367, Idea Group Reference, London, UK

Ahmad, A. M. A., & Lee, S.-Y. (2008). Fast and Robust Object-extraction Framework for Object-based Streaming System. *International Journal of Virtual Technology and Multimedia*, Vol.1, No.1, (Feburary 2008), pp. 39-60, ISSN 1741-1874

Alben, L. (1996). Quality of Experience. *Interactions*, Vol.3, No.3, (May 1996), pp. 11-15, ISSN 1072-5520

Apple Inc. (September 2011). HTTP Live Streaming, In: *Apple Inc.*, 2.09.2011, Available from http://tools.ietf.org/html/draft-pantos-http-live-streaming-06

Arhippainen, L., Tähti, M. (2003). Empirical Evaluation of User Experience in Two Adaptive Mobile Application Prototypes. *Proceedings of 2nd International Conference on Mobile and Ubiquitous Multimedia*. pp. 27-34, Norrköping, Sweden

Bradeanu, O., Munteanu, D., Rincu, I., & Geanta, F. (2006). Mobile Multimedia End-user Quality of Experience Modeling. *Proceedings of International Conference on Digital Telecommunications, ICDT '06*, pp. 49-52, Cap Esterel, Cote d'Azur, France

Buchinger, S., & Hlavacs, H. (2008). A Low Start for Mobile Video Patching. *Proceedings of Euro FGI IA.7.6 Workshop on Socio-Economoic Aspects of Future Generation*, Karlskrona, Sweden

Buchinger, S., Kriglstein, S., Brandt, S., & Hlavacs, H. (2011). A Survey on User Studies and Technical Aspects of Mobile Multimedia Applications. *Entertainment Computing, In Press*, ISSN 1875-9521

Buchinger, S., Kriglstein, S., & Hlavacs, H. (2009). A Comprehensive View on User Studies: Survey and Open Issues for Mobile TV. *Proceedings of 7th European Conference on Interactive Television*. pp. 179-188, Leuven, Belgium

Buchinger, S., Nezveda, M., Robitza, W., Hummelbrunner, P., & Hlavacs, H. (2009). Mobile TV Coding, *Proceedings of Workshop on IPTV Technology and Multidisciplinary Application*. Zagreb, Croatia.

Carlsson, C., Carlsson, J., Puhakainen, J., & Walden, P. (2006). Nice Mobile Services do not Fly: Observations of Mobile Services and the Finnish Consumers. *Proceedings of 19th Bled eCommerce Conference*, Bled, Slovenia

Carlsson, C., & Walden, P. (2007). Mobile TV-to Live or Die by content, *Proceedings of 40th Annual Hawaii International Conference on System Sciences (HICSS)*, pp. 51-57

Chang, S.-F., & Vetro, A. (2005). Video adapation: Concepts, Technologies, and Open Isses. *Proceedings of The IEEE*, Vol.93, No.1, (27 June 2005), pp. 148-158, ISSN 0018-9219

Chen, Q., Song, L., Yang, X., & Zhang, W. (2007). Robust Region-of-Interest Scalable Coding with Leaky Prediction in H.264/AVC, *2007 IEEE Workshop on Signal Processing Systems*, pp. 357-362

Chikkerur, S., Sundaram, V., Reisslein, M., & Karam, L. J. (2011). Objective Video Quality Assessment Methods: A Classification, Review, and Performance Comparison. *IEEE Transactions on Broadcasting*, Vol.57, No.2, (June 2011), pp. 165-182, ISSN 0018-9316

Chipchase, J., Yanqing, C., & Jung, Y. (2006). Personal Television: A Qualitative Study of Mobile TV Users in South Korea, *Proceedings of Mobile HCI 2006*, Espoo, Finland

Claypool, M., & Tripathi, A. (2004). Adaptive Video Streaming Using Content-aware Media Scaling, (Janurary 7, 2004), pp. 20, Worcester, Massachusetts, USA: Worcester Polytechnic Institute

Cranley, N., Murphy, L., & Perry, P. (2004). Content-based Adaptation of Streamed Multimedia, *Proceedings of 7th International Conference on Management of Multimedia Networks and Services*. pp. 39-49, ISSN 0302-9743, San Diego, CA, Oct 03-06, 2004

Cranley, N., Perry, P., & Murphy, L. (2006). Dynamic Content-based Adaptation of Streamed Multimedia. *Journal of Network and Computer Applications*, Vol.30, No.3, pp. 983-1006, ISSN 1084-8043

de Koning, T. C. M., Veldhoven, P., Knoche, H., & Kooij, R. E. (2007). Of MOS and Men: Bridging the Gap between Objective and Subjective Quality Measurements in Mobile TV. *Proceedings of Multimedia on Mobile Devices 2007, IS&T/SPIE Symposium on Electronic Imaging*, San Jose, CA, USA, 28 Janurary 2007

De Moor, K., Ketyko, I., Joseph, W., Deryckere, T., De Marez, L., Martens, L., et al. (2010). Proposed Framework for Evaluating Quality of Experience in a Mobile, Testbed-oriented Living Lab Setting. *Mobile Networks and Applications*, Vol.15, No.3, (29 January 2010), pp. 378-391, ISSN 1383-469x

Eichhorn, A., & Ni, P. (2009). Pick Your Layers Wisely - A Quality Assessment of H.264 Scalable Video Coding for Mobile Devices. *Proceedings of IEEE International Conference on Communications*, pp.1019-1025, ISBN 978-1-4244-3435, June 14-18, 2009

Engelke, U., & Zepernick, H.-J. (2009). Optimal Region-Of-Interest Based Visual Quality Assessment. *Proceedings of Human Vision and Electronic Imaging XIV*, Vol.7240, No. 11, (Janurary 2009), pp. 1-12,

Eronen, L. (2001). Combining quantitative and qualitative data in user research on digital television. *Proceedings of 1st Panhallenic Conference PC HCI'01*. pp. 51-56, Patras, Greece, December 7-9, 2001

Fiedler, M., Hossfeld, T., & Tran-Gia, P. (2010). A Generic Quantitative Relationship between Quality of Experience and Quality of Service. *IEEE Network: The Magazine of Global Internetworking - Special issue on improving quality of experience for network services*, Vol.24, No.2, (March/April 2010), pp. 36-41, ISSN 0890-8044

Forlizzi, J., & Ford, S. (2000). The Building Blocks of Experience: An Early Framework for Interaction Designer. *Proceedings of Dis 2000*, pp. 419-423, ISBN 1-58113-219-0, Brooklyn, New York, n. d.

Geerts, D., De Moor, K., Ketyko, I., Jacobs, A., Van den Bergh, J., Joseph, W., et al. (2010). Linking an Integrated Framework with Appropriate Methods for Measuring QoE. *Proceedings of second International Workshop on Quality of Multimedia Experience (QoMEX 2010)*, pp. 158-163, Trondheim, Norway, June 21-23, 2010

Ghazal, M., Amer, A., & Ghrayeb, A. (2007). A Real-Time Technique for Spatio-Temporal Video Noise Estimation.*IEEE Transactions on Circuits and Systems for Video Technology*, Vol.17, No.12, (December 2007), pp. 1690-1699, ISSN 1051-8215

Girod, B., Kalman, M., Liang, Y. J., & Zhang, R. (2002). Advances in Channel-adaptive Video Streaming. *Proceedings of International Conference on Image Processing*, pp. I9-12, ISSN 1522-4880, Rochester, New York, USA, 22-25 September, 2002

Guixu, L., Shibao, Z., & Jianling, H. (2008). A Two-stage ρ-domain Rate control Scheme for H.264 Encoder. *Proceedings of 2008 IEEE International Conference on Multimedia and Expo*, pp. 713-716, ISBN 978-1-4244-2570-9, Hannover, Germany , June 23-26, 2008

Hassenzahl, M., & Tractinsky, N. (2006). User Experience - A Research Agenda. *Behaviour & Information Technology*, Vol.25, No.2, (March-April 2006), pp. 91-97, ISSN 0144-929x

Hemami, S. S., & Reibman, A. R. (2010). No-reference Image and Video Quality Estimation: Applications and Human-motivated Design. *Signal processing: Image communication*, Vol.25, No.27, (2010), pp. 469-481, ISSN 0923-5965

Huber, J., Steimle, J., & Mühlhäuser, M. (2010). Toward More Efficient User Interfaces for Mobile Video Browsing: An In-depth Exploration of the Design Space. *Proceedings of 16th international conference on Multimedia (ACM MM'10)*, pp. 341-350, Firenze, Italy, October 25-29, 2010

Hussain, Z., Lechner, M., Milchrahm, H., Shahzad, S., Slany, W., Umgeher, M., et al. (2008). User Interface Design for a Mobile Multimedia Application: An Iterative Approach. *Proceedings of International Conference on Advances in Computer-Human Interaction - ACHI'08*, pp. 189-194, Sainte Luce, Martinique, February 10-15, 2008

IIS (2011). Smooth Streaming. In: *ISS.net*, 2.09.2011, Available from
http://www.iis.net/download/SmoothStreaming

ISO (2010). Ergonomics of Human-system Interaction -- Part 210: Human-centred Design for Interactive Systems, *9241-210: 2010*. In: *International Organization for Standardization (ISO)*, Switzerland

ITU-R Recommendation BT. 500-11: (2004). Methodology for the Subjective Assessment of Quality for Television Pictures. In: *International Telecommunication Union*

ITU-T (1999). Subjective Video Quality Assessment Methods for Multimedia Applications. In: *International Telecommunication Union*

ITU-T (2007). Quality of Service and Performance – Generic and User-related Aspects: Opinion Model for Video-telephony Applications (ITU-T   Recommendation G.1070). In: *International Telecommunication Union*

ITU-T Study Group 12 (2007). Definition of quality of experience, *Reference: TD 109rev2 (PLEN/12)*. In: *International Telecommunication Union*

Jerbi, A., Wang, J., & Shirani, S. (2005). Error-resilient region-of-interest video coding. *IEEE Transactions on Circuits and Systems for Video Technology*, Vol.15, No.9, (September 2005) pp. 1175-1181, ISSN 1051-8215

Jordan, P. W. (2002). *Designing Pleasurable Products: An Introduction to the New Human Factors*. Taylor & Francis, ISBN 0-203-30568-X, London, English

Joskowicz, J., & Ardao, J. C. L. (2010). A Parametric Model for Perceptual Video Quality Estimation. *Telecommunication System*, Vol.46, (June 2010), pp. 14, ISSN 1018-4864

Jumisko-Pyykkö, S., & Häkkinen, J. (2005). Evaluation of Subjective Video Quality on Mobile Devices. *Proceedings of 13th ACM International Conference on Multimedia*. pp. 535-538, Singapore, 6-12 November, 2005

Jumisko-Pyykkö, S., Häkkinen, J., & Nyman, G. (2007). Experienced Quality Factors-Qualitative Evaluation Approach to Audiovisual Quality. *Proceedings of SPIE Multimedia on Mobile Devices*

Jumisko-Pyykkö, S., & Hannuksela, M. M. (2008). Does Context Matter in Quality Evaluation of Mobile Television? *Proceedings of 10th International Conference on Human Computer Interaction with Mobile Devices and Services*. pp. 63-72, ISBN 978-1-59593-952-4, Amsterdam, The Netherlands, September 2–5, 2008

Jumisko-Pyykkö, S., Ilvonen, V. P., & Väänänen-Vainio-Mattila, K. A. (2005). Effect of TV Content in Subjective Assessment of Video Quality on Mobile Devices. *Proceedings of Multimedia on Mobile Devices*. pp. 243-254, San Jose CA, 17-18 January 2005

Jumisko-Pyykkö, S., Vadakital, V. K. M., & Hannuksela, M. M. (2008). Acceptance Threshold: A Bidimensional Research Method for User-oriented Quality Evaluation Studies. *International Journal of Digital Multimedia Broadcasting*, Vol.2008, pp. 20, ISSN 1687-7578

Jumisko-Pyykkö, S., Weitzel, M., & Strohmeier, D. (2008). Designing for User Experience: What to Expect from Mobile 3D TV and Video? *Proceedings of 1st International Conference on Designing Interactive User Experiences for TV and Video*, pp. 183-192, ISBN 978-1-60558-100-2, Silicon Valley, California, USA, October 22–24, 2008

Kaasinen, E., Kulju, M., Kivinen, T., & Oksman, V. (2009). User Acceptance of Mobile TV Services. *Proceedings of Mobile HCI 09*. pp. 1-10, ISBN 978-1-60558-281-8, Bonn, Germany, September 15 - 18, 2009

Ketyko, I. n., De Moor, K., Joseph, W., Martens, L., & De Marez, L. (2010). Performing QoE-Measurements in an Actual 3G Network. *Proceedings of 2010 IEEE International Symposium on Broadband Multimedia Systems and Broadcasting (BMSB)* pp. 1-6. Shanghai, China, March 24-26, 2010

Khan, A., Sun, L., Jammeh, E., & Ifeachor, E. (2010). Quality of Experience-driven Adaptation Scheme for Video Applications over Wireless Networks. *IET Communications*, Vol.4, No.11, (July 2006), pp. 1337-1347, ISSN 1751-8628

Kim, J.-G., & Suh, J.-W. (2009). An Efficient MB Layer Rate Control for H.264/AVC Based on Adaptive QP Decision. *Proceedings of Advances in Multimedia Information Processing-PCM 2009*, pp. 1058-1067 ISBN 978-3-642-10466-4 Bangkok, Tailand, December 15-18, 2009

Kim, S.-H., Heo, J., & Ho, Y.-S. (2010). Efficient Entropy Coding Scheme for H.264/AVC Lossless Video Coding. *Signal Processing: Image Communication* Vol.25, No.9, (October 2010), pp. 687-696

Knoche, H., & McCarthy, J. D. (2004). Mobile Users' Needs and Expectations of Future Multimedia Services. *Proceedings of Wireless World Research Forum (WWRF)12.* pp. 1-8, Toronto, Canada, n.d.

Knoche, H., McCarthy, J. D., & Sasse, M. A. (2005). Can Small be Beautiful?: Assessing Image Resolution Requirements for Mobile TV. *Proceedings of 13th annual ACM international conference on Multimedia.* pp.829-838, ISBN 1-59593-044-2, Hilton, Singapore, November 6–11, 2005

Knoche, H., Papaleo, M., Sasse, M. A., & Vanelli-Coralli, A. (2007). The Kindest Cut: Enhancing the User Experience of Mobile TV through Adequate Zooming. *Proceedings of 15th international conference on Multimedia.* pp. 87-96, ISBN 978-1-59593-701-8, Augsburg, Bavaria, Germany, September 23–28, 2007

Knoche, H., & Sasse, M. A. (2008). Getting the Big Picture on Small Screens: Quality of Experience in Mobile TV. In: *Multimedia Transcoding in Mobile and Wireless Networks,* A. M. A. Ahmad & I. K. Ibrahim (Eds.), pp. 31-46, Information Science Reference, ISBN 1-59904-984-8, New York, USA

Kun, T., Richard, R., & Shih-Ping, L. (2001). Content-sensitive Video Streaming over Low Bitrate and Lossy Wireless Network. *Proceedings of 9th ACM international conference on Multimedia.* pp. 512-515, ISBN 1-58113-394-4, Ottawa, Canada, September 30 - October 5, 2001

Lambert, P., Schrijver, D. D., Deursen, D. V., Neve, W. D., Dhondt, Y., Walle, R. V. d. (2006). A Real-time Content Adaptation Framework for Exploiting ROI Scalability in H.264/AVC, *Proccedings of 8th International Conference of Advanced Concepts for Intelligent Vision Systems,* pp. 442-453, Antwerp, Belgium, September 18-21, 2006

Law, E. L.-C., Roto, V., Hassenzahl, M., Vermeeren, A. P. O. S., & Kort, J. (2009). Understanding, Scoping and Defining User Experience: A Survey Approach. *Proceedings of 27th international conference on Human factors in computing systems.* pp. 719-728, ISBN 978-1-60558-246-7, Boston, MA, USA, April 4-9, 2009

Leontaris, A., & Reibman, A. (2005). Comparison of Blocking and Blurring Metrics for Video Compression. *Proceedings of IEEE International Conference on Acoustics, Speech and Signal Processing (ICASSP'05),* pp. 585-589, ISSN 1520-6149, Philadelphia, USA, 23-23 March 2005

Liu, S., & Kuo, C. C. J. (2003). Joint Temporal-spatial Rate Control for Adaptive Video Transcoding. *Proceedings of 2003 International Conference on Multimedia and Expo, ICME '03,* pp. II-225-228, ISBN 0-7803-7965-9, July 6-9, 2003

Liu, Y., Li, Z. G., & Soh, Y. C. (2008). Region-of-Interest Based Resource Allocation for Conversational Video Communication of H.264/AVC. *IEEE Transaction on Circuits and Systems for Video Technology,* Vol.18, No.1, (January 2008), pp. 134-139, ISSN 1051-8215

Lu, Z., Lin, W., Li, Z., Lim, K. P., Lin, X., Rahardija, S., et al. (2005). Perceptual Region-of-interest (ROI) Based Scalable Video Coding, In: *Joint Video Team (JVT) of ISO/IEC 15th meeting,* pp. 16-22, Busan, KR, 16-22 April, 2005

MacLean, K. E. (2008). Using Haptics for Mobile Information Display, *Proceedings of Pervasive Mobile Interaction Devices (PERMID'08), Workshop at 6th International Conference on Pervasive Computing*, pp. 175-179, Sydney, Australia, May 19, 2008

Mäki, J. (2005). Finnish Mobile TV Pilot, In: *Research International Finland*, Augst 2005.

Marziliano, P., Dufaux, F., Winkler, S., & Ebrahimi, T. (2002). A No-reference Perceptual Blur Metric. *Proceedings of 2002 International Conference on Image Process*, pp. 57-60, ISSN 1522-4880, Rochester, New York, USA, September 22-25, 2002

Masry, M., & Hemami, S. S. (2002). Perceived Quality Metrics for Low Bit Rate Compressed Video. *Proceedings of 2002 International Conference on Image Processing*. pp. 49-52, ISSN 1522-4880, Rochester, New York, USA, September 22-25, 2002

McCarthy, J., & Wright, P. (2004). *Technology as experience*. MIT Press, Cambridge MA.

McCarthy, J. D., Sasse, M. A., & Miras, D. (2004). Sharp or Smooth?: Comparing the Effects of Quantization vs. Frame Rate for Streamed Video. *Proceedings of SIGCHI Conference on Human Factors in Computing Systems*. pp. 535-542, ISBN 1-58113-702-8, Vienna, Austria, April 24–29, 2004

Menkovski, V., Oredope, A., Liotta, A., & Sánchez, A. C. (2009). Predicting Quality of Experience in Multimedia Streaming. *Proceedings of the 7th International Conference on Advances in Mobile Computing and Multimedia*. pp. 52-59, ISBN 978-1-60558-659-5, Kuala Lumpur, Malaysia, December 14–16, 2009

Miyauchi, K., Sugahara, T., & Oda, H. (2008). Relax or Study?: A Qualitative User Study on the Usage of Mobile TV and Video. *Proceedings of the 6th EuroITV*, pp. 128-132, ISBN 978-3-540-69478-6, Salzburg, Austria, July 3-4, 2008

Moller, S., Engelbrecht, K. P., Kuhnel, C., Wechsung, I., & Weiss, B. (2009). A taxonomy of Quality of Service and Quality of Experience of Multimodal Human-machine Interaction. *Proccedings of International Workshop on Quality of Multimedia Experience, (QoMEx 2009)*, pp. 7-12, Trondheim, Norway, 29-31 July 2009

Muntean, G. M., Ghincea, G., & Sheehan, T. N. (2008). Region of Interest-based Adaptive Multimedia Streaming Scheme. *IEEE Transactions on Broadcasting*, Vol.54, No.2, (June 2008) pp. 296-303, ISSN 0018-9316

Murillo, J. O., Ransburg, M., & Graciá, E. M. (2010). Towards User-driven Adaptation of H.264/SVC Streams. *Proceedings of EuroITV2010*. ISBN 978-1-60558-31-5, Tampere, Finland, June 9-11, 2010

Nokia (2004). Quality of Experience (QoE) of Mobile Services: Can It be Measured and Improved? In: Nokia, 30.08.2009, Available from www.nokia.com/NOKIA_COM_1/Operators/Downloads/Nokia_Services/white paper_qoe_net.pdf

Norman, D. A. (2004). *Emotional Design: Why We Love (Or Hate) Everyday Things*. Basic Book, New York

Obrist, M., Meschtscherjakov, A., & Tscheligi, M. (2010). User Experience Evaluation in the Mobile Context. In: *Mobile TV: Customizing Content and Experience*, A. Marcus et al. (Ed.), pp. 195-204, ISBN 978-1-84882-701-1, Springer-Verlag, London, UK

Orgad, S. (2006). This Box was Made for Walking, In: *Department of Media and Communications, London School of Economics and Political Science*.

Pinson, M. H., & Wolf, S. (2004). A New Standardized Method for Objectively Measuring Video Quality. *IEEE Transactions on Broadcasting,* Vol.50, No.3, (September 2004), pp. 312-322, ISSN 0018-9316

Reguant, V. D., Prats, F. E., de Pozuelo, R. M., Margalef, F. P., & Ubiergo, G. F. (2008). Delivery of H264 SVC/MDC Streams over WiMAX and DVB-T Networks. *ISCE 2008. IEEE International Symposium on Consumer Electronics,* pp. 1-4, ISBN 978-1-4244-2422-1, April 14-16, 2008

Ries, M., Nemethova, O., & Rupp, M. (2008). Video Quality Estimation for Mobile H.264/AVC Video Streaming. *Journal of Communications,* Vol.3, No.1, (Juanuary 2008), pp. 41-50, ISSN 1796-2021

Robitza, W., Buchinger, S., Hummelbrunner, P., & Hlavacs, H. (2010). Acceptance of Mobile TV Channel Switching Delays. *Proceedings of Workshop on Quality of Multimedia Experience.* pp. 236-241, Trondheim, Norway, June 21-23, 2010

Roto, V. (2006a). User Experience Building Block. *Proceedings of NordiCHI'06.* pp. 1-4, Oslo, Norway, October 14-18, 2006

Roto, V. (2006b). *Web Browsing on Mobile Phones - Characteristics of User Experience.* Unpublished Doctoral Dissertation, Helsinki University of Technology, Finland.

Saad, M. A., Bovik, A. C., & Charrier, C. (2010). A DCT Statistics-Based Blind Image Quality Index. *IEEE Signal Processing Letters,* Vol.17, No.6, (June 2010), pp. 583-586, ISSN 1070-9908

Sadaka, N. G., Karam, L. J., Ferzli, R., & Abousleman, G. P. (2008). A No-reference Perceptual Image Sharpness Metric based on Saliency-weighted Foveal Pooling, *Proceedings of 15th IEEE International Conference on Image Processing.* pp. 369-372, ISSN 1522-4880, San Francisco, California, USA, October 12-15, 2008

Sasse, M. A., & Knoche, H. (2006). Quality in Context-an Ecological Approach to assessing QoS for mobile TV. *Proceedings of 2nd ISCA/DEGA Tutorial & Research Workshop on Perceptual Quality of System.* Berlin, Germany, September 3-5, 2006

Schatz, R., & Egger, S. (2008). Social Interaction Features for Mobile TV Services. *Proceedings of 2008 IEEE International Symposium on Broadband Multimedia Systems and Broadcasting.* pp. 1-6, Las Vegas, NV, USA, March 31 - April 2 2008

Schatz, R., Egger, S., & Platzer, A. (2011). Poor, Good Enough or Even Better? Bridging the Gap between Acceptability and QoE of Mobile Broadband Data Services. *Proceedings of IEEE International Conference on Communications ICC 2011.* pp. 1-6, ISBN 978-1-61284-232-5, Kyoto, Japan, 5-9 June 2011

Seo, K., & Kim, C. (2006). A Context-aware Video Display Scheme for Mobile Devices *Proceedings of Multimedia on Mobile Devices II.* pp. 278-287, San Jose, CA, USA

Seshadrinathan, K., & Bovik, A. C. (2010). Motion Tuned Spatio-temporal Quality Assessment of Natural Videos. *IEEE transactions on image processing,* Vol.19, No.2, (February 2010), pp. 335-350, ISSN 1057-7149

Seshadrinathan, K., Soundararajan, R., Bovik, A. C., & Cormack, L. K. (2010). Study of Subjective and Objective Quality Assessment of Video. *IEEE Transaction on Image Processing,* Vol.19, No.6, (June 2010), pp. 1427-1441, ISSN 1057-7149

Sheikh, H. R., & Bovik, A. C. (2006). Image Information and Visual Quality, *IEEE Transactions on Image Processing,* Vol.15, No.2, (Februray 2006), pp. 430-444, ISSN 1057-7149

Shenghong, H., Yufu, J., & Shenglong, T. (2010). Content Aware Retargeting of Soccer Video, *Proceedings of 2010 International Conference on Information Science and Engineering (ICISE),* pp. 1-4, ISBN 978-1-4244- 7618-3, Hangzhou, China, December 4-6, 2010

Shi, Y., Yue, S., & Yin, B. (2008). A Novel Rate Control Scheme with Region-of-Interest Concern, *Proceedings of the 5th International Conference on Visual Information Engineering, VIE 2008,* pp. 634-637, ISSN 0537-9989, July 29-Auguset 1, 2008.

Södergård, C. (2003). Mobile Television-technology and User Experiences, In: *Report on the Mobile-TV project. VTT, Finland,* VTT Information Technology.

Song, W., & Tjondronegoro, D. (2010). A Survey on Usage of Mobile Video in Australia, *Proceedings of OZCHI 2010.* pp. 5-8, ISBN 978-1-4503-0502-0, Brisbane, Australia, 22-26 Nov 2010

Song, W., Tjondronegoro, D., & Azad, S. (2010). User-centered video quality assessment for scalable video coding of H.264/AVC standard, *Proceedings of 16th International Multimedia Modeling Conference.* pp. 55-65, Chongqing, China, Januray 6-8, 2010

Song, W., Tjondronegoro, D., & Docherty, M. (2010). Exploration and Optimisation of User Experience in Viewing Videos on A Mobile Phone. *International Journal of Software Engineering and Knowledge Engineering,* Vol.8, No.20, (December 2010), pp. 1045-1075, ISSN 0218-1940

Song, W., Tjondronegoro, D., & Docherty, M. (2011). Saving Bitrate vs. Pleasing Users: Where is the Break-even Point in Mobile Video Quality?, *Proceedings of ACM Multimedia 2011.* pp. 403-412, Scottscale, Arizona, USA.

Song, W., Tjondronegoro, D., Wang, S.-H., & Docherty, M. (2010). Impact of Zooming and Enhancing Region of Interests for Optimizing User Experience on Mobile Sports Video, *Proceedings of ACM Multimedia 2010,* pp. 321-330, ISBN 978-1-60558-933-6, Firenze, Italy, October, 25-29, 2010

Sun, Y., Ahmad, I., & Zhang, Y. Q. (2006). Region-based Rate Control, and Bit Allocation for Wireless Video Trasmission. *IEEE Transactions on Multimedia,* Vol.8, No.1, (Februray 2006), pp. 1-10, ISSN 1520-9210

Tasaka, S., Yoshimi, H., & Hirashima, A. (2008). The Effectiveness of a QoE-based Video Output Scheme for Audio-video IP Transmission, *Proceedings of ACM Multimedia Information System.* pp. 259-268, ISBN 978-1-60558-303-7, Vancouver, Canada, October 26-31, 2008.

The Nielsen Company (2011). Telstra Smartphone Index. In: *The Nielsen Company,* 10.07.2011, Available from http://sensisdigitalmedia.com.au/Files/Mobile/Nielsen_Telstra_Smartphone_Index_June2011_Presentation.pdf

Tominaga, T., hayashi, T., Okamoto, J., & Takahashi, A. (2010). Performance Comparisions of Subjective Quality Assessment Methods for Mobile Video. *Proceedings of 2nd International Workshop on Quality of Multimedia Experience (QoMEX 2010).* pp. 82-87, Trondheim, Norway, June 21-23, 2010

Trefzger, J. (2005). Mobile TV Launch in Germany: Challenges and Implications, In: *Institute for Broadcasting Economics Cologne University.*

Tripathi, A., & Claypool, M. (2002). Improving Multimedia Streaming with Content-aware Video Scaling, *Proceedings of 2nd International Workshop on Intelligent Multimedia Computing and Networking (IMMCN),* Durham, North Carolina, USA, March 8-12, 2002

Vangenck, M., Jacobs, A., Lievens, B., Vanhengel, E., & Pierson, J. (2008). Does Mobile Television Challenge the Dimension of Viewing Television? An Explorative Research on Time, Place and Social context of the Use of Mobile Television Content, *Proceedings of EuroITV 2008,* pp. 122-127, Salzburg, Austria, July 3-4, 2008

Wang, Z., Bovik, A. C., Sheikh, H. R., & Simoncelli, E. P. (2004). Image Quality Assessment: From Error Visibility to Structural Similarity. *IEEE Transaction on Image Processing,* Vol.13, No.4, (April 2004), pp. 600-612, ISSN 1057-7149

Wang, Z., Sheikh, H. R., & Bovik, A. C. (2004). Objective Video Quality Assessment. In *Handbook of Video Databases Design and Applications,* B. Furht & O. Marques (Eds.), pp. 1041-1078, CRC Press LLC, ISBN 9780849370069

Wang, Z., Simoncelli, E. P., & Bovik, A. C. (2003). Multiscale Structural Similarity for Image Quality Assessment, *Proceedings of 37th Asilomar Conference on Signals, Systems and Computers, 2003.* pp. 1398-1402, Pacific Grove, CA, USA, November 9-12, 2003

Wiegand, T., Sullivan, G. J., Bjontegaard, G., & Luthra, A. (2003). Overview of the H.264/AVC Video Coding Standard. *IEEE Transactions on Circuits and Systems for Video Technology,* Vol.13, No.7, (July 2003), pp. 560-576, ISSN 1051-8215

Winder, J. (2001). Net Content: From Free to Fee. In: *Harvard Business Publishing,* 19.08.2011, Available from http://hbr.harvardbusiness.org/2001/07/net-content-from-free-to-fee/ar/1

Winkler, S., & Faller, C. (2005). Maximizing Audiovisual Quality at Low Bitrates. *Proceedings of Workshop on Video Processing and Qaulity Metrics for Consumer Electronics,* pp. 23-25, Scottsdale, Arizona, USA, Juanuray 2005

Wu, W., Arefin, A., Rivas, R., Nahrstedt, K., Sheppard, R., Yang, Z. (2009). Quality of Experience in Distributed Interactive Multimedia Environments: Toward a Theoretical Framework. *Proceedings of 17th ACM international conference on Multimedia.* pp. 481-490, Beijing, China, October 19–24, 2009

Yang, L., Zhang, L., Ma, S., & Zhao, D. (2009). A ROI Quality Adjustable Rate Control Scheme for Low Bitrate Video Coding. *Proceedings of 27th conference on Picture Coding Symposium,* pp. 441-444, n.d.

Yun-Chung, C., Jung-Ming, W., Bailey, R. R., Sei-Wang, C., & Shyang-Lih, C. (2004). A Non-parametric Blur Measure Based on Edge Analysis for Image Processing Applications, *Proceedings of 2004 IEEE Conference on Cybernetics and Intelligent Systems,* pp. 356-360, December 1-3, 2004

Zhang, Q. (2005). Video Delivery over Wireless Multi-hop Networks. *Proceedings of 2005 International Symposium on Intelligent Signal Processing and Communication Systems.* pp. 793-796, Hong Kong, China, December 13-16, 2005

Zhenghua, Y., & Wu, H. R. (2000). Human Visual System based Objective Digital Video Quality Metrics. *Proceedings of 5th International Conference on Signal Processing (WCCC-ICSP)*. pp. 1088-1095, Beijing, China, n.d.

Zhou, W., Bovik, A. C., & Evan, B. L. (2000). Blind Measurement of Blocking Artifacts in Images, *Proceedings of 2000 International Conference on Image Processing*, pp. 981-984, ISBN 0-7803-6297-7, Vancouver, BC , Canada, September 10-13, 2000

Zinner, T., Hohlfeld, O., Abboud, O., & Hossfeld, T. (2010). Impact of Frame Rate and Resolution on Objective QoE Metrics. *Proceedings of 2nd International Workshop on Quality of Multimedia Experience (QoMEX 2010)*. pp. 29-34, Trondheim, Norway, June 21-23, 2010

Part 2

Network and Coding Technologies

3

Recent Advances and Challenges in Wireless Multimedia Sensor Networks

Denis do Rosário, Kássio Machado, Antônio Abelém,
Dionne Monteiro and Eduardo Cerqueira
Federal University of Pará (UFPA)
Brazil

1. Introduction

Wireless Sensor Networks (WSNs) Akyildiz et al. (2002), Zhao & Guibas (2009) are formed of spatially distributed autonomous sensor nodes (motes). They are deployed in an environment where they can be used to monitor environmental conditions in collaboration, and communicate with each other through the wireless links. Several applications that are used in different areas have been outlined in the literature, such as, medical applications for monitoring patients Shnayder et al. (2005), monitoring mission critical environments, e.g., volcanic eruptions Werner-Allen et al. (2005), monitoring the structural integrity of buildings/towers Ceriotti et al. (2009) and several other multimedia applications.

WSNs can be deployed in an environment that covers a large area with hundreds or thousands of motes that are able to sense physical values and send them to either one or a set of Base-Stations (BSs), or end-systems (including end-users).

WSN is part of a new network paradigm, called of Internet of Things (IoT) Atzori et al. (2010), that is becoming very popular in wireless communication systems. The principle of this paradigm is that objects or things interact and cooperate with each other to ensure ubiquitous communications. These objects or things might be Radio-Frequency IDentification (RFID) tags, WSNs, actuators, applications, mobile phones, among others.

In the context of future WSN/IoT systems, Wireless Multimedia Sensor Networks (WMSNs) Gurses & Akan (2005), Almalkawi et al. (2010) are attracting considerable attention from both academic and industrial research groups. WMSN provide a wide range of potential applications in both civilian and military areas, which require visual and audio information, such as a surveillance sensor network, environmental and industrial monitoring, intelligent traffic congestion control, health-care, and others multimedia digital entrainment, or green city applications. In all of these, the multimedia content has the potential to enhance the level of information collected, by for example, allowing multi-resolution views (making comparisons with the measurements of scalar data).

A typical multimedia mote (e.g., TelosB MEMSIC (2011c), MICAz MEMSIC (2011b) and IRIS MEMSIC (2011a)) is equipped with a radio transceiver or other wireless communication devices, a small microcontroller, an energy source (i.e., a battery), some scalar sensors (i.e., temperature, humidity, and others), and multimedia sensors (camera and/or audio). A mote might vary in size from that of a shoebox down to the size of a speck of dust. Due to recent technological advances, involving the rapid improvement and miniaturization of hardware, it has become possible to develop single and usually small devices equipped with an audio and video camera. An example of this device is the CMUcam Rowe et al. (2002), an embedded camera with a CIF Resolution (352 x 288) RGB color that can be interfaced with an IEEE 802.15.4 compliant radio transceiver (e.g., TelosB mote).

Basically, the WSN/WMSN stack consists of four layers (Physical, Link, Network, and Application), as shown in Figure 1. The lower layers (Physical and Link Layers) are defined by the IEEE 802.15.4 standard IEEE-TG15.4 (2006). However, no standard exists for the upper layers although they have some features which can be expected. The responsibilities of each layer outlined as follows: (i) the Physical layer is responsible for providing access techniques; (ii) the Link layer works on medium access control, (iii) the purpose of the Network layer is to route the data in a network, and finally, (iv) different types of applications can be built and used on the Application layer.

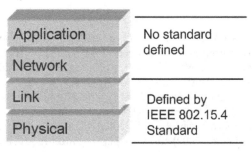

Fig. 1. WMSN Stack Layers

With regard to applications, multimedia sensing is expected to be wide-ranging. New WMSN network-based solutions must be specified, implemented and validated to support the requirements of multimedia applications in fixed and mobile sensor systems. Additionally, the sensor nodes have a limited power supply and are constrained in terms of bandwidth. All of these mentioned constraints impose a challenge in terms of the routing protocol in WMSN.

As mentioned earlier, the sensor nodes are usually deployed in a field that covers a large area and has hundreds or thousands of nodes. Thus, the nodes that are far away from the BS are unable to send their packets in a one-hop communication. Hence, it is necessary to use a multi-hop approach to provide a end-to-end communication.

From the perspective of the Network Layer, one of the main research problems is to ensure an efficient routing protocol with high-quality multimedia support for the WMSNs. This is hard to achieve because of the restrictions imposed by the WMSN features, which distinguish it from other wireless networks.

As presented in Al-Karaki & Kamal (2004), these new features are: (i) since the WSN has a large number of nodes and these are deployed in a wide area, it is difficult to have a global addressing system ; (ii) multiple sources send their data to the BS; (iii) the WSN has some restrictions with regard to energy, processing, and storage capacity; (iv) in some scenarios, the nodes are either static or mobile; (v) the location of a mote is important since the data collection is normally based on its location; and (vi), a WSN is usually composed of many motes and there is a high degree of probability that the collected data will have some redundancy.

This Chapter focuses on routing approaches for WMSNs and provides an overview of the most significant challenges and tendencies with regard to routing protocols for WMSNs, multimedia and network performance. Owing to the importance of the routing schemes and multimedia-awareness delivery in optimization operations, a particular attention will be given in this area. A number of different approaches to multimedia routing will be discussed to explain the nature of these challenges.

A use case will be discussed in this Chapter. The scenario selected is a multimedia-aware fire detection application in a rainforest area. Serious fires are common during the summer in the Amazon rainforest, and several research groups are attempting to monitor a fire alarm system. By using this system, it must be possible to collect information, such as temperature, humidity and multimedia data from the region and send it to the BS (or another end-system).

The BS will then forward the data to an end-system (e.g., desktop or mobile phone), where it will be analyzed and the possible occurrence of fire can be predicted. An integrated approach based on sensor data and physical models will be used to estimate the potential risks and hazards. This information can then be used to notify people and the local government can take appropriate measures to minimize the impact on the environment and save lives. A generic scenario of the use case is shown in Figure 2.

Fig. 2. A Recommended Generic Architecture for Fire Detection in the Rainforest Area

In the scenario outlined above, the nodes are deployed in a field (in this case in a rainforest) to carry out the sensing task, e.g., periodically collecting scalar data (temperature or humidity). The network is structured as follows: the architecture should have been designed in a hierarchical architecture, query-based, and with heterogeneous nodes (nodes with different capabilities).

The network architecture is hierarchical-based, as recommended for WMSNs in Akyildiz et al. (2007). Thus, the nodes are grouped in clusters, and a head node is assigned to each cluster, that is called the Cluster-Head (CH). In this scenario, the CH is a powerful mote that is equipped with a power supply and audio/video sensors. The main advantage of using a hierarchical-based architecture is its scalability and the fact that it is energy-efficient.

The nodes collect information about temperature and humidity, and send it to its CH which then forwards it to the BS by using multi-hop communications. The BS receives the data, and combines them with the aid of physical models, (e.g., the Angstrom index which is defined in Langholz & Schmidtmayer (1993)). The index is used to estimate the probability of a fire in a particular region.

The network can be classified as query-based, because after the BS detects the index value at a certain threshold, it will query/request multimedia data from the CH where the incident occurs. Thus, this application can be regarded as event-driven. The multimedia data is used to confirm the presence of fire, and then detect the impact of the disaster and assist the rescue operations.

The remainder of this Chapter is structured as follows. Section 2 provides a taxonomy of routing protocols, and addresses the main challenges and trends in designing a routing protocol for WMSN. Section 3 introduces the main features and drawbacks of routing protocols for WMSNs. Finally, Section 4 offers some final considerations on this Chapter.

2. Research directions and relevant issues in the design of routing protocols for WMSN

Owing to the small size of the sensor node, the WMSN nodes have limited resources, such as energy, bandwidth, memory, buffer size and processing capability. At the same time, the multimedia content (video stream, image or audio data) requires a high bandwidth, processing and storage capacity and this raises an additional challenge for the WMSNs. Additionally, the existing routing protocols for WSNs are not suitable for WMSNs. Thus, the design for routing protocols must take these constraints into consideration in order to overcome these drawbacks.

The multimedia content adds further restrictions to the design of routing protocols and makes it difficult to meet the application-specific Quality-of-Service (QoS) requirements and network conditions, e.g. ensuring that the end-to-end delay is within an acceptable range. Thus, providing an efficient routing scheme for the WMSNs, is a complex issue.

The following qualities are sought by most of the proposed routing protocols: (i) to be energy-efficient, and maximize the network lifetime; (ii) to be scalable, since the network must be composed of a large number of sensor nodes; (iii) to be fault-tolerant, due to the problem of sensor damage and battery exhaustion; and (iv) to have real-time, since in some applications the data has a real-time feature and has to take account of latency, throughput and delay. However, to the best of our knowledge, none of the proposed routing protocols for WMSN provides all of these features.

A routing protocol, usually aims to provide an efficient means of communication for a specific application, or similar applications. Thus, in designing the routing protocol, the researcher/developer must take into account important issues regarding the network structure, and which is the best approach for routing data.

In the following section, there is a taxonomy for routing protocols in WMSNs, which classifies the protocols according to the requirements of the network structure and protocol operation. Finally, there is a discussion of the main challenges and trends for the designing of a routing protocol.

2.1 A taxonomy for routing protocols

As mentioned earlier, WSN/WMSN has many features that distinguish it from other wireless or ad-hoc networks. Thus, several algorithms have been proposed to solve the problem of routing data in this network. These protocols must be developed by taking into account the characteristics of the sensor nodes and their applications, as well as the requirements of the network structure and architecture.

In Al-Karaki & Kamal (2004) there is a taxonomy for routing protocols in WSNs that can be extended to WMSNs, as shown Figure 3. According to this taxonomy, the protocols can be divided into two main groups: network structure and protocol operations; it is important to highlight that these groups are complementary. Depending on the network structure, the routing protocols can be classified into flat, hierarchical, or location-based networks. From the standpoint of the protocol operation, they can be classified into multipath, query, negotiation, QoS, or coherent-based protocols.

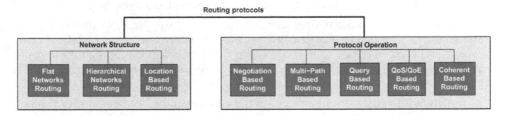

Fig. 3. Taxonomy for Routing Protocols

The way the routing protocol can be classified depends on how the source node finds routes to the destination node. In this context, the protocols are proactive, reactive or hybrid. In proactive protocols, all the paths are computed before they are really needed. In reactive protocols, the routes are computed on demand. Hybrid protocols use a combination of both proactive and reactive schemes. For static nodes, the best choice is to use a reactive protocol, since it implements a table-driven routing protocol and thus reduces energy consumption. In reactive protocols, the routes are computed on demand, which implies that a significant amount of energy is consumed in this task (route discovery and setup).

More detailed information will now be given about each of the categories of Figure 3. First, there is a classification based on the network structure of the routing protocols.

- **Flat networks:** all of the nodes have the same roles or functionalities, and collaborate with each other to carry out the sensing task, e.g., a sensor network deployed in an environment where all the nodes sense the temperature and humidity, so that they can send the information to the BS.

- **Hierarchical network:** the nodes are grouped in clusters and will play different roles in the network. The clusters are formed dynamically and a node in each cluster is elected as a leader; this node is called the Cluster-Head (CH). The main advantage of using this architecture is that it includes scalability and efficient communication issues. In this context, the nodes with higher energy are used to process and send information, while others with lower energy are used to carry out the sensing task.

- **Location network:** the node positions are used to route the data in a network. The relative location of the nodes can be estimated on the basis of the RSSI (Received Signal Strength Indicator) value of a received packet and by employing a radio propagation model. Alternatively, location information can also be obtained by communicating with a satellite, e.g., GPS (Global Positioning System).

Complementary, routing protocols can also be classified on the basis of the protocol operation, which varies depending on which approach is adopted. It should be underlined that some of the routing protocols may fall below one or more of the above routing categories. In the following section, there will be an examination of the detailed information of the network classification based on the protocol operation.

- **Multipath protocol:** to improve the performance of the system and ensure reliability, some protocols use multiple paths rather than a single path. Thus, alternate routes are established between a source and a destination node. Periodical messages are exchanged to maintain these alternate paths and these increase the network overhead.

- **Query protocol:** the protocol operation is based on request and reply queries through the network; these queries are usually described in either natural or high-level query languages. For example, a node sends a query to a specific node through the network, requesting sensing data (e.g., temperature), and the receiver replies to the sender with the data which matches the query.

- **Negotiation protocol:** the main purpose of this class of protocols is to eliminate duplicate information and prevent redundant data from beginning, by conducting a series of negotiation messages before the real data transmission. Additionally, communication decisions are taken based on available resources.

- **QoS/QoE protocol:** multimedia and mission-critical applications are sensitive to delay, jitter, loss, and other user- perceived metrics, such as blur and noise. This means that the QoS routing protocols must select routes that meet the quality level requirements of these applications. As a result, the use of QoS metrics is not enough to evaluate the quality of a video. Thus, recently a user perception scheme has been used to classify the multimedia content transmitted through the network. These user perception approaches are called Quality-of-Experience (QoE)-aware.

- **Coherent and non-coherent protocol:** this category of routing is focused on data processing techniques. The routing protocols can be classified as coherent and non-coherent data processing-based routing. If the nodes process the raw data before sending it, the routing protocol is classified as non-coherent data processing routing. Otherwise it is called coherent routing.

2.2 Challenges and trends for routing in WMSN

The main goal of a routing protocol is to carry out data communication while maximizing data delivery, extending the network lifetime, and preventing connectivity degradation. These goals can be achieved by employing data aggregation, energy management, and efficient control of path selection techniques. Additionally, there are restrictions of the nodes, and multimedia content which impose additional challenges. Thus, all these issues should be addressed at the time of the conception of a routing protocol for WMSN.

The performance of routing protocols for WMSN is affected by several complex factors. All of these must be overcome to provide an efficient communication system. In this subsection, there will be an examination of a list of issues which affects the performance of routing protocols, together with the way that they have been explored in the recent literature. Additionally, the use case examined in Section 1, will be used to show how these issues can be solved through the example of a multimedia-aware fire detection application in a rainforest area.

2.2.1 Data sensing and delivery model

This Section is related to the way that the nodes sense data (scalar or multimedia) and report to the CH/BS. The model can vary, depending on the nature of each kind of application. The delivery models can be classified as follows: continuous, event-driven, query-driven, and hybrid.

In a continuous model, the nodes are continually collecting data and transmitting it to CH/BS. This model is suitable for applications that require periodic sensing data. The event-driven and query-driven models are similar, in so far as the data are transmitted after an event occurs or when a BS requests a query. In some applications a hybrid model is employed, which is a combination of the previously used schemes.

- **Challenges:** the data sensing and delivery model affect the performance of the routing protocols. Especially with regard to energy consumption and route changes, i.e. if a node is continually capturing a video content and sending it to a CH/BS, the node in question will consume more energy. Thus, it reduces its own lifetime and, consequently that of the whole system as well. Depending on the type of the routing protocol, the data transmission will continually cause a route change. A similar kind of behavior occurs with scalar data transmissions.

- **Trends:** one of the possible means of tackling this problem is to consider employing an event-driven or query-driven sensing and delivery model. By using one of these techniques, the protocol will reduce the amount of transmitted data and will improve the network lifetime. The reason for this is that the data are transmitted only when an event occurs or is requested.

  Returning to the use case, some nodes collect scalar data in order to detect or predict an event, in this case a fire. The multimedia content will only be sent when an event occurs.

  Other studies in the literature, use the same means of solving the problem, as shown by Kandris et al. (2011), and Czarlinska & Kundur (2008). In the works referred to, once the sensor nodes detect an event in a certain region, the node(s) that is nearest to the event captures the multimedia content and sends it to the sink.

2.2.2 Node deployment

This can be categorized as being either deterministic or randomized. In the case of the deterministic deployment, the nodes are deployed manually in an environment where data transmission is routed through pre-determined paths. In contrast, for random deployment, the motes create an ad-hoc infrastructure with random location.

The choice of deterministic or random deployment depends on the type of sensors employed, as well as the applications and environment. Deterministic deployment is recommended and even necessary for expensive sensors or when their operation is significantly affected by their position, which includes being in a populated area, underwater applications, or nodes equipped with imaging or video sensors. On the other hand, random deployment is the best choice for harsh environments, such as a battle-field or disaster zone Younis & Akkaya (2008).

- **Challenges:** the distance between two nodes affects the link quality. In the case of a network, in which some nodes have a small number of neighborhoods, this node will rapidly exhaust its battery. Additionally, for a not uniform distribution, an optimal position of the CH/BS is necessary to allow the connectivity required that can enable an energy-efficient network operation to be carried out.

  Since multimedia sensors are sensitive to direction of acquisition and have limited coverage, the multimedia node must be deployed in the best place to optimize the coverage and avoid obstacles.

- **Trends:** with regard to the use case, some nodes are equipped with a camera and there is a need to study the best place to deploy them to ensure a better coverage. The other nodes (without cameras) can be deployed in a random way, although with a uniform distribution.

  In the literature, most of the applications assume that the nodes are randomly deployed in an environment that creates an ad-hoc infrastructure, such as that shown in Kandris et al. (2011), Politis et al. (2008), and others.

  With regard to the optimization of the node deployment, there are some WSN schemes proposed in the literature and which can be adapted to work in WMSN. Two techniques are highlighted here: (i) optimization of node location Kulkarni & Venayagamoorthy (2010), and Wang et al. (2008); and (ii) optimization of the Base Station location Akkaya et al. (2007).

2.2.3 Node capabilities

Depending on the application, some sensor nodes can have a different role or capability, which is related to the capacity of the nodes in terms of computation, communication, power and multimedia support. The network can be classified as either homogeneous or heterogeneous.

Most of the applications use homogeneous nodes, which have equal capabilities in terms of computation, communication and power, or are produced by the same manufacturer. However, in some applications the network is considered to be heterogeneous, because some/all of the nodes have different capabilities or roles. In this context, they are able to perform special functions, such as sensing, aggregation, or the retrieval of multimedia content.

- **Challenges:** in the case of the heterogeneous network, the node that is able to perform a lot of tasks, e.g., sensing, aggregation, or retrieval of multimedia content is likely to end up its source of energy in a short period of time.

  Most of the nodes used in the literature are constrained in terms of their processing capability, which makes it difficult for them to carry out many tasks. Additionally, due to the fact that each manufacturer uses the standard IEEE 802.15.4 for the lower layer, (although not the upper layers), each of them recommend their own implementation, which means that the motes from different manufacturers are not able to communicate with each other.

- **Trends:** the use of a heterogeneous network can be an alternative means of overcoming the problems arising from multimedia content and the restrictions of the sensor node.

Concerning the use case, the nodes are heterogeneous, and can be divided into: (i) Common nodes that are used to perform simple tasks, with limited battery supply, and restricted in terms of processing and memory; and (ii) Powerful nodes, used for data aggregation and the retrieval of multimedia content. These nodes are equipped with multimedia equipment, and solar power. Thus, they are not restricted in terms of battery and are more powerful in terms of memory and processing.

In the approaches Akyildiz et al. (2007) and Kim et al. (2011), common nodes (resource-constrained and low-power) are able to perform simple tasks, e.g., detecting scalar data, whereas powerful nodes are able to accomplish more complex tasks, e.g., data aggregation or capturing multimedia content.

2.2.4 Link Quality Estimators (LQEs)

The wireless links are unreliable and unpredictable in WSN/WMSN. This is mainly due to the fact that the nodes use low-power radios, which are very sensitive to noise, interference, and multipath distortion. In this context, it is important for the nodes to be able to quantify a value for the quality of communication between neighborhoods. This value is obtained through a Link Quality Estimator (LQE). A path is considered to be good when a link has the highest value.

Most of the routing protocols rely on LQEs as a mechanism for selecting the most stable routes, and the accuracy of the selected LQE has an impact on their performance. Thus, LQE is a fundamental building block in the design of routing protocols for WSN/WMSN Baccour et al. (2011).

- **Challenges:** LQEs which rely on a single link property, provide only a partial view of the link quality. Thus, they are not accurate, and as mentioned above, the accuracy of LQEs greatly affects the efficiency and performance of the routing protocols.

- **Trends:** Recently, two new LQEs were devised that combine four link quality metrics: (i) F-LQE: A Fuzzy Link Quality Estimator for Wireless Sensor Networks (F-LQE) Baccour et al. (2010), which combines four link quality properties, namely packet delivery, asymmetry, stability, and channel quality. The overall quality is computed as a fuzzy rule which returns the membership of the link in the fuzzy subset of good links; and (ii) Holistic Packet Statistics (HoPS) Renner et al. (2011), which incorporates four quality metrics (Short-term, Long-term, Absolute Deviation, and Trend Estimation) that provide a holistic assessment of the link and its dynamic behavior.

  Another interesting mechanism that can be used to estimate the overall quality of a link, is introduced in Butt et al. (2010). This study suggests computing and transmitting the overall quality of a link between the source and sink, and defined two thresholds to choose the best route: (i) a LQI (Link Quality Indicator) threshold which characterizes a link as a Weak Link; and (ii) a hop count threshold that determines whether or not a route is reliable enough to replace an old route.

  In the use case, the network architecture is hierarchical-based and uses a multi-hop communication between the CHs and BS. For the CH to reach the BS with higher reliability, it should select the best routes. The routing protocol uses the F-LQE as a mechanism to estimate the overall quality of a path to route its data.

  Additionally, the network must create cluster, and it also elects the CHs and non-cluster-head. Each non-cluster-head must choose the best CH to become its leader.

The choice of the best CH is made by using some LQE metrics. In this context, LQI (provided by a physical layer) is the best metric. Since the nodes have to select the CH with the minimal overhead communication, and for each received packet the nodes can obtain the LQI.

2.2.5 Mobility

Mobility Chen & Ma (2006) is one of the key challenges in wireless communications. Some nodes in a network are assumed to be either physically or logically moving closer to each other. Physical mobility refers to changes in the geographical location of the nodes during the time, i.e., movement of vehicles, animals, and humans. On the other hand, logical mobility refers to changes in network topology, e.g. adding or removing some nodes.

Mobility can be categorized as either static or dynamic. The network is considered to be dynamic if some nodes are moving in a logical way during a period of time. Otherwise, the network is considered to be static. The mobility scenario refers to the sensed phenomenon event that depends on the application. A dynamic event can be a target detection/tracking application. Forest monitoring for fire detection is an example of a static event. Most of the routing protocols assume that the network is composed of sensor nodes that are fixed in a certain position (static network).

- **Challenges:** mobility raises the problem of routing messages through the network, since the paths/routes are continually changing; this leads to an important issue regarding optimization, as well as make improvements in energy saving and bandwidth.

- **Trends:** basically most of the works in the literature take account of the mobility of the nodes or of the sink. In Deng et al. (2011) and Tan et al. (2009) are exploit the node mobility, the works consider considering an hierarchical network and a reactive node mobility to improve the target detection performance in WSN.

  The nodes near to the sink are responsible for delivering the data to the BS, which makes the lifetime of the network strongly dependent on the energy of these nodes. To overcome this problem, some works consider that the mobile sink is a way to increase the network lifetime, such as the suggestion made by Kim et al. (2010) and Yu et al. (2010)

2.2.6 Scalability

WMSN are usually composed of hundreds or thousands of nodes, which are densely deployed either inside the phenomenon or very close to it. The density in a region of interest, can range from a few to a hundred sensor nodes, to cover the whole area. Using higher density leads to more valuable information, but implies that there is more information to transmit and process.

In this context, scalability is one of the main design attributes of the sensor networks, and this must be encompassed by the protocols. The routing protocol should be scalable enough to enable it to work with a large number of nodes, and continually ensure the correct behavior of the application. Additionally, it must be adapted to scalability changes in a transparent way, i.e., without requiring the intervention of the user.

- **Challenges:** scalability must be taken into account to achieve efficient data processing, aggregation, storage and querying in WMSNs, especially when this involves a huge amount of data.

- **Trends:** as mentioned before, the use case employs a hierarchical architecture. This architecture offers considerable advantages with respect to a flat architecture in terms of scalability, lower costs, better coverage, higher functionality, and greater reliability.

2.2.7 Multimedia content

As mentioned earlier, multimedia content produces a huge amount of data. The data is compacted by employing a compress technique, such as, MPEG, H.263 and H.264 which can be classified as predictive coding techniques. The video is compressed once by the encoder (sender) and uncompressed by the decoder (receiver).

For MPEG are defined three types of frames (I, P, B-frames) are defined, where: (i) Intra, or I-frames, is the reference for all the other frames which provide a reference point for decoding a received video stream; (ii) Predictive-coded, or P-frames, provide an increased rate of compression compared to the I-frames, with a P-frame normally being 20 to 70 % the size of an associated I-frame; and (iii) Bi-directionally predictive-coded, or B-frames, use the previous and next I-frame or P-frame as their reference points for motion compensation. B-frames provide further compression, typically 5 to 40 % the size of an associated I-frame Greengrass et al. (2009).

The nodes in a WMSN are able to capture and transmit multimedia content, which can either be a snapshot or streaming content. A snapshot contains data from an event that was triggered in a short time period, e.g. an image. Streaming multimedia content is generated over a longer time period, e.g. video and audio streaming.

- **Challenges:** the nominal transmission rate for WSN/WMSN is 250 kbit/s which is defined by the IEEE 802.15.4 standard. Thus, transmitting video which requires a high data rate over the WSN/WMSN link is extremely difficult. The limitations of the sensor nodes require video coding/compression that has a low complexity, produces a bandwidth with a low output, can tolerate loss, and consumes as little power as possible.

  Furthermore, the predictive schemes for video coding techniques are not suitable for WMSN as they require complex encoders, powerful processing algorithms, and entail a high rate of energy consumption.

- **Trends:** in the use case, a multipath can be adopted to increase the bandwidth. The multimedia content will only be sent when events occur to reduce the amount of data.

  There are some works in the literature that adopt a multi-channel and multi-path approach to increase the available bandwidth. In Hamid et al. (2008) there is a design for a QoS aware routing protocol which uses multiple paths and multiple channels to ensure bandwidth and end-to-end delay requirements. In Maimour (2008) another suggested solution is shown, where multi-path routing is used to provide a sufficient bandwidth for multimedia applications.

  Currently, there are studies that aim to scale down the complexity of the computation and consumption of power that is a feature of the motion estimation and compensation of the predictive schemes. This scheme that has been suggested is classified as distributed source coding and aims to reduce the complexity at the encoder. By using this technique, the encoder can be simple and low-powered, while the decoder will be complex and loaded with most of the processing and energy burden. Examples of distributed source coding are Wyner-Ziv Aaron et al. (2004) and PRIZM Puri & Ramchandran (2002).

2.2.8 Energy considerations

The motes are usually equipped with a small battery as an energy source, which restricts the supply of energy. The best way of overcoming this drawback would be to have nodes that are energetically self-sustainable, e.g. equipped with battery recharge/replacement or solar power, but in some cases this may not be feasible, or at least, inappropriate.

The nodes consume energy in tasks such as sensing, communication, and data processing. However, they use up more energy in data communication, which involves both data transmission and reception. As has been shown throughout this section, all of the discussed topics raise serious issues regarding energy consumption. This will have to be solved in the future by reducing the amount of work done by the node and in particular, by reducing the number of transmitted packets.

It should be pointed out that it is desirable to find methods for discovering an energy-efficient route, and route data from the sensor nodes to the BS, in order to improve the network lifetime.

- **Challenges:** as mentioned earlier, multimedia content produces a huge amount of data which has to be delivered over the network. Hence, there is a risk that the node that is transmitting or routing multimedia data might quickly drain its energy. The main difficulty is to achieve reliability in data delivery packets, with a minimal consumption of energy, while increasing the lifetime of the network.

- **Trends:** by focusing on the use case, the multimedia nodes will consume more energy which is needed to capture and transmit multimedia content. To overcome this problem, these nodes will be equipped with solar power to increase the energy source. As mentioned before, the application is event-trigger so that it can reduce the amount of multimedia data. This will prevent these nodes from consuming more energy and using up its energy resources.

  Additionally, the CHs will use the remaining energy of its neighborhoods to the CHs and select the best route to reach the BS. This scheme prevents a node with higher LQEs and low remaining energy from becoming the best route. Otherwise, this node will always be selected as the best route and will use up all its energy.

  Recently, there have been some studies that have demonstrated that the nodes must be energetically self-sustainable, i.e., equipped with battery recharge, as shown in Abu-Baker et al. (2010). Another proposal takes into account the energy required for the route selection, such as is shown in PEMuR Kandris et al. (2011). These studies compute the difference between the residual energy of a CH and the energy required to route a message between two sequential CHs. The path with the highest value is selected as the best route.

2.2.9 Quality-of-Service (QoS)

Traditionally, the main goal of QoS is to provide a set of measurable services at network/packet layer in terms of delay, jitter, available bandwidth, and packet loss, with the aim of assessing the quality level of multimedia from the perspective of the network.

Due to the difference between WMSN and other wireless networks, the QoS requirements are different for WMSN. For Chen & Varshney (2004), some QoS parameters are required to measure the delivery of data in an efficient and effective way. Moreover, for Alves et al. (2009) QoS should be seen and addressed from a more extensive and holistic perspective, and instantiated in a wider range of properties, such as heterogeneity, energy-sustainability, timeliness, scalability, reliability, mobility, security, cost-effectiveness and invisibility.

- **Challenges:** sensed data (multimedia or scalar) should be delivered at the sink within a certain period of time, otherwise, the data will be useless. Thus, during the design of a routing protocol, QoS metrics such as end-to-end delay, jitter, loss, and throughput should be taken into account.

- **Trends:** to provide higher throughput and minimal end-to-end delay for multimedia data, the protocol can use packet differentiation in a way that allows multimedia packet to be given a higher priority than scalar data. Additionally, the packets must be assigned a deadline, since any data arriving later than the deadline are simply useless. Thus, before forwarding a packet, the nodes look for the deadline, and drop them if the deadline has expired.

In Hamid et al. (2008) a QoS-aware routing protocol is shown for WMSN, which provides packet delivery over multi-path and multi-channel. The main purpose of this proposal is to support a high data rate while meeting the required deadline. Thus, the multimedia packets can be delivered to the destination with their bandwidth and delay requirements.

In addition, there are some protocols that have been inspired by ant colonies, such as in ASAR: an ant-based service-aware routing algorithm for multimedia sensor networks Sun et al. (2008), which provides a QoS routing model for WMSN. It chooses appropriate paths for different QoS requirements from different types of services based on ant colonies.

2.2.10 Quality-of-Experience (QoE)

Recently, QoE has grown in importance in the wireless networks and is now able to provide mechanisms to overcome the drawbacks of the QoS schemes regarding the subjective aspects of human perception. QoE metrics have employed important role to measure the quality level of multimedia content based on the perspective of the user Rowe & Jain (2005), De Vleeschauwer et al. (2008), and Serral-Gracià et al. (2010).

Several objective QoE metrics have been formulated to estimate/predict (based on mathematical models) the quality level of multimedia services in the perception of the user. The main objective metrics are as follows: Peak Signal to Noise Ratio (PSNR), Structural Similarity (SSIM) and Video Quality Metric (VQM).

The PSNR is the most traditional objective metric and compares (frame by frame) the quality of the video received by the user with the original video. The value of PSNR is expressed in dB (decibels). For a video to be considered of good quality, it should have an average PSNR of at least 30dB.

The SSIM is a measurement of the structural distortion of the video, which trying to obtain a better correlation with the user's subjective impression, where the values vary between 0 and 1. The closer the metric gets to 1, the better the video quality.

The VQM metric measures the "perception damage" the video experienced, by drawing on the Human Visual System (HVS) characteristics, including distinct metric factors such as blurring, noise, color distortion and distortion blocks. VQM obtains values between 0 and 5, where the closer to 0, means a better video quality.

- **Challenges:** the main problems are related to how to devise a new real-time and non-reference metrics to evaluate the quality level of multimedia content in WMSNs. In addition, it is also expected that there will be further routing protocol extensions with user perception.
- **Trends:** new CODECs will be developed to allow the distribution of multimedia content in WMSNs with quality level support and low energy consumption Misra et al. (2008). Cluster-based routing solutions with QoE will be used to provide high quality video distribution with energy-efficient assurance. QoE-awareness in routing protocols will create a new multimedia era in WMSNs.

2.3 Concluding remarks

From our perspective, there is no doubt that the main challenge in designing a routing protocol for WMSNs is to find an optimal trade-off between energy consumption, multimedia transmission, and the ability to meet QoS/QoE requirements (e.g., by using LQE). Additionally, the routing protocol must be sufficiently scalable, be able to work with heterogeneous environments, and, in the case of node mobility, be self-organized with a low consumption of energy.

3. State of the art for routing protocols in WMSNs

Several routing protocols were proposed for the WSNs, but the new characteristics and constraints imposed by the multimedia content made them unsuitable for WMSNs. Thus, routing protocols for WMSNs are still an open and hot field for researchers.

The recent proposals for WMSN aim to meet the QoS requirements, by applying modifications to the previous protocols for WSN or offering new solutions/mechanisms. In the following section, some promising routing protocols for WMSN will be examined. They are either a modification to an existing scheme or a new scheme.

3.1 Extensions of proposed routing protocols for WSN

Researchers have often suggested making extensions to existing protocols to overcome some of the drawbacks and improve the network performance. In the following section, some of these studies are explained in detail.

3.1.1 Multimedia streaming in large-scale sensor networks with mobile swarms

The study in Gerla & Xu (2003) aims to support high quality multimedia streams in a sensor network, by adopting the Landmark Ad-Hoc Routing (LANMAR) protocol Gerla et al. (2000). The network architecture is a kind of hierarchical architecture, where the nodes are divided into groups (called swarm groups), and each group has a leader (a swarm node) which is selected in a dynamic way. Each group is formed of nodes that are physically close to each other, and usually share the same mobility pattern.

In terms of node capabilities, the swarm nodes are powerful and equipped with high quality video cameras, long-range radio and a high channel bandwidth. Additionally, they can be equipped with satellites, and move at a relatively high speed. An example of a swarm node is a tank or Unmanned Aerial Vehicle (UAV). The other nodes carry out simple, and basic functionalities, such as, detecting intruders and monitoring changes in the environment.

The sensor nodes are deployed in an environment that covers a very large scale field, as illustrated in Figure 4. They detect intruders or monitor environmental changes, and can be characterized as an event-trigger application. If a sensor node detects an event in a given area, one or more mobile swarms are directed to that area to help forward the multimedia streams with high quality.

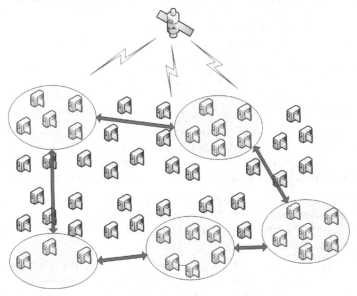

Fig. 4. Overview of a large-scale sensor network enhanced by mobile swarms

A normal radio installed in a swarm node, is sometimes not powerful enough to reach other swarms. To overcome this problem, this study recommends the adoption of a Mobile Backbone Network (MBN) for multiple swarms. This will allow the mobile swarms to communicate and exchange information with each other by using satellite communication or MBN.

This idea also suggests the use of the LANMAR routing protocol integrated with MBN, where the packets are routed through the nearest backbone node. Furthermore, this node forwards the packet through a MBN to a remote backbone node near the remote swarm node. The remote backbone node sends the data to the remote swarm node or directly to the destination if it is within its scope. This will greatly reduce the number of hops.

The study uses an event-driven approach which reduces energy consumption. However it uses satellite communication to transmit multimedia data of a high quality. This is inappropriate since this kind of communication can consume more energy, and satellite communication is out of the approach of WMSN.

3.1.2 Delay-constrained high throughput protocol for multi-path transmission over Wireless Multimedia Sensor Networks

The work proposed in Li et al. (2008) is an extension of the Directed Diffusion (DD) Intanagonwiwat et al. (2000) routing protocol which was proposed for WSN. DD has been used for sensor networks because of its scalability and energy efficiency. However, DD is a single path routing protocol, which means that the path with the lowest delay is selected as the best route. As already mention in the previous section, a single path is not suitable for multimedia transmission.

The aim of the proposed extension of DD is to provide support for multimedia streaming over WSNs. To achieve this goal, the protocol uses a multipath with a high quality link and low latency. This study considers a flat network, with stationary nodes or with a reduced mobility, that uses the same channel to communicate and where all the links are symmetrical.

In addition, the scheme does not take specific multimedia QoS requirements into account, such as throughput or loss which are used to guide the routing decision process, or prioritized packet scheduling to avoid a fast depletion of energy in the sensor nodes. However, the work considers a deadline, since any data arriving later than the deadline are simply useless.

The main goal of this proposal is to find multiple disjoint paths with a high throughput and low end-to-end delay. To maximize throughput and minimize delay, a metric was proposed to select the best route, which is called of $Cost_p$. This replaces the "pure delay" that was used in DD. $Cost_p$ can be defined as a product of expected transmission count (ETX) and delay.

A further point is that the closest nodes interfere with each other's communication. A node with a poor Signal-to-Noise Ratio (SNR), which is indirectly used to estimate ETX, implies a low value of $Cost_p$. In this case, with the use of the proposed metric, the node is less likely to be selected as the best path.

Another suggested alteration for DD is to reinforce multiple paths to the sink to obtain a disjoint path from the source to the sink and match the multipath requirements. The proposed protocol is able to find more than the required number of paths, because some paths may not be reinforced if a disjoint node is not found or the deadline has expired. If two nodes try to reinforce a path that converges to the same node, the first one that reinforces it will be selected.

Although the work uses multi-paths to increase the available bandwidth, the proposal adopts the continuous data sensing and delivery model, with a flat network, and as well as this, all the nodes are equipped with a camera. The nodes are continually capturing multimedia data, and can forward them. Thus, it makes the protocol not energy-efficient.

3.1.3 Power Efficient Multimedia Routing (PEMuR)

In Kandris et al. (2011) a Power Efficient Multimedia Routing (PEMuR) is proposed, which is an extension of the Scalable Hierarchical Power Efficient Routing (SHPER) protocol Kandris et al. (2009). PEMuR aims to provide an efficient video communication over WMSNs and is based on a combination of hierarchical routing and video packet scheduling models. The proposal ensures low power consumption in all the sensor nodes and a high perceived video.

This study examines a hierarchical network which assumes the coexistence of a BS and a set of homogeneous sensor nodes. They are randomly distributed within a delimited area. The base station is located at a position that is far from the sensor field. All the nodes (BS and nodes) are stationary, as can be seen in Figure 5. However, the network nodes are intended to be energy constrained.

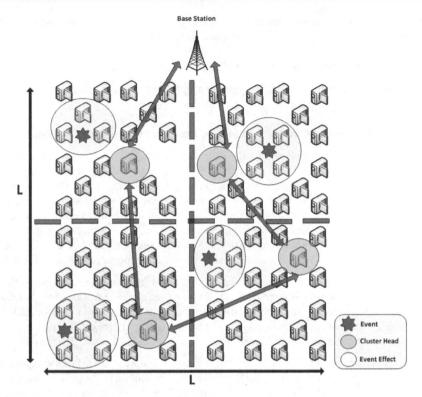

Fig. 5. Architecture scheme adopted by PEMuR

The proposed algorithm combines the benefits of the use of energy-efficient hierarchical routing with a distortion prediction model to drop packets. A time slot is assigned to each node, and the transmission only occurs when an event is detected.

The video sequence is encoded in accordance with the H.264/AVC standard. The protocol provides a packet scheduling algorithm that allows the reduction of the video transmission rate with a minimum possible increase of distortion. This algorithm is useful, because there are some cases in which the transmission bandwidth required from the sensor node exceeds the capacity limit of the shared wireless channel. Thus, each sensor node decides which video packets should be dropped so that it can reduce its current transmission rate.

To select the best route, PEMuR enables a selection of the most energy-efficient paths, by managing the network load according to the residual energy of the nodes and prevents unnecessary data transmissions by adopting a proposed energy threshold. The nodes compute the difference between the residual energy of the CH and the energy required to route a message between two sequential CHs. The path with the highest value is selected as the best route.

However, the protocol only uses the remaining energy to estimate the best routes. This means that the proposal is neither reliable nor energy-efficient. This scheme should involve a combination of some LQEs with remaining energy to find the best routes. Multi-path and multi-channel approaches should be adopted by the protocol to increase the available bandwidth that is required to transmit multimedia content.

3.2 New solutions for routing protocols in WMSN

In the following section, some important examples of new routing protocols will be investigated.

3.2.1 ASAR: An ant-based service-aware routing algorithm for multimedia sensor networks

In Sun et al. (2008) an ant-based algorithm, described as ASAR, is recommended for routing in WMSNs. The protocol provides support for three kinds of services: (i) event-driven (R-service), where the applications tend to be delay and error intolerant. This service should meet higher real-time and reliability requirements; (ii) data query (D-service), are services with both error intolerant and query-specific delay tolerant applications. It needs to be supplied with relevant data that is as reliable as possible. However, it tolerates query-specific delay; and (iii) stream query (S-service), are services with delay intolerant, but query-specific error tolerant applications. Additionally, packet losses can be tolerated within a certain limit.

The proposed routing protocol takes into account three different types of services (R/D/S), and four QoS requirements (latency, packet loss, energy consumption and bandwidth). Thus, it aims to maximize the use of the network and improve its performance. An ant-based algorithm was recommended to select an optimal path, together with an Ant-based Service-Aware Routing algorithm (ASAR).

The ASAR algorithm is running in all of the CH, and three available paths are periodically found for three types of services. The R-service requires less bandwidth and a path with lower traffic and higher SNR is an attractive solution. For D-service, a path can be used with significant congestion and a higher SNR on each link. Finally, a path with less traffic and lower SNR may be better for S-service. However, all of these kinds of services have the same goal, which is to reduce energy consumption and extend the network lifetime. Moreover, the selection of three paths for each service can prevent link congestion, when multiple kinds of services reach a node at the same time.

When selecting the paths, each CH generates ants for each type of services that depends on a proposed objective function, and a pheromone value for each path. Different paths from the CH to the BS are found which meet different QoS requirements. The pheromone value on the sink is quantified to decrease the transmission frequency of reverse ants, and this leads to a more rapid convergence of the algorithms and helps to optimize the network resources.

A system which uses bio inspirat schemes, e.g., ant colonies, is not usually explored in real applications. This is because it involves exchanging a lot of messages to discovery routes. Thus, it increases the communication overhead, and decreases the network lifetime. Another problem is the lack of multi-paths and multi-channels.

3.2.2 Design of a QoS-aware routing mechanism for Wireless Multimedia Sensor Networks

The work Hamid et al. (2008), presents a QoS-aware routing protocol to support a high data rate for WMSNs. The routing protocol works in a distributed manner to ensure bandwidth and end-to-end delay requirements of real-time data, and maximize the throughput of the non-real-time data.

The protocol targets applications of the WMSNs, where the nodes produce multimedia contents from the deployed area to deal with both the critical and general data. This study takes into account the fact that it is a static, flat and heterogeneous network, as shown in Figure 6.

The nodes are able to perform a wide range of tasks, e.g., sensing multimedia and scalar data. However, a subset of nodes has higher processing capabilities, which allows it to perform in-network processing, such as data aggregation and to discard redundant data. The sensor nodes are equipped with a multi-channel radio, which means that the nodes are capable of transmitting or receiving data on one channel at a given time.

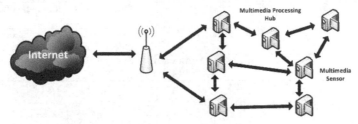

Fig. 6. The network model adopted

The proposal takes account of real-time and non-real-time data of multimedia and scalar content. The data originated from various types of events and has different levels of importance. The incoming packets are classified according to their degree of importance at each node, and then are sent to the appropriate queue. As well as this, there is a scheduler which is used to schedule the packets according to delay and bandwidth requirements.

The proposed routing protocol uses multi-path and multi-channel techniques, to increase the bandwidth. The routing decisions for real-time and non-real-time traffics are taken according to Path-length-based Proportional Delay Differentiation (PPDD). To meet the bandwidth requirements, a QoS packet scheduling technique was employed to provide a dynamic bandwidth adjustment. The PPDD device was used to meet the delay requirements.

The nodes choose the paths/channels to route their packets and meet the bandwidth and delay requirements. Additionally, each sensor node knows its next 2-hops available path, and the collision-free channel assignment. Throughout the network, the real-time packets that do not meet the deadline requirement are discarded. For best-effort traffic, alternative paths are used to balance the traffic, and the processing hubs perform data aggregation to reduce the amount of data that is transmitted through the network.

The main drawback of this is that it involves the use of a flat network. As mentioned before, in this architecture, all the nodes can forward packets, and multimedia data generates a lot of packets that have to be forwarded. Thus, this proposal is not energy-efficient.

3.3 Final considerations of proposed routing protocols

This section addresses important issues related to relevant routing protocols for WMSNs. They represent new solutions or extensions/improvements of existing protocols. The protocols that have been outlined rely on an ant colony, multipath, multi-channel, and cost function to define the best routes. The protocols attempt to provide QoS and efficient video transmission over WMSNs, as summarized in Table 1. However, they are inefficient in terms of providing reliable communication and maximizing the lifetime of the network.

Protocols	Mobility	Architecture	Multi-Path Multi-Channel	Data sensing and delivery model	Node Capabilities	Bio inspirat
LANMAR Gerla & Xu (2003)	Some mobile nodes	Hierarchical	No	Event-driven	Heterogeneous	No
DD-Extension Li et al. (2008)	Static or reduced mobility	Flat	Multi-path	Continuous	Homogeneous	No
PEMuR Kandris et al. (2011)	Static	Hierarchical	No	Event-driven	Homogeneous	No
ASAR Sun et al. (2008)	Static	Hierarchical	No	Event-driven Query-driven	Homogeneous	Ant-colony
QoS-aware Hamid et al. (2008)	Static	Flat	Multi-path Multi-channel	Event-driven	Heterogeneous	No

Table 1. Main Features of Routing Protocols

In general, the routing solutions inspired in ant colonies, are not explored in real applications because these schemes have a long adaptation time to react to changes in the topology and also during the setup phase. Additionally, in some cases, they are not energy-efficient since they involve exchanging a lot of messages to discovery routes.

At the same time, there is no doubt that multi-paths and multi-channels are the best approaches to increase the network bandwidth in WMSNs, although, these schemes affect the other layers, such as MAC and transport layers. Further proposals must be designed so that they can find a satisfactory solution to this problem and cover routing, transport, and MAC layers.

As mentioned in the previous section, QoS is not accurate enough to achieve higher video quality in wireless multimedia transmissions. Thus, QoE is the most suitable scheme to overcome the main drawbacks of QoS regarding user perception. This approach has been used in wireless communication, e.g., mesh network, and its implementation in WMSNs is now being studied.

Finally, this last comment also applies to network topology and the nodes feature. The best network architecture for WMSN is hierarchical/cluster-based. This kind of architecture offers considerable benefits, such as, scalability, lower cost, better coverage, higher functionality, and greater reliability. The multimedia nodes should be more powerful and self-sustainable in terms of energy, since retrieving multimedia content requires higher processing and energy.

4. Final considerations

In wireless sensor network, the access and distribution of multimedia applications/services with quality level continue to be an attractive research area, since they allow the emergence of a wireless multimedia sensor network. WMSN is a network of wirelessly interconnected sensor nodes equipped with multimedia devices, and can be expected to offer a wide range of potential applications in both civilian and military areas.

In most of the applications in WMSN, the nodes are densely deployed in a large field. Thus, some nodes need to use multi-hop communication. In this context, the nodes rely on a routing protocol to deliver the multimedia content and scalar data to BS. WMSN has several characteristics that distinguish it from other wireless networks. Thus, there are some challenges to overcome during the design of a reliable, fairness and energy-efficient routing protocol for WMSNs.

The objective of this Chapter was to highlight important topics in WMSN, namely the challenges and current trends in routing protocols. The main issues that affect the designer when designing the routing protocol are explored to provide an energy-efficient, reliable and fair distribution of resources as well as a quality level of support.

We hope that this chapter will help to improve the understanding of the issues and challenges that lie ahead in WMSN and the examination of the routing issues will serve as a stimulus for designers, engineers, and researchers to seek innovative solutions in the future.

5. Acknowledgments

This work is supported by CNPq and FAPESPA.

6. References

Aaron, A., Rane, S., Setton, E., Girod, B. et al. (2004). Transform-domain wyner-ziv codec for video, *Proc. SPIE Visual Communications and Image Processing*, Vol. 5308, Citeseer, pp. 520–528.

Abu-Baker, A., Huang, H., Johnson, E. & Misra, S. (2010). Green Diffusion: Data Dissemination in Sensor Networks Using Solar Power, *Proceedings of IEEE Consumer Communications and Networking Conference (CCNC 2010)*, IEEE.

Akkaya, K., Younis, M. & Youssef, W. (2007). Positioning of base stations in wireless sensor networks, *IEEE Communications Magazine* 45(4): 96 –102.

Akyildiz, I., Melodia, T. & Chowdhury, K. (2007). A survey on wireless multimedia sensor networks, *Computer Networks* 51(4): 921–960.

Akyildiz, I., Su, W., Sankarasubramaniam, Y. & Cayirci, E. (2002). Wireless sensor networks: a survey, *Computer networks* 38(4): 393–422.

Al-Karaki, J. & Kamal, A. (2004). Routing techniques in wireless sensor networks: a survey, *IEEE Wireless Communications* 11(6): 6–28.

Almalkawi, I., Guerrero Zapata, M., Al-Karaki, J. & Morillo-Pozo, J. (2010). Wireless Multimedia Sensor Networks: Current Trends and Future Directions, *Sensors* 10(7): 6662–6717.

Alves, M., Baccour, N., Koubâa, A., Severino, R., Dini, G., Pereira, N., Sá, R., Savino, I. & de Sousa, P. G. (2009). Quality-of-Service in Wireless Sensor Networks: state-of-the-art and future directions, *Technical report*, CISTER, ISEP.

Atzori, L., Iera, A. & Morabito, G. (2010). The Internet of Things: A survey, *Computer Networks* .

Baccour, N., Koubâa, A., Jamâa, M., Rosário, D., Youssef, H., Alves, M. & Becker, L. (2011). RadiaLE: a Framework for Designing and Assessing Link Quality Estimators, *Ad Hoc Networks* .

Baccour, N., Koubâa, A., Youssef, H., Jamâa, M. B., Rosário, D., Becker, L. B. & Alves, M. (2010). F-LQE: A Fuzzy Link Quality Estimator for Wireless Sensor Networks, *Proceedings of the 7th European Conference on Wireless Sensor Networks (EWSN 2010)*, University of Coimbra, Coimbra, Portugal, pp. 240–255.

Butt, M., Javed, M., Akbar, A., Taj, Q., Lim, C. & Kim, K. (2010). LABILE: Link quAlity-Based LexIcaL Routing MEtric for Reactive Routing Protocols in IEEE 802.15. 4 Networks, *5th International Conference on Future Information Technology (FutureTech 2010)*, IEEE, pp. 1–6.

Ceriotti, M., Mottola, L., Picco, G., Murphy, A., Guna, S., Corra, M., Pozzi, M., Zonta, D. & Zanon, P. (2009). Monitoring heritage buildings with wireless sensor networks: The Torre Aquila deployment, *Proceedings of the International Conference on Information Processing in Sensor Networks (IPSN) - SPOTS track*, IEEE Computer Society, pp. 277–288.

Chen, C. & Ma, J. (2006). Mobile enabled large scale wireless sensor networks, *The 8th International Conference in Advanced Communication Technology (ICACT 2006)*, Vol. 1, IEEE, pp. 333–338.

Chen, D. & Varshney, P. (2004). QoS support in wireless sensor networks: A survey, *International Conference on Wireless Networks*, Citeseer, pp. 227–233.

Czarlinska, A. & Kundur, D. (2008). Reliable Event-Detection in Wireless Visual Sensor Networks Through Scalar Collaboration and Game-Theoretic Consideration, *IEEE Transactions on Multimedia* 10(5): 675–690.

De Vleeschauwer, B., De Turck, F., Dhoedt, B., Demeester, P., Wijnants, M. & Lamotte, W. (2008). End-to-end QoE optimization through overlay network deployment, *International Conference on Information Networking (ICOIN 2008)*, IEEE, pp. 1–5.

Deng, S., Li, J. & Shen, L. (2011). Mobility-based clustering protocol for wireless sensor networks with mobile nodes, *IET Wireless Sensor Systems* 1(1): 39–47.

Gerla, M., Hong, X. & Pei, G. (2000). Landmark routing for large ad hoc wireless networks, *Global Telecommunications Conference, 2000. GLOBECOM'00. IEEE*, Vol. 3, IEEE, pp. 1702–1706.

Gerla, M. & Xu, K. (2003). Multimedia streaming in large-scale sensor networks with mobile swarms, *ACM SIGMOD Record* 32(4): 72–76.

Greengrass, J., Evans, J. & Begen, A. (2009). Not all packets are equal, part i: Streaming video coding and sla requirements, *Internet Computing, IEEE* 13(1): 70–75.

Gurses, E. & Akan, O. (2005). Multimedia communication in wireless sensor networks, *Annales des Télécommunications*, Vol. 60, Citeseer, p. 872.

Hamid, M., Alam, M. & Hong, C. (2008). Design of a QoS-aware Routing Mechanism for Wireless Multimedia Sensor Networks, *IEEE Global Telecommunications Conference (GLOBECOM 2008)*, IEEE, pp. 1–6.

IEEE-TG15.4 (2006). 802.15.4: Wireless Medium Access Control (MAC) and Physical Layer(PHY) Specifications for Low-Rate Wireless Personal Area Networks (LR-WPANs), *IEEE standard for Information Technology* .

Intanagonwiwat, C., Govindan, R. & Estrin, D. (2000). Directed diffusion: A scalable and robust communication paradigm for sensor networks, *Proceedings of the 6th annual international conference on Mobile computing and networking*, ACM, pp. 56–67.

Kandris, D., Tsagkaropoulos, M., Politis, I., Tzes, A. & Kotsopoulos, S. (2011). Energy efficient and perceived qos aware video routing over wireless multimedia sensor networks, *Ad Hoc Networks* 9(4): 591 – 607. Multimedia Ad Hoc and Sensor Networks.

Kandris, D., Tsioumas, P., Tzes, A., Nikolakopoulos, G. & Vergados, D. (2009). Power conservation through energy efficient routing in wireless sensor networks, *Sensors* 9(9): 7320–7342.

Kim, J., In, J., Hur, K., Kim, J. & Eom, D. (2010). An intelligent agent-based routing structure for mobile sinks in wsns, *IEEE Transactions on Consumer Electronics* 56(4): 2310–2316.

Kim, J., Seo, H. & Kwak, J. (2011). Routing protocol for heterogeneous hierarchical wireless multimedia sensor networks, *Wireless Personal Communications* pp. 1–11. 10.1007/s11277-011-0309-4.

Kulkarni, R. & Venayagamoorthy, G. (2010). Bio-inspired algorithms for autonomous deployment and localization of sensor nodes, *IEEE Transactions on Systems, Man, and Cybernetics, Part C: Applications and Reviews* 40(6): 663 –675.

Langholz, H. & Schmidtmayer, E. (1993). Meteorologische verfaren zur abschatzung des waldbrandrisikos, *Allgemeine Forstzeitschrift* 48(8): 394–396.

Li, S., Neelisetti, R., Liu, C. & Lim, A. (2008). Delay-constrained high throughput protocol for multi-path transmission over wireless multimedia sensor networks, *In International Symposium on a World of Wireless, Mobile and Multimedia Networks (WoWMoM 2008)* pp. 1–8.

Maimour, M. (2008). Maximally radio-disjoint multipath routing for wireless multimedia sensor networks, *Proceedings of the 4th ACM workshop on Wireless multimedia networking and performance modeling*, ACM, pp. 26–31.

MEMSIC (2011a). Iris datasheet. Available at: `http://memsic.com/support/documentation/wireless-sensor-networks/category/7-datasheets.html?download=135%3Airis` and access at 01 feb. 2011.

MEMSIC (2011b). Micaz datasheet. Available at: `http://memsic.com/support/documentation/wireless-sensor-networks/category/7-datasheets.html?download=148%3Amicaz` and access at 01 feb. 2011.

MEMSIC (2011c). Telosb datasheet. Available at: `http://memsic.com/support/documentation/wireless-sensor-networks/category/7-datasheets.html?download=152%3Atelosb` and access at 01 feb. 2011.

Misra, S., Reisslein, M. & Xue, G. (2008). A survey of multimedia streaming in wireless sensor networks, *Communications Surveys & Tutorials, IEEE* 10(4): 18–39.

Politis, I., Tsagkaropoulos, M., Dagiuklas, T. & Kotsopoulos, S. (2008). Power efficient video multipath transmission over wireless multimedia sensor networks, *Mobile Networks and Applications* 13(3): 274–284.

Puri, R. & Ramchandran, K. (2002). Prism: A new robust video coding architecture based on distributed compression principles, *PROCEEDINGS OF THE ANNUAL ALLERTON CONFERENCE ON COMMUNICATION CONTROL AND COMPUTING*, Vol. 40, Citeseer, pp. 586–595.

Renner, C., Ernst, S., Weyer, C. & Turau, V. (2011). Prediction accuracy of link-quality estimators, *In Proceedings of the 8th European Conference on Wireless Sensor Networks (EWSN'11)* pp. 1–16.

Rowe, A., Rosenberg, C. & Nourbakhsh, I. (2002). A low cost embedded color vision system, *International Conference on Intelligent Robots and Systems (IEEE/RSJ 2002)*, Vol. 1, IEEE, pp. 208–213.

Rowe, L. & Jain, R. (2005). ACM SIGMM retreat report on future directions in multimedia research, *ACM Transactions on Multimedia Computing, Communications, and Applications (TOMCCAP)* 1(1): 3–13.

Serral-Gracià, R., Cerqueira, E., Curado, M., Yannuzzi, M., Monteiro, E. & Masip-Bruin, X. (2010). An overview of quality of experience measurement challenges for video applications in ip networks, *In Proc. of International Conference on Wired/Wireless Internet Communications (WWIC 2010)* .

Shnayder, V., Chen, B.-r., Lorincz, K., Jones, T. R. F. F. & Welsh, M. (2005). Sensor networks for medical care, *Proceedings of the 3rd international conference on Embedded networked sensor systems (SenSys 05)*, New York, NY, USA, pp. 314–314.

Sun, Y., Ma, H., Liu, L. & Zheng, Y. (2008). ASAR: An ant-based service-aware routing algorithm for multimedia sensor networks, *Frontiers of Electrical and Electronic Engineering in China* 3(1): 25–33.

Tan, R., Xing, G., Wang, J. & So, H. (2009). Exploiting reactive mobility for collaborative target detection in wireless sensor networks, *IEEE Transactions on Mobile Computing* pp. 317–332.

Wang, Y.-C., Hu, C.-C. & Tseng, Y.-C. (2008). Efficient placement and dispatch of sensors in a wireless sensor network, *IEEE Transactions on Mobile Computing* 7(2): 262 –274.

Werner-Allen, G., Johnson, J., Ruiz, M., Lees, J. & Welsh, M. (2005). Monitoring volcanic eruptions with a wireless sensor network, *Proceeedings of the Second European Workshop on Wireless Sensor Networks (EWSN 2005)*, pp. 108–120.

Younis, M. & Akkaya, K. (2008). Strategies and techniques for node placement in wireless sensor networks: A survey, *Ad Hoc Networks* 6(4): 621–655.

Yu, F., Park, S., Lee, E. & Kim, S. (2010). Elastic routing: a novel geographic routing for mobile sinks in wireless sensor networks, *IET Communications* 4(6): 716–727.

Zhao, F. & Guibas, L. (2009). Wireless sensor networks, *Communications Engineering Desk Reference* p. 247.

4

Recent Advances in Future Mobile Multimedia Networks

Paulo Bezerra, Adalberto Melo, Billy Pinheiro, Thiago Coqueiro,
Antônio Abelém, Agostinho Castro and Eduardo Cerqueira
Federal University of Pará (UFPA)
Brazil

1. Introduction

The increase in the number of wireless devices and multimedia applications, coupled with the desire to connect them to the ever-growing Internet, is leading to a mobile multimedia Internet, where the support for the mobility of devices will soon be taken for granted. In addition to the global connectivity support, it is also expected that the management of intra and inter-domain handovers (heterogeneous scenarios), in a seamless and multimedia-awareness manner, is a way to increase user satisfaction and profits for mobile multimedia providers. However, heterogeneous wireless network structures, severe channel impairments, unavailable multimedia quality level controllers and complex traffic patterns make mobile scenarios much more unpredictable than wired networks.

Existing mobility control proposals, such as Mobile IP version 4 (MIPv4) Gunasundari & Shanmugavel (2009) and MIP version 6 (MIPv6) Dinakaran & Balasubramanie (2011), Hierarchical MIPv6 (HMIPv6) Harini (2011), Fast Handovers for IPv6 (FMIPv6) Zhang & Pierre (2009), bi-directional tunnelling based on MIP, and the remote-subscription technique were developed to control mobility applications in homogeneous networks. Other recent wireless access technologies, based on IEEE 802.11 De Moor et al. (2010), IEEE 802.16 Ahmadi (2009) and LTE Ergen (2009), aim to provide handovers, but fail in the Quality of Service (QoS), Quality of Experience (QoE), and in seamless heterogeneous support.

With regard to heterogenic control, the IEEE 802.21, wherein is proposed the Media Independent Handover (MIH) Taniuchi et al. (2009), enables vertical handover, detects target networks in advance, and allows the integration and seamless mobility among heterogeneous systems. Recent advances in wireless radio resource management, as proposed by the IEEE 802.11k Meschke et al. (2010) Working Group, are aimed at improving the distribution of multimedia content within a network, where the mobile user can connect to the access point (AP) that provides the best QoS/QoE support and not only the strongest signal. Other approaches have been proposed to support seamless mobility for multimedia applications, such as pre-fetch and cache-based multimedia schemes, self-adaptive handover management solutions for mobile streaming continuity, and content-oriented mobility schemes. For example, the last application mentioned performs handovers, by exploring the characteristics of the available wireless resources, predicted user perception, and on-going multimedia content.

To follow, a traditional handover process is described where two MIP (v4 and v6) are designed for network-layer handover and hide mobility from upper layers. On a macro movement (Layer 3 handover), a Foreign Agent (FA) or a Dynamic Host Configuration Protocol (DHCP) server distributed an FA Care-of-Address (CoA) or a uniquely put CoA to a mobile device. The mobile device then performs location update at its Home Agent (HA) with the latter binding between its Home Address (HoA) and CoA. When a Correspondent Host (CH) sends data packets of the mobile device to the HoA, its HA receives the packets and tunnels them to the CoA.

Afterwards, the FA or the MH itself decapsulates the tunnelled packets, depending on the CoA type. If MIP with Route Optimization (MIP-RO) Shahriar et al. (2010) is applied, the HA may send a Binding Update (BU) message to the CH on intercepting the first incoming packet. This functionality allows the CH to tunnel directly the following session packets to the CoA associated with the mobile device. However, as presented, it is evident that novel mobile multimedia mechanisms are needed to provide seamless, QoS/QoE, green communication, cross-layer and multimedia-awareness in future heterogeneous multimedia networks Seshadrinathan & Bovik (2011).

In future mobile multimedia systems, it is very important to develop (or extend) novel handover controllers to allow intra and inter mobility, while keeping ongoing mobile applications with an excellent quality level and optimizing the usage of wireless resources. The base station selection procedure should be done, by controlling and adapting QoE performance indicators which represent service integrity, such as throughput, delay, jitter, packet loss, bit error rate (BER), peak signal-to-noise ratio (PSNR), structural similarity (SSIM), video quality metric (VQM), and mean opinion score (MOS)-related metrics Zinner et al. (2010). In addition, buffer and caching mechanisms, together with mobility prediction and session context transfer approaches, must be integrated in order to provide seamless mobile multimedia handover in future wireless networks Klein & Klaue (2009) Zhou et al. (2010).

To conclude, an overview of the most relevant challenges and trends for future mobile multimedia networks will be addressed, Mobility was concentrated in the k, v, and r mechanisms of the IEEE 802.11 standard, heterogeneity and quality level support. These will be discussed in detail. Moreover, seamless handover and user experience mobility approaches will be presented in the context of future Internet scenarios. In order to introduce the benefits of traditional and novel mobile multimedia solutions, simulation experiments will be carried out to demonstrate the impact of handover schemes on the performance of the networks.

2. Design of Mobile IP

The IP Mobile is a standard protocol which aims at connectivity to the level of the IP layer, irrespective of the physical location of the mobile gadget. A node in the roaming may have access to the internet by the encapsulation of its data through the IP protocol, without, however, changing the IP address of its home network, leaving the mobility transparent for the application and protocols of the layer TCP and UDP of transport.

Before mobility of IP the users of mobile nodes had to be satisfied entirely with the portability of the equipment. This is because at first when a node was moved from one network to another, the data transactions which had access were interrupted and a new data transaction with a NE network was initiated. With the coming of the MIP a node can have almost uninterrupted and continual connectivity with the applications provided it among the networks keeping its original IP address.

One of the main technical problems that have to be dealt with for mobility support is the manner in which the addressing IP has to be used. The Unicast internet traffic is routed to a specific locality in the field of the address destination of the IP header. The IP destination address specifies the address for the networks and , therefore, the traffic it is carrying for this network. This is not appropriate for the mobile noder, which wants to mantain its original IP address irrespective of its present location and without that of the internet network node. The MIP resolved the problem by making the mobile node use two IP addresses, the home Address (HA) and Foreign Agent (FA), as shown in Figure 1.

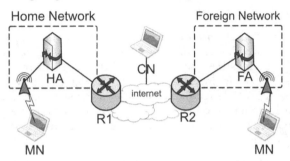

Fig. 1. Basic Topology of MIP

The Mobile IP was conceived to allow the movement of nodes from one IP subnet to another. Although its arquitecture suits this purpose, the process of transition from one node among IP subnets with the change in the access point, called handoff or handover, presents two factors which harm the applications in real time, i.e. interactives or those sensitive to delays. The first is a great latency in the process, which generates a long period of time without receiving the packages. The second refers to the great number of discarded or delayed packages due to the change in the point of access.

2.1 Mobile IPv4 overview

The Mobile protocol IP4 (MIPv4) was proposed by the IETF work group in Mobile IP. The mobility of IP in the IPv4 as specified in Gunasundari & Shanmugavel (2009), has objectives such as presenting the functional entities of the MIPv4(MobileIPv4), presenting support operations for mobility, presenting the extensions for the optimizing of the routing of the MIPv4 (Mobile IPv4) and identifying the problems which affect communication during the handover.

2.1.1 Functional entities of the MIPv4

The Mobile IP is formed by the following functional entities Le-Trung et al. (2010):

1. **Mobile Node (MN):** represents a host or a router that alters its point of access when it migrates from one network or subnet to the other. It can change location without modifying its IP address and may continue to communicate with other nodes of the internet in any place using its IP address (constant), assuming that a connection of the level of the looping to an access point is available.

2. **Home Agent (HA):** represents a router in the home network (HN) of a MN that does tunneling of datagrams in order to deliver to the MN when it is away from home, in addition to keeping information on the actual location of the MN.

3. **Foreign Agent (FA):** represents a router in the network visited by the MN, also known as the foreign network, which provides the service of routing to the MN while it is registered. The FA delivers to the MN datagrams received through the tunnel configures with the HA. For the datagrams sent by the MN, the FA can serve as a default router for registered MNs.

Apart from these entities, the hosts with which the MN communicates are known as CNs. These hosts can be movable or stationary.

2.1.2 Optimizing of routing for the MIPv4

As specified in Shahriar et al. (2010), the extensions of routing optimizing offer provide means for the nodes to make cache binding of the MN. Mobility binding is mobility information associated to the MN, such as HA and CoA. This then tunnels its own datagrams directly to the CoA indicated by the binding, thus diverting the traffic of the HA to the MN. These extensions also make it possible for the datagrams in transit to move and the datagrams sent based on an invalid binding to be sent directly to the MN in its new CoA. The routing optimizing is divided into two parts, updating of the cache binding and management of the smooth handover among FAs.

In relation to the cache binding, each of the nodes has the means of maintaining a cache and CoA binding containing a CoA of one or more MNs. When it sends a datagram to an MN, if there has been an entry in the cache binding to the MN destination, the datagrama can be tunneled directly to the CoA indicated in the cache binding. In the absence of an entry, the datagramas destined for the MN must be routed to the HN of the MN in the traditional way of IP routing, then to be tunneled by the HA to the CoA of the MN. These entries have an associated valid time limit that is specified in the Binding Update message received by the node for updating the cache binding. After the validity has expired the binding is erased from the cache.

2.1.3 Handover in the MIPv4

The handover in the MIPv4 is typically determined when the MN receives a new Agent Advertisement message. When in a new FN, the MN executes the standard procedure for registering of the new CoA in its HA. The register is done through the exchange of RR and RR messages, via FA or directly ,depending on the CoA obtained. When the register is completed , the HA cancels the tunnel established with the former CoA, in order to establish a new tunnel with the new CoA. After this process, the HA begins to send the datagrams destined for the MN via the new tunnel.

Although the handover occurs in a manner which maintains communication between the MN and the CNs, this process does not cater for the characteristics of the real time and sensitive applications to the delays due to the latency of the process itself Le-Trung et al. (2010).

The latency in detection of the movement is due to the necessity to detect the movement in a reliable way for the new network (without the ping-pong effect). This occurs as a result of the frequency of messages announcing routers, as well as their range.

The latency in obtaining the CoA depends on type of CoA obtained. If the collocated CoA mode was utilized, together with DHCP, the latency will be high and unacceptable. The latency of the process occurs due to the necessity of exchanging signal messages with external components of the network.

The delays associated with the operations of the looping layer are specific to the technology used and contribute to the performance of the handover. For example, in the IEEE802.11, the handover operation typically involves sweeping of the access points in all the channels available. The selection of the appropriate access point, and its association with this access point, may even involve access control operations as specified in the IEEE802.1x De Moor et al. (2010).

Another factor which jeopardizes some applications during the handover is the loss of datagramas. In the MIPv4, the MN remains without receiving datagrams until the registration procedure is completed and the tunnel between the HA and the new CoA is established. Once this exists, during the time of the process described, there occurs a complete loss of datagrams in transit through the tunnel established between the HA and the former CoA.

Even with the utilization of the smooth handover, as the datagrams in the optimization of the MIPv4, MN remains without receiving the datagrams until the notification of the binding update is sent to the former FA and the tunnel between the former FA and the new CoA is established for sending the datagramas. Thus being the case, during the time of the process described, there occurs a partial loss of datagrams in transit through the tunnel established between the CN and the former FA.

2.2 Mobile IPv6 Overview

As presented in Dinakaran & Balasubramanie (2011), the support to the IP mobility in the IPv6 (Mobile IPv6) has benefitted from the experiences obtained in the development of the MIPv4 (MIPv4) and from the facilities provided by the IPv6. For this reason, the mobile IPv6 shares many operational characteristics of the Mobile IPv4. However, it is integrated to the IPv6 and offers other improvements. Some of the main differences between the MIPv4 and MIPv6 are listed below:

2.2.1 Functional entities of the MIPv6

The mobile MIPv6 is formed by the same functional entities defined in the MIPv4, with the exception of the FA. As stated Yu et al. (2008), any IPv6 router with a foreign link can function as a default router of the MN in a foreign locality. This router is responsible for providing the prefix of the foreign network and the Care-of-Address CoA for the MN. There is not any special configures requirement for the router, as this is merely a routable unicast address associated to the MN during its visit in the foreign link whose subnet prefix of the IP is a prefix of the foreign subnet CoA an equivalent to the collocated Care-of-Address of the MIPv4). In particular, the CoA registered in the HA of the MN is associated with its home address, being called the primary Care-of-Address.

2.2.2 Routing optimizing for the MIPv6

The optimizing of the routing requires that the MN register its current binding in the CN. For this it is necessary that the CN supports mobility binding and that the MN executes the registry procedure in the appropriate manner. As part of this procedure the test called Return Routability, which is described in Yu et al. (2008), must be executed to authorize the configures of the binding. This test supplies necessary security information to the MN to build a binding update message that must be sent to the CN to update the binding of the MN.

In the routing optimizing mode , the packets of the CN can be routed directly to the CoA of the MN. When packets are sent to any IPv6 destination, the CN searches for an entry into its cache binding destination address for the packet. If this is found the node utilizes a new IPv6 routing header, called type routing header Yu et al. (2008), to rout the packet to the MN through the CoA indicated in the binding. For correct routing the CN fills out the destination address in the IPv6 header with the CoA of the MN and the new type of header with the home address of the MN. This router shortens the communication means being used and also eliminates congestioning in the HA of the MN and in the home link. Even as a consequence, the impact of possible failures associated with the HA or with the networks on route between the MN and the HA is reduced.

In a similar way the packets of the MN can be routed directly to the CNs. For this, the MN fills out the original address of the IPv6 header of the packet with its CoA and the destination address with the address of the CN. Following this, the MN adds a new option, called IPv6 home address destination to carry its home address. The inclusion of the home address in these packets makes the use of CoA transparent to the layers of upper networks (for example, at the level of transport).

The MIPv6 also offers support to the multiple HAs, and limited support for reconfigures of the HN. In these cases, the MN cannot know the IP address of its own HA, and even the prefixes of the home subnets can change over time. One known mechanism, such as dynamic home agent address discovery allows for a MN to dynamically discover, the IP address of a HA in its home link even when the MN is outdoors. The MNs also can learn new information on the prefixes of the home subnet through the mobile prefix discovery mechanism.

2.2.3 Handover in the MIPv6

The MIPv6 Yu et al. (2008) specification considers the primary objective of movement detection is to detect handovers of the third level (L3 handovers) describing a generic method which utilizes the facilities of the IPv6 Neighbor Discovery Dinakaran & Balasubramanie (2011), including the Router Discovery and the Neighbor Unreachability Detection.

This generic detection of movement utilizes the Neighbor Unreachability Detection to detect when the default router is unreachable in a bidirectional manner, the moment in which the MN must discover a new router (usually in a new link). However, this detection only occurs when the MN has packets to send. This being the case, in the absence of a continual message of router advertisement or indices of the data link layer, the L3 handover can be noticed by the MN. For this reason, it is recommended that the MN supplements this method with some other information whenever the it is available (for example, from the protocols of the lower layers).

When a L3 handover is perceived, the MN must execute the Duplicate Address Detection procedure Dinakaran & Balasubramanie (2011) for its local link address, select a new router with the Router Discovery procedure , and then execute the Prefix Discovery procedure with the new router in order to form the new CoA. After this, the MN must register the new CoA primary with the HA in order to update its information mobility (mobility binding) of the CNs which operate in the same routing optimization mode.

Just as with the MIPv4 , although the handover occurs in a manner that maintains communication between the MN and the CNs, this process does not address the characteristics of the real time and sensitive applications to the delays, for the same reasons already explained for the MIPv4, in other words, its great latency.

The loss of the datagrams during the handover also occurs in a similar manner to the MIPv4. In the tunnel bidirectional mode of operation, the MN remains without receiving datagrams until the registration procedure is completed and the bidirectional tunnel between the HA and the new CoA is established for the sending of datagrams. Thus being the case, during the time of the process described , there occurs the complete loss of datagrams in transit through the bidirectional tunnel established between the HA and the old CoA.

Even with the utilization of the routing optimization mode of operation the MN remains without receiving datagrams, until the Binding Update notification is sent to all the CNs. Thus, until the updating of the mobility binding, associated with the MN in the CNs, there occurs a complete loss of datagrams sent by the unupdated CNs with the old CoA.

In light of these exposed problems, the scientific community seeks to improve the support for mobility in the IP through optimization proposals which come to reduce the loss of datagrams and the latency of handovers, thereby minimizing the time without receiving datagrams, with the objective of offering a transparent handover (seamless handover).

2.3 Optimizing for the handover

As stated before, one of the problems affecting MIPv4 and MIPv6 communication is the latency as it relates to rendering the new CoA register effective. This operation is slow because it involves the exchange of signal messages with components outside the network, particularly with the HA and with the CNs that support routing optimization.

Here is presented some of the main optimizations proposed for the MIPv6. The main objective of these proposals is to minimize the latency of the handover and to reduce the delay and the loss of datagrams during this operation. In a general way the proposals seek solutions for: i) minimizing the register time for CoA; ii) minimize the time for changing the access point; iii) to avoid delays and loss of datagrams.

The hierarchical handover scheme described below was defined for the MIPv4, as was presented in Romdhani & Al-Dubai (2007) and will not be presented here.

2.3.1 Hierarchical Mobile IPv6 Mobility Management (HMIPv6)

The hierarchical handover scheme divides mobility into two categories, with the aim of minimizing the latency, being the primary layer of micromobility (generally intra-domain)and the second layer being the macromobility (generally inter-domain). The central element of this scheme is the entity concept called Mobility Anchor Point (MAP) Pack et al. (2007), that defines a domain MAP formed by one or more networks. The movement of a MN between networks of the different MAP domains determines a macromobility.

Each of the networks of a MAP domain has an Access Router (AR) which corresponds to the router default of the MNs in its reachable (scope) region. The presence of the MAP domain to which the AR belongs is announced in a message of Router Advertisement. Thus, the change of a MAP domain is perceived by the MN when a new advertisement with information from a new MAP is received by the MN.

As specified in Khan & Rehana (2010), in a new MAP domain, the MN makes a binding of its CoA obtained in the local network, known as Local CoA (LCoA),with an address in the subnet of the MAP, known as Regional CoA (RCoA), and that usually is the address of the very MAP. Acting with a local HA, the MAP intercepts all the packets destined to the MN and encapsulates them and sends them directly to the LCoA. If the MN changes to another network of the same domain MAP only the register of the new LCoA is made, together with MAP with a binding update message. And then, only the RCoA needs to be registered, through another binding update message, in the HA and in the CNs with which the MN communicates. This RCoA is not modified if the movement of the MN is along the same MAP domain. This makes the micromobility of the MN transparent in relation to HA and the CNs. Figure 2 illustrates the hierarchical MIPv6 scheme.

With the objective of accelerating the handover between MAPs and reducing the loss of packets, the MN must send a binding update message to its previous MAP, specifying its new LCoA. The packets that were in transit to the previous MAP will then be passed on to the new LCoA. It is also allowed that MNs send binding update messages containing the LCoA (instead of the RCoA) to CNs which are present in the same network visited. In this way the packets will be routed directly without crossing the MAP.

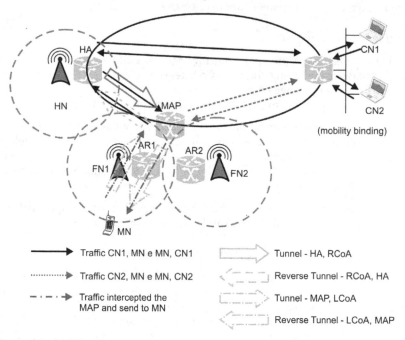

Fig. 2. Hierarchical MIPv6 Scheme

2.3.2 Fast handovers for Mobile IPv6 (FMIPv6)

As described in Han et al. (2007), the ability of immediately sending packets from a new subnet link depends on the latency of the IP connectivity, which itself depends on the latency of movement detection and the latency of configures of the new CoA. Once the IP capacity of the MN is restored the binding update message can be sent to its HA and all the CNs. From the successful processing of the binding update by its CNs, which typically involves the execution of the return routability procedure Yu et al. (2008), the MN can receive packets of the new CoA. Thus, the ability to receive new packets from the CNs directly to its new CoA depends on the latency of the binding update and the latency of the IP connectivity.

The protocol defined in Tabassam et al. (2009) makes it possible for the MN to rapidly detect its movement to a new network as it supplies information on the new Access Point (AP) and on the associated subnet prefix while the MN still finds itself connected to its actual subnet, whose default router comes to be called the Previous Access Router (PAR). For example, a MN can discover the available APs using mechanisms of the data link layer (for example, scan operation in WLAN) and then request information from the corresponding subnet to one or more of the APs discovered. This requisition is done with the sending of the Router Solicitation for Proxy Advertisement (RtSolPr) to its access router.

The result of the identifier resolution associated with an AP is the tupla [AP-ID, ARInfo], where AP-ID is the AP identifier and AR-Info is composed of the L2 address of the router, IP address of the router and a valid prefix in the subnet to which the AP is connected. This response is sent by the AR to the MN in the Proxy Router Advertisement (PrRtAdv) message.

With the information obtained, the MN formulates a secondary new CoA (NCoA) and sends an AFSt binding update message (FBU) when a specific handover link event occurs .This message has the purpose of authorizing the PAR to make PCoA binding (Previous CoA) for the NCoA, in a way that the packets which arrive could be tunneled to the new MN location. Whenever possible, the FBU must be sent from the PAR link. When this is not possible the FBU is sent from the new link. With the execution of this procedure the latency related to the discovery of the new prefix subsequent to the handover is eliminated. As confirmation of receipt of the FBU, the PAR must send the Fast Binding Acknowledgment (FBack) message, whether or not the FBack message is received in the previous link. The scenario in which the MM sends a FBU message and receives a FBACK message in the PAR link is characterized as an operation in pre-indicated mode or anticipated (predictive), as illustrated in Figure 3.

The scenario in which the MN sends a FBU message from the NAR link is characterized as an operation in the reactive mode, as is illustrated in Figure 4. This mode also deals with cases in which the FBU message is sent from the PAR link , but a FBack message was not yet received.

Finally, the PrRtAdv can be sent unsolicited, i.e. without a previous RtSolPr message. This operation makes it possible for the MN to be kept informed about the geographically adjacent networks, thus reducing the quantity of traffic necessary to obtain the topological map of the neighborhood links and subnets. Nevertheless, the HI and HACK messages can still be utilized for transference of relevant information in the context of the network, such as access control, QoS and header compression along with the handover.

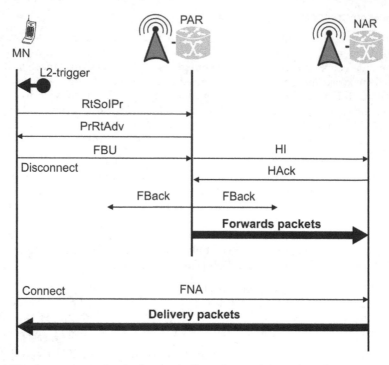

Fig. 3. Fast Handover: operation in the pre-indicated or anticipated mode

2.4 Media Independent Handover - MIH

The Media Independent Handover (MIH) IEEE 802.21 Draft Standard defines methods and specifications for transparent handovers in layer 2 (Handover L2) among networks with different technologies Taniuchi et al. (2009). The envisaged standard helps in the determination and initialization of a handover, but leaves unspecified details about how to treat the handover.

In order to provide such functions, the IEEE802.21 defines the MIH Function (MIHF) positions between layers 2 and 3, which offer three basic services: i) Events Service, through the Media Independent Event Service (MIES); ii) The Command Service, through the Media Independent Command Service (MICS); and iii) The Information service, through the Media Independent Information Service (MIIS). The architecture of the MIHF is illustrated in Figure 5.

The MIES supplies a classification of events, filtering of events and a report of events that correspond to the dynamic changes which occur in the link in relation to characteristics, state and quality. As shown in Figure 6, the MIH Function must be registered in the data link layer in order to receive the link events, while the upper links interested in MIH events must be registered in the MIH Function to receive these events. The events can be generated by remote battery of the Point of Access (PoA) which is acting as a Point of Service (PoS). The link events and MIH events are divided into five categories: administrative, change of state, link parameter, pre-indicated (predictive) link synchronization, and link transition.

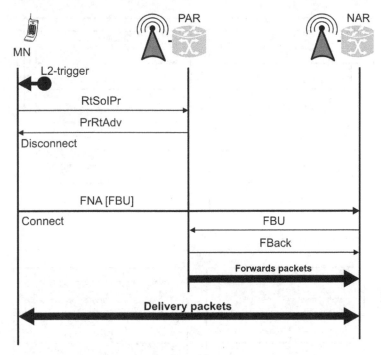

Fig. 4. Operation in the reactive mode

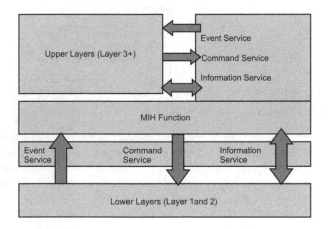

Fig. 5. Architecture of MIH Function

The MICS allows MIH users to be able to manage and control relevant link characteristics for handover and mobility. As illustrated in Figure 7, the MIH commands originate in the upper layers in direction to the MIH Function. In this, these commands become a remote MIH command for a remote battery and/or follow the lower layers as a link command of the MIH Function. The link commands are specific to the access network in use and are only local.

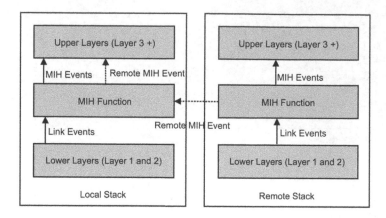

Fig. 6. Functioning of the MIES

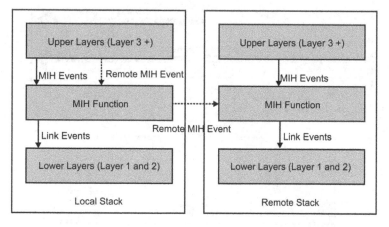

Fig. 7. Functioning of the MICS

The MIIS provides the capacity to obtain information necessary for the handovers such as neighborhood maps, information about the data link layer and available services. In short, this service offers a two-way route for all the layers to share Information elements that help in the handover decision-making process. These information elements are divided into five groups: General Information (e.g. area operators); Network Access (e.g. cost, security, QoS); Information on PoA (e.g. information about the subnet); and Other Information (e.g. specific to the supplier).

3. Wireless networks and multimedia communications

The networks of the next generation, such as the fourth generation wireless networks (4G), represent a total convergence of voice and data. There is also consideration of the convergence of wireless networks such as the standards (IEEE 802.11; IEEE 802.16; IEEE 802.15.4; IEEE 802.22; 3GPP-LTE; 3G; and G4), and of the integration of fixed and mobile networks.

3.1 Wireless networks

According to the Institute of Electrical and Electronics Engineers (IEEE) Wireless networks are classified into Wireless Personal Area Network (WPAN); Wireless Local Area Network (WLAN); Wireless Metropolitan Area Network (WMAN); and Wireless Regional Area Network (WRAN). For each classification IEEE defines the parameter standard. A different set of characteristics are included in the technologies of each determined wireless network service. These technologies were described in the above classification. Thus each classification needs to work with its specific IEEE standard as these are the standards which represent the classification.

3.1.1 The IEEE 802.11 Standard

When one uses mobility in the IEEE802.11 standard for WLAN network infrastructure the connection point of the device for the Internet network remains the same during its mobility. This means that a mobile node dislocating itself within its own network, with various points of connection making use of the same configures parameters, can have its data received in that new location De Moor et al. (2010). This mobility seeks to increase the action raduis of a node within a determined area (intra-domain). Over time, and like the other standards, the 802.11also experienced evolutions from which emerged the k, v, and r standards that will be mentioned below.

1. **The IEEE 802.11k Standard**
   The k extension of the 802.11 standardizes various types of information on characteristics of the 802.11 radio which can be measured, as well as the messages used in these, and allows transparent transitions of the Basic Set of Services (BSS). This standard also implements QoS. The main objectives of the 802.11k extension are Yu et al. (2008) Hermann et al. (2007):

   - To allow the station to measure the specific parameters of the 802.11radio;
   - To standardize requisitions and report messages with the results of these measures; and
   - To make available access of this information to all the upper layers of the pile of protocols.

2. **The 802.11v Standard**
   The v extension of the 802.11 is characterized by the management of wireless networks, and allows the configures of devices of clients connected to the networks similar to those used in mobile networks IEEE802.11v (2011)Ciurana et al. (2011).

3. **The 802.11r Standard**
   The r extension of the 802.11, standardizes rapid handover when a wireless client associates with another AP in the same network during a locomotion process Khan & Rehana (2010) Tabassam et al. (2009).

3.1.2 The IEEE 802.16 Standard

The IEEE 802.16 Standard defines, among other characteristics, the air interface specification, the additional functionalites in the physical layer, and the changes in the layer of access control of the device for metropolitan wireless networks, also known as fixed systems, without broad band connection Li et al. (2007). The system, based on the 802.16 standard, is basically composed of a base station and terminal stations, known also as CPE (Customer Premises

Equipment). A station base is the central place that collects all the data of and for the terminal stations within a cell. The station bases have antennas with relatively wide beams, divided into one or various sectors to supply 360 degree coverage. A subscriber unit, or CPE, consists basically of an external unit with a radio and an antenna connected to an internal unit, basically a modem, which makes the interface with the end-user.

3.1.3 The IEEE 802.15.4 Standard

The IEEE 802.15.4 Standard, called Low-Rate Wireless Personal Area Networks (LR-WPAN), has as its objective to establish a network with characteristics of low complexity, low costs and low energy consumption Ramachandran et al. (2007). The scope of this standard is to define the physical layer and sub-layer of access control of the MAC device, as the IEEE 802 workgroups traditionally do in network solution standards.

3.1.4 The IEEE 802.22 Standard

The development of the IEEE 802.22 standard (WRAN), destined for the use of cognitive radio technology, is to allow for the sharing of locally idle spectrum attributed to the TV diffusion service in a regime of non-interference, and to take wideband access to regions of difficult access, areas of low population density, and rural environments. For this it is timely and has the potential for ample applicability in the whole world Stevenson et al. (2009).

3.2 Multimedia communications

The applications for Long Term Evolution (LTE) Ergen (2009), third-generation (3G) and fourth-generation (4G), have presented increasing integration and convergence of multimedia services linked directly the increase in demand for data and mobility. As a result the 4G technology is gaining much attention.

4G environments are a fully integrated all-IP packet-switched system that promises to support the following features: a highly efficient spectral system, support for all types of multimedia content, access speeds up to 1 Gigabit/second for low mobility, such as local wireless access, and up to 100 Mbits/s for high mobility, such as vehicular scenarios, seamless handoff and global roaming across multiple heterogeneous networks, better scheduling and call admission control schemes, terminal heterogeneity, and several other interesting features Tong et al. (2008).

In addition, 4G networks also provide high usability for end users, enabling them to customize their multimedia applications and receive their content with QoE assurances. 4G systems are expected to play a fundamental role in supporting truly ubiquitous multimedia communications in coming years. However, to satisfy the skyrocketing demand for multimedia service access over heterogeneous wireless network infrastructures at any-time, from anywhere and any device, several challenges need to be addressed at the network, device, and application levels.

It is well known that multimedia transmissions over wireless communication links need to also take into account the characteristics of the links in contrast to wired networks. Packet losses in wired networks are primarily due to congestions, whereas in the case of wireless networks they are caused mainly by corruption of packets due to low Signal to Noise Ratio (SNR), interferences from nearby transmissions, or multi-path signal fading Bouras et al. (2008). Past efforts to mitigate delays and packet losses caused by wireless links have primarily focused on cross-layer design optimization techniques, where dependencies between protocol layers are exploited to improve the end-to-end performance delivered to end-users. Some of the recent cross-layer design architectures that have been proposed specifically for multimedia transmissions include Huusko et al. (2007)Bobarshad et al. (2010). Most of these cross-layer approaches provide additional support through the implementation of new interfaces used for sharing information between adjacent layers or by adjusting parameters that span across different transmission layers.

The layers exploited by several proposed cross-layer designs typically involve all or a subset of the application layer (even a user-based layer), the Media Access Control (MAC) layer, and the physical layer. For instance, proposed a cross-layer design aimed at improving the quality of H.264 video over IEEE 802.11e-based networks Chilamkurti et al. (2010). The design takes advantage of the characteristics of both application and MAC layer information to improve the video transmission quality of H.264 video. As described in Kovács et al. (2010) proposed an approach that classifies multimedia packets into different classes, and depending on the underlying network conditions, only specific packets are transmitted. Their cross-design approach also exploits information from the MAC layer and the transport layer to optimize MPEG-4 video delivery and quality. Several other multimedia cross-layer designs for multimedia transmissions using different types of adaptation strategies (such as the integrated, the MAC-centric, or the top-down approaches) have been proposed in the literature.

Advances in wireless QoS/QoE models and portable devices have been allowing the distribution of high quality multimedia content to fixed and mobile users. New strategies in routing, admission control, resource reservations, re-registration, and authorization, among others have been discussed in literature and implemented by service providers, and are creating ubiquitous wireless multimedia systems.

In addition to network-based efforts, mobile wireless devices are also attracting a lot of attention. Nowadays, it is possible to see fairly complex multi-function terminals capable of handling different media types. Mobile users are using such devices for different purposes, including the storage of personal information (e.g., an address book), to conduct various forms of interactions (e.g., voice, email, video phone), entertainment (e.g., gaming, on-demand video streaming), and information access (through web browsers) Cerqueira et al. (2008).

Wireless multimedia devices are placing increasing demands on designers and manufacturers to provide higher processing capabilities, a larger number of functions and usage modes, displays with higher resolutions, user-friendly/multimodal interaction modes, and the support of multiple wireless interfaces that can connect to different types of wireless networks. In the context of future multimedia systems, fast detection of available access networks and selection of the "most appropriate" network interface based on factors such as user preference, costs, seamless and application requirements are becoming increasingly important for many portable devices.

Another important design consideration for future mobile multimedia devices is their conformance to well-known standards Cerqueira et al. (2008) (open application framework, standard interfaces, etc.) relieving end-users of the need to spend time learning proprietary technologies. By providing such design flexibility to end-users, software development on these platforms will be made much easier and more modular.

4. Challenges for future multimedia networks

In recent years, several solutions have been proposed in academic and industry environments regarding mobile multimedia networks assessment, content distribution, and optimization over heterogeneous wireless and wired networks and seamless multimedia mobility.

In future multimedia systems, new QoE-based application, transport and network levels optimization mechanisms (whether a cross-layer approach is used or not) are still needed, such as routing, inter/intra-session adaptation, resource reservation, traffic controller, seamless multimedia mobility and base station selection/user experience and IEEE 802.11k, v and r schemes mobility. Additionally, the multi-homing capability of current devices can also provide an improved performance for multimedia applications by taking advantage of the multiple connectivity levels of each wireless device.

4.1 Mobile multimedia systems

Seamless multimedia mobility will be one of the dominating factors for the success of next generation systems. Besides the basic connectivity needed by any type of application, multimedia applications have stringent requirements from the network, which include bounds on the end-to-end delay, loss rate, and delay jitter. Considering voice services: they commonly have generally low bandwidth requirements, which depend on the codec being used; but, on the other hand, voice is very sensitive to losses. Video services need a large amount of available bandwidth and compression is mandatory for such applications. While jitter and delay are still an issue, some losses are bearable due to the recovery capabilities of the compression mechanisms, such as MPEG-4. Overall, multimedia applications require that the quality of the communication has acceptable levels, which are naturally dependent on the nature of each application.

Due to the innate characteristics of wireless mobile technologies that have a limited capacity and are prone to interference, as well as to the challenges associated with mobility, the support of multimedia in such scenarios has raised work at several levels from, the technology dependent layers up to application adaptation, such as the compression mentioned before and base station selection.

The end-to-end support of multimedia applications requires the maintenance of the transmission quality level when multiple heterogeneous technologies are used and devices/users are mobile. One can imagine a Wireless LAN access and a WiMAX backhaul within a city scenario, a WiMAX access in rural areas with connection to some satellite or wired Internet access technology, or a train travelling across a country or between different countries. Besides the QoS capabilities of each technology, there is the need to guarantee an end-to-end quality level with QoE support.

Nowadays, mobility usually occurs between different access points, but within the same technology, which is known as horizontal handover. However, as devices become empowered with different technologies, which naturally vary in their quality and costing procedures, there is a need to develop mechanisms for handovers between different technologies, known as vertical handover. This situation raises the issue of inter-technology mobility, which poses additional challenges when multimedia applications are at stake.

4.2 Mobile scenario

The proposal of the scenario is based, Figure 8 shows on a mobility profile model, by forecasting the user centered path, and having as its main objective a resource reserve for multi-media traffic in WLAN networks. This scenario has as its intuition to present an analysis on the IEEE 802.11 technology utilizing some innovative concepts which combine the IEEE 802.11k,r and v mechanisms, having in view user mobility within a WLAN domain (BSS) and from this to minimize delays in the handover.

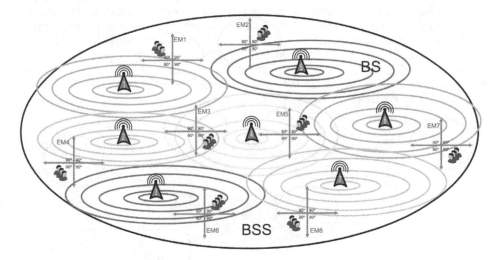

Fig. 8. Basic Scenario

4.2.1 Proposed model

The model seeks to minimize the reserve resource and in this way, maximize the resources for other EM mobiles in the domain. This model considers that 360° (degrees) of the possible direction of an EM mobile can be analyzed either in parts or in each of the four 90° (degree) quadrants and, in this way, can achieve the reserve resource in the neighboring APs of each quadrant, as can be illustrated as follows.

Taking account of the basic scenario of Figure 8, it is possible to observe a BSS with 7 Access Points (AP) and 8 Mobile Equipments (EP). A detailed description of the scheme can be undertaken for the analysis, by examining the AP2, AP4, EM3 and EM5 respectively.

The user of the EM3 is connected to the AP2 and in normal conditions, the reserve resource can be carried out in all the other 6 APs of the BSS, taking into account the fact that the user is able to follow the 360° (degrees) of the possible directions within the domain. Thus, by setting out with the proposed model and on the basis of the User Mobility Profile, (which was defined after the analysis of the k Standard Reports that identified the second quadrant [90°-180° degrees] as the probable path of the EM3), it can be stated that the AP2 is able to evaluate the neighboring APs within the coverage radius of the first quadrant, which are 5, 7 and 8 APs. It can also achieve the reserve resource for the EM5 which has one of the three APs as a prediction of the path.

In another analysis, the EM5 user is connected to the AP4 and in normal conditions, the reserve resource can also be carried out in all the other 6 APs of the BSS, by taking account of the 360° (degrees) possible direction that the user can follow within the domain. Thus, on the basis of the proposed model and taking the User Mobility Profile as a basis (which was defined after an analysis of the K Standard Report that identified the first quadrant [0°-90° degrees] as the probable path for the EM5), it can be considered that the AP4 is able to evaluate the neighboring APs within the coverage radius of the first quadrant (which are AP 5 and 6) and to achieve the reserve resource for the EM5 which has one of the two APs as the prediction of the path. After the reserve resource has been achieved in the determined APs, another process of great importance is initiated for multimedia traffic, which is related to the handover process. Figure 9 shows the handover concept in the IEEE 802.11k standard. When the STA configures the handover for the current AP, it evaluates its neighbors and makes a selection of the AP candidate through graphic or cache of the neighbor. A neighbor report is requested and soon after furnishes a response that finds and makes a selection of the AP. This model supplies the knowledge about the location of the neighboring APs.

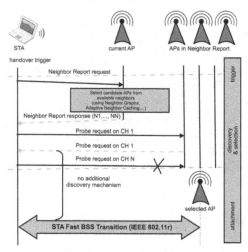

Fig. 9. The Handover Concept using IEEE 802.11k with neighbor reports

Figure 10 shows the concept handover based on neighbor reports and LCI (Location Configuration Information) . Position and velocity can be computed for each STA, which allows the exclusion of the neighboring APs from the list of candidates , thereby reducing latency in relation to the previous model. However, the 802.11k standard is not defined.

Managing BSS transactions in the IEEE 802.11v allows APs to set off handovers with a Management of BSS Transaction request at the specific moment, which is not defined by the IEEE 802.11v. This can happen automatically, or after being requested through checking on the management of the BSS Transaction of a STA. Figure 11 shows this mechanism in detail.

Figure 12 shows that in this mechanism there is an increase in functionality with the combination of the IEEE mechanisms 802.11k and 802.11v, although it uses IEEE802.11v through the management of BSS Transaction. Despite greater control of overload it forecasts the minimum of latency in the handover

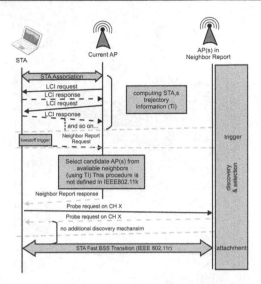

Fig. 10. Concept Handover using IEEE802.11k with neighbor reports and LCI

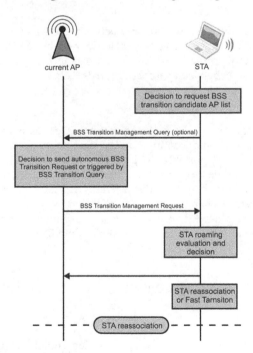

Fig. 11. Management of BSS Transaction IEEE 802.11v

After being collected, the information of the network APs of the mobility profile model with prediction of the user-centered path, will be define. The actual AP, where the user is

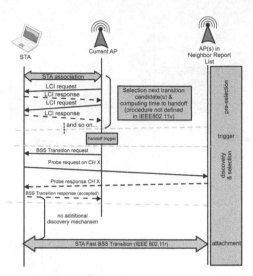

Fig. 12. The Handover Concept, using IEEE 802.11v with BSS Transaction Management and LCI

connected, will have a confidential relationship between the APs (Trusting AP and Trusted AP). Depending on the number and geographical location of the subscribers (STA), the reserve resources will be balanced, so that there can be no bias in the general performance of the network favoring handovers between neighboring APs.

5. Conclusions

Multimedia networks continue to be a strong research area, as it has been for more than a decade. This tendency should continue as the new challenges, such as the results of new services, mobility, novel portable devices, changes in user demands and terminals, network infra-structure, and heterogeneous devices arise. This chapter focuses on presenting important concepts of mobility based on IEEE 802.11k, v, and r. User-centric mobility models are required to allow seamless handover with QoE, including for high resolution multimedia such as 3D videos among others. This chapter has contributed to the understanding of the questions and challenges for the next generation of multimedia networks.

6. Acknowledgments

This work is supported by CNPq and FAPESPA.

7. References

Ahmadi, S. (2009). An overview of next-generation mobile wimax technology, *IEEE Communications Magazine* 47(6): 84–98.
Bobarshad, H., van der Schaar, M. & Shikh-Bahaei, M. (2010). A low-complexity analytical modeling for cross-layer adaptive error protection in video over wlan, *Multimedia, IEEE Transactions on* 12(5): 427–438.

Bouras, C., Gkamas, A. & Kioumourtzis, G. (2008). Challenges in cross layer design for multimedia transmission over wireless networks, *Proceedings of WWRF-21st Meeting WG3–Future Architecture, Stockholm, Sweden, October*, Citeseer.

Cerqueira, E., Zeadally, S., Leszczuk, M., Curado, M. & Mauthe, A. (2008). Recent advances in multimedia networking, *Multimedia Tools and Applications* pp. 1–13.

Chilamkurti, N., Zeadally, S., Soni, R. & Giambene, G. (2010). Wireless multimedia delivery over 802.11 e with cross-layer optimization techniques, *Multimedia Tools and Applications* 47(1): 189–205.

Ciurana, M., Barceló-Arroyo, F. & Martín-Escalona, I. (2011). Comparative performance evaluation of ieee 802.11v for positioning with time of arrival, *Computer Standards & Interfaces* 33(3): 344 – 349.

De Moor, K., Joseph, W., Ketykó, I., Tanghe, E., Deryckere, T., Martens, L. & De Marez, L. (2010). Linking users' subjective qoe evaluation to signal strength in an ieee 802.11 b/g wireless lan environment, *EURASIP Journal on Wireless Communications and Networking* 2010: 6.

Dinakaran, M. & Balasubramanie, P. (2011). Performance analysis of various mipv6 protocols, *European Journal of Scientific Research* 49(3): 403–414.

Ergen, M. (2009). *Mobile broadband: including WiMAX and LTE*, Springer Verlag.

Gunasundari, R. & Shanmugavel, S. (2009). Performance comparison of mobile ipv4 and mobile ipv6 protocols in wireless systems, *First International Communication Systems and Networks and Workshops, 2009. COMSNETS 2009.*, IEEE, pp. 1–8.

Han, Y., Jang, H., Choi, J., Park, B. & McNair, J. (2007). A cross-layering design for ipv6 fast handover support in an ieee 802.16 e wireless man, *Network, IEEE* 21(6): 54–62.

Harini, P. (2011). A novel approach to improve handoff performance in hierarchical mobile ipv6 using an enhanced architecture, *IJCST* 2(1).

Hermann, S., Emmelmann, M., Belaifa, O. & Wolisz, A. (2007). Investigation of ieee 802.11 k-based access point coverage area and neighbor discovery, *32nd IEEE Conference on Local Computer Networks, 2007. LCN 2007*, IEEE, pp. 949–954.

Huusko, J., Vehkapera, J., Amon, P., Lamy-Bergot, C., Panza, G., Peltola, J. & Martini, M. (2007). Cross-layer architecture for scalable video transmission in wireless network, *Signal Processing: Image Communication* 22(3): 317–330.

IEEE802.11v (2011). Ieee standard for information technology–telecommunications and information exchange between systems–local and metropolitan area networks–specific requirements part 11: Wireless lan medium access control (mac) and physical layer (phy) specifications amendment 8: Ieee 802.11 wireless network management, *IEEE Std 802.11v-2011 (Amendment to IEEE Std 802.11-2007 as amended by IEEE Std 802.11k-2008, IEEE Std 802.11r-2008, IEEE Std 802.11y-2008, IEEE Std 802.11w-2009, IEEE Std 802.11n-2009, IEEE Std 802.11p-2010, and IEEE Std 802.11z-2010)* pp. 1 –433.

Khan, K. & Rehana, J. (2010). Wireless handoff optimization: a comparison of ieee 802.11 r and hokey, *Networked Services and Applications-Engineering, Control and Management* pp. 118–131.

Klein, A. & Klaue, J. (2009). Performance evaluation framework for video applications in mobile networks, *Second International Conference on Advances in Mesh Networks, 2009. MESH 2009*, IEEE, pp. 43–49.

Kovács, Á., Gódor, I., Rácz, S. & Borsos, T. (2010). Cross-layer quality-based resource reservation for scalable multimedia, *Computer Communications* 33(3): 283–292.

Le-Trung, Q., Engelstad, P., Skeie, T., Eliassen, F. & Taherkordi, A. (2010). Mobility management for all-ip mobile networks: Spanning manet domain, *Book chapter proposal for the call: Emerging Wireless Networks, CRC Press, Taylor & Francis, USA* .

Li, B., Qin, Y., Low, C. & Gwee, C. (2007). A survey on mobile wimax [wireless broadband access], *Communications Magazine, IEEE* 45(12): 70–75.

Meschke, R., Krohn, M., Daher, R., Gladisch, A. & Tavangarian, D. (2010). Novel handoff concepts for roadside networks using mechanisms of ieee 802.11 k & ieee 802.11 v, *International Congress on Ultra Modern Telecommunications and Control Systems and Workshops (ICUMT), 2010*, IEEE, pp. 1232–1238.

Pack, S., Kwon, T. & Choi, Y. (2007). A performance comparison of mobility anchor point selection schemes in hierarchical mobile ipv6 networks, *Computer Networks* 51(6): 1630–1642.

Ramachandran, I., Das, A. & Roy, S. (2007). Analysis of the contention access period of ieee 802.15. 4 mac, *ACM Transactions on Sensor Networks (TOSN)* 3(1): 4–es.

Romdhani, I. & Al-Dubai, A. (2007). Mobile ip conditional binding update.

Seshadrinathan, K. & Bovik, A. (2011). Automatic prediction of perceptual quality of multimedia signals-a survey, *Multimedia Tools and Applications* pp. 1–24.

Shahriar, A., Atiquzzaman, M. & Ivancic, W. (2010). Route optimization in network mobility: Solutions, classification, comparison, and future research directions, *IEEE Communications Surveys & Tutorials* 12(1): 24–38.

Stevenson, C., Chouinard, G., Lei, Z., Hu, W., Shellhammer, S. & Caldwell, W. (2009). Ieee 802.22: The first cognitive radio wireless regional area network standard, *Communications Magazine, IEEE* 47(1): 130–138.

Tabassam, A., Trsek, H., Heiss, S. & Jasperneite, J. (2009). Fast and seamless handover for secure mobile industrial applications with 802.11r, *Local Computer Networks, 2009. LCN 2009. IEEE 34th Conference on*, IEEE, pp. 750–757.

Taniuchi, K., Ohba, Y., Fajardo, V., Das, S., Tauil, M., Cheng, Y., Dutta, A., Baker, D., Yajnik, M. & Famolari, D. (2009). Ieee 802.21: media independent handover: features, applicability, and realization, *IEEE Communications Magazine* 47(1): 112–120.

Tong, W., Sich, E., Zhu, P. & Costa, J. (2008). True broadband multimedia experience, *Microwave Magazine, IEEE* 9(4): 64–71.

Yu, C., Pan, M. & Wang, S. (2008). Adaptive neighbor caching for fast bss transition using ieee 802.11 k neighbor report, *International Symposium on Parallel and Distributed Processing with Applications, 2008. ISPA'08*, IEEE, pp. 353–360.

Zhang, L. & Pierre, S. (2009). Intelligent fast handover scheme for mobile ipv6-based wireless local area networks, *IJCSNS* 9(8): 60.

Zhou, Z., Peng, Z., Cui, J., Shi, Z. & Bagtzoglou, A. (2010). Scalable localization with mobility prediction for underwater sensor networks, *IEEE Transactions on Mobile Computing* .

Zinner, T., Hohlfeld, O., Abboud, O. & Hoßfeld, T. (2010). Impact of frame rate and resolution on objective qoe metrics, *Second International Workshop on Quality of Multimedia Experience (QoMEX), 2010*, IEEE, pp. 29–34.

5

Source Coding and Channel Coding for Mobile Multimedia Communication

Hammad Dilpazir[1], Hasan Mahmood[1], Tariq Shah[2] and Hafiz Malik[3]
[1]*Department of Electronics, Quaid-i-Azam University, Islamabad*
[2]*Department of Mathematics, Quaid-i-Azam University, Islamabad*
[3]*Department of Electrical and Computer Engineering,*
University of Michigan - Dearborn, Dearborn, MI
[1,2]*Pakistan*
[3]*USA*

1. Introduction

In the early era of communications engineering, the emphasis was on establishing links and providing connectivity. With the advent of new bandwidth hungry applications, the desire to fulfill the user's need became the main focus of research in the area of data communications. It took about half a century to achieve near channel capacity limit in the year 1993, as predicted by Shannon (Shannon, 1948). However, with the advancement in multimedia technology, the increase in the volume of information by the order of magnitude further pushed the scientists to incorporate data compression techniques in order to fulfill the ever increasing bandwidth requirements. According to Cover (Cover & Thomas, 2006), the separation theorem stated by Shannon implies that it is possible for the source and channel coding to be accomplished on separate and sequential basis while still maintaining optimization. In the context of multimedia communication, the former represents the compression while the latter, the error protection. A major restriction, however, with this theorem is that it is applicable only to asymptotically lengthy blocks of data and in most situations cannot be a good approximation. So, these shortcomings have tacitly led to devising new strategies for joint-source channel coding.

This chapter addresses the major issues in source and channel coding and presents the techniques used for efficient data transmission for multimedia applications over wireless channels. The chapter highlights the strategies and notions of the source, channel, and joint source-channel coding. The remaining chapter is divided into two parts. The first part provides a brief description of digital image storage and transmission process, and the second part provides a brief description of digital video storage and transmission process.

1.1 Source coding

The process by which information symbols are mapped to alphabetical symbols is called *source coding*. The mapping is generally performed in sequences or groups of information and alphabetical symbols. Also, it must be performed in such a manner that it guarantees the exact recovery of the information symbol back from the alphabetical symbols otherwise it will destroy the basic theme of the source coding. The source coding is called *lossless compression* if the information symbols are exactly recovered from the alphabetical symbols otherwise it is called *lossy compression*. The Source coding also known as compression or bit-rate reduction process. It is the process of removing redundancy from the source symbols, which essentially reduces data size. Source coding is a vital part of any communication system as it helps to use disk space and transmission bandwidth efficiently. The source coding can either be lossy or lossless. In case of lossless encoding, error free reconstruction of source symbols is possible, whereas, exact reconstruction of source symbols is not possible in case of lossy encoding. The minimum average length of codewords as function of entropy is restricted between an upper and lower bound of the information source symbols by the Shannon's source coding theorem (Shannon, 1948). For a lossless case, entropy is the maximum limit on the data compression, which is represented by $H(\chi)$ and is defined as

$$H(\chi) = \sum_i p_x(i) \log p_x(i) \tag{1}$$

where $p_x(.)$ is the probability distribution of the information source symbols.

The Huffman algorithm is basically used for encoding entropy and to compress data without loss. In order to choose a particular representation for each symbol, Huffman coding makes use of a particular method that leads to a prefix code also called as *prefix-free code*. This method uses a minimum number of bits in the form of strings to represent mostly used and common source symbols and vice versa. Furthermore, Huffman coding uses a code table of varying length in order to encode a source symbol. The table is made on the basis of the probability calculated for all the values of the source symbol that have the possibility to occur. This scheme is optimal in terms of obtaining code words of minimum yet possible average length.

The coding concept of Shannon-Fano (Shannon, 1948) is used to construct prefix code using a group of symbols along with the probabilities by which they are measured or calculated. This technique, however, is not the optimum as it does not guarantee the code word of minimum yet possible average length as does the Huffman coding. In contrast, this coding technique always achieves code words lengths that lie within one bit range of the theoretical and ideal $\log P(x)$.

Shannon-Fano-Elias coding, on the other hand, works on cumulative probability distribution. It is a precursor to arithmetic coding, in which probabilities are used to determine codewords. The Shannon-Fano-Elias code is not an optimal code if one symbol is encoded at time and is a little worse than, for instance, a Huffman code. One of the limitation of these coding techniques is that all the methods require the probability density function or cumulative density function of the source symbols which is not possible in many practical applications. The universal coding techniques are proposed to address this dilemma. For instance, Lempel-Ziv (LZ) coding (Ziv & Lempel, 1978) and Lempel-Ziv-Welch (LZW) coding. The LZ coding algorithm is a variable-to-fixed length, lossless coding method.

A high level description of the LZ encoding algorithm is given as,

1. Initializing the dictionary in order to have strings/blocks of unity length.

2. Searching the most lengthy block W in the dictionary that matches the current input string.

3. Encode W by the dictionary index and remove W from the input.

4. Perform addition of W which is then followed by the a next symbol as input to the dictionary.

5. Move back to step 2.

The compression algorithm proposed in (Ziv & Lempel, 1978), shows that this technique asymptotically achieves the Shannon limit (Shannon, 1948). More details on existing source coding methods and their properties can be found in (Cover & Thomas, 1991) and references therein.

The rate distortion theory highlights and discusses the source coding with losses, i.e., data compression. It works by finding the minimum entropy (or information) R for a communication channel in order to approximately reconstruct the input signal at the receiver while keeping a certain limit of distortion D. This theory actually defines the theoretical limits for achieving compression using techniques of compression with loss. Today's compression methods make use of transformation, quantization, and bit-rate allocation techniques to deal with the rate distortion functions. The founder of this theory was C. E. Shannon (Shannon, 1948). The number of bits that are used for storing or transmitting a data sample are generally meant as *rate*. The distortion is the subject of discussion in these lines. The Mean Squared Error (MSE) commonly used distortion measure in the rate-distortion theory. Since most of lossy compression techniques operate on data that will be perceived by human consumers (listening to music, watching pictures and video), therefore, the distortion measure should be modeled on human perception. For example, in audio compression, perceptual models are comparatively very promising and are commonly deployed in compression methods like MP3 or Vorbis. However, they are not convenient to be taken into account in the rate distortion theory. Also, methods that are perception dependent are not considered promising for image and video compression so they are in general used with Joint Picture Expert Group (JPEG) and Moving Picture Expert Group (MPEG) weighting matrix.

Some other methods such as Adam7 Algorithm, Adaptive Huffman, Arithmetic Coding, Canonical Huffman Code, Fibonacci Coding, Golomb Coding, Negafibonacci Coding, Truncated Binary Encoding, etc., are also used in different applications for data compression.

1.2 Channel coding

The channel coding is a framework of increasing reliability of data transmission at the cost of reduction in information rate. This goal is achieved by adding redundancy to the information symbol vector resulting in a longer coded vector of symbols that are distinguishable at the output of the channel.

Channel coding methods can be classified into the following two main categories:

1. *Linear block coding* maps a block of k information bits onto a codeword of n bits such that $n > k$. In addition, mapping of k information bits is distinct, that is, for each sequence of k information bits, there is a distinct codeword of n bits. Examples of linear block codes include Hamming Codes, Reed Muller Codes, Reed Solomon Codes, Cyclic Codes, BCH Codes, etc. A Cyclic Redundancy Check (CRC) code can detect any error burst up to the length of the CRC code itself.

2. *Convolutional coding* maps a sequence of k bits of information onto a codeword of n bits by exploiting knowledge of the present k information bits as well as the previous information bits. Examples include Viterbi-decoded convolutional codes, turbo codes, etc.

The major theme of channel coding is to allow the decoder to decode the valid codeword or codeword with noise which means some bits would be corrupted. In ideal situation, the decoder knows the codeword that is sent even after corruption by noise. C. E. Shannon in his landmark work (Shannon, 1948) proposed a framework of coding the information to be transmitted over a *noisy channel*. He also provided theoretical bounds for reliable communication over a noisy channel as a function of the channel capacity.

1.3 Joint source-channel coding

The joint source-channel coding corresponds to the process of mapping (or encoding) the source data such that it can be compressed and protected against transmission errors over a noisy channel. Shannon's separation theorem states that source coding (compression by redundant bit removal) and channel coding (bit interleaving for error protection) can be performed separately and sequentially, while maintaining optimality. However, when operating under a *delay-constraint* on a *time-varying* channel, sequential optimality of two coders does not guarantee joint optimality. In order to achieve joint optimality, the source coding and the channel coding can be achieved through Joint Source-Channel Coding (JSCC). Thus, considerable interest is developed in various schemes of JSCC. For example, Gray and Ornstein (Gray & Ornstein, 1976) proposed sliding-block codes based on discrete-time-invariant nonlinear filtering to achieve JSCC. Gray and Ornstein provided theoretical bound for overall symbol error probability $\epsilon > 0$ for the proposed time-invariant finite-length sliding-block encoder and decoder in terms of channel capacity C and entropy rate $H(U) < C$, where U denotes discrete ergodic source.

A technique of using joint source channel coding was proposed in (Modestino et al., 1981), where the author exploits the trade off between compression and error correction. The performance of the proposed framework was tested using 2D Discrete Cosine Transform (DCT) for source coding and convolutional codes for channel coding together. In (Ayanoglu & Gray, 1987), a design of joint source and channel trellis waveform coding was proposed. Effectiveness of the proposed method has been experimentally demonstrated. Another important result of the article was to show that the jointly optimized codes achieve performance either near or better than separately optimized codes. Farvardin and Vaishampayan (Farvardin & Vaishampayan, 1987) have also proposed a scheme for joint source-channel coding optimization, however, this scheme is based on the optimal quantizer design. Similarly, Goodman (Goodman et al., 1988) have also modeled the joint source-channel coding as a joint optimization problem. Sayood (Sayood et al., 1988) have provided a Maximum A Posteriori (MAP) based approach for jointly optimizing the problem of communication over an unreliable link. Effectiveness of their scheme has been demonstrated using image transmission over wireless channel. Wyrwas and Farrell (Wyrwas & Farrell, 1989) have shown that the joint source channel coding is more efficient for low resolution graphics transmission.

2. Image

Still images contain both spatial and psycho-visual redundancy. For efficient transmission or storage, all redundancy should be removed. However, transmission of compressed images over a noisy channel makes it very sensitive to the channel noise. Channel coding is generally used to combat these errors. This section provides an overview of image compression and its transmission over a wireless channel.

2.1 Image compression using JPEG

JPEG is among the most popular and widely used image compression methods. JPEG supports both lossy and lossless compression.

The JPEG compression scheme is divided into the following stages:

1. Transform the image into an optimal color space.
2. Down sample chrominance components by averaging groups of pixels together.
3. Apply a forward 2D DCT to blocks of pixels to remove redundancies from the image data.
4. Quantize each block of DCT coefficients using weighting functions which are optimized for the human eye.
5. Encode the resulting coefficients (image data) using entropy coding based on Huffman variable word-length algorithm to further remove redundancies in the quantized DCT coefficients.

Fig. 1 shows the block diagram of the JPEG encoder.

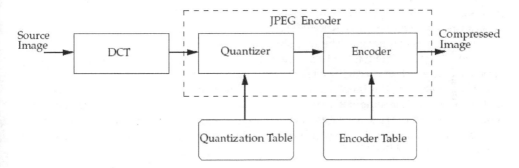

Fig. 1. JPEG encoder.

The gray-scale image contains a 2D set of pixels that correspond to the intensities (shades). There are 255 intensity levels, so pixel values are between 0 to 255. Since JPEG works on pixel values between -128 to 127, the values of source image are shifted to this scale. The image after scaling is decomposed into 8×8 block. DCT is performed using standard method. In case of color images, the method is the same, however, color images are in the beginning decomposed into either three sets, for example, Red, Green, Blue (RGB) or Brightness, Hue, Saturation (BHS) or in four components Cyan, Magenta, Yellow, Black (CMYK). Hence, without the loss of generality, we can proceed with gray scale image.

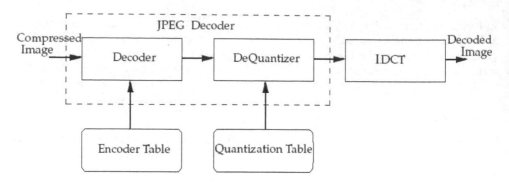

Fig. 2. JPEG decoder.

The image reconstruction, that is, the decoding of the compressed image is achieved by following encoding steps in reversed order. Fig. 2 shows the block diagram of a the decoder.

Up till now, the baseline requirements for JPEG were discussed. However, few extensions of JPEG standard also exists, such as attaining the progressive image buildup, arithmetic encoding and decoding for improved compression ratio and lossless compression scheme etc. Though these features are not essential for many JPEG implementations and hence are called extensions of JPEG standard.

The baseline JPEG image data is first received and decoded and then is reconstructed and displayed, therefore, baseline mode cannot be used for applications that demand for receiving the data stream and displaying it in a run. Instead of transmitting the image in lines the progressive buildup supports the layered based transmission. The layered based transmission is performed by sending a succession of image buildup, starting with an approximation of the image to the original image. The first scan is low quality JPEG image. Subsequent scans improve the quality gradually to refine the image. It can be observed that the first image appears to be rough but recognizable estimate of the original image but within an instance a refine image appears, this is because we need less data to produce the original image from the first estimate. Higher computational complexity is one of the limitations of progressive JPEG mode as with the progressive nature, every scan needs a full JPEG decompression cycle. For a fixed data transmission rates, faster JPEG decoder is required for efficient use of progressive transmission for real time applications.

Higher computational complexity is one of the limitations of progressive JPEG mode as each scan takes essentially a full JPEG decompression cycle to display. Therefore, with typical data transmission rates, a very fast JPEG decoder is needed to make effective use of progressive transmission to real time application.

Other JPEG extensions include arithmetic coding, lossless JPEG compression, variable quantization, selective refinement, image tiling, etc.

The JPEG standard became very popular after its publication, however, it has few shortcomings. This standard does not provide significant improvement for SNR scalability.

To overcome this problem, JPEG2000 standard was developed which contains some extra features like object and region based representation.

The JPEG2000 compression scheme is divided into the following stages:

1. *Color components transformation*: Transform the image into an optimal color space.

2. *Wavelet transform*: These color tiles are then transformed via a Discrete Wavelet Transform (DWT) to an arbitrary depth. The JPEG2000 uses two different wavelet transforms:
   - **irreversible**: The CDF 9/7 wavelet transform is said to be "irreversible" because it introduces quantization noise that depends on the precision of the decoder.
   - **reversible**: a rounded version of the bi-orthogonal CDF 5/3 wavelet transform. It uses only integer coefficients, so the output does not require rounding (quantization) and so it does not introduce any quantization noise. It is used in lossless coding.

3. *Quantization*: The wavelet coefficients are scalar-quantized to reduce the number of bits to represent them, at the expense of quality using weighting functions optimized for the human eye.

4. *Encoding*: The coefficients of each sub-band of every transformed block are arranged into rectangular blocks, also know as code blocks, which are coded individually, one bit plane at a time. Starting from the most significant bit plane with a nonzero element, each bit plane is processed in three passes. Each bit in a bit plane is coded in three passes only, which are called *significant propagation*, *magnitude refinement*, and *cleanup*. The output is arithmetically codded and grouped with similar passes from the other code blocks to form *layers*. These layers are partitioned into packets which are the fundamental units of the encoded stream.

Fig. 3 shows the block diagram of the JPEG2000 encoder. The JPEG2000 decoder simply applies the inverse operations of the encoder in reverse order. The JPEG2000 decoder simply inverts the operations of the encoder.

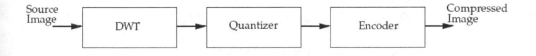

Source Image ▶ DWT ▶ Quantizer ▶ Encoder ▶ Compressed Image

Fig. 3. JPEG2000 encoder.

2.2 Channel coding of images

When digital images are transmitted over a wireless channel, channel coding is generally used to combat errors due to noise in wireless channels. This section provides an overview of channel encoding for still image communication over the channel. Recent developments in the wireless communication and mobile computing have sparked interest in the area of multimedia communication over wireless channels (Modestino & Daut, 1979), (Modestino et al., 1981), (Sabir et al., 2006). The state-of-the-art encoding and decoding methods rely on joint source channel coding for optimal communication performance.

For example, Cai et al. (Cai & Chen, 2000) presented a scheme of transmitting images over a wireless channel. Fig. 4 shows the proposed encoding and decoding framework.

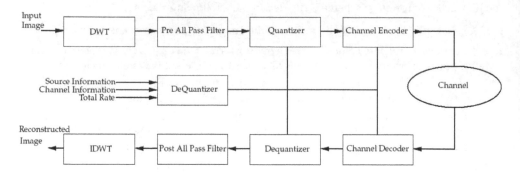

Fig. 4. Encoder-decoder framework presented in (Cai & Chen, 2000).

Similarly, Wu et al. (Wu et al., 2005) have developed a theoretical framework for image transmission over a wireless channel. This work exploits the error resilience property of JPEG2000 and achieves optimal distortion performance. Fig. 5 shows the semantic description of the proposed method. The problem is considered as a constraint optimization problem, i.e., minimizing the distortion by keeping the constraints on rate (or length of codewords), which can be expressed as,

$$\min_{b} \sum E[D_b(V_b)] = \min_{b} \sum D_{b,0} - E[\triangle D_b(V_b)] \quad \text{s.t.} \quad \sum_{b} L_b(V_b) \leq L_T \tag{2}$$

where $E[D_b(V_b)]$ is the expected value of distortion D_b where V_b denotes the code. The term $D_{b,0}$ is distortion when channel noise is zero, the term $E[\triangle D_b(V_b)]$ is the expected reduction in distortion when a code V_b is adopted. L_b is the length of bit stream of code block b. For noisy channel Equation 2 reduces to

$$\min_{b} \sum -E[\triangle D_b(V_b)] \quad \text{s.t.} \quad \sum_{b} L_b(V_b) \leq L_T \tag{3}$$

which can be minimized through constrained optimization as,

$$\min \left\{ \sum_{b} -E[\triangle D_b(V_b)] + \lambda \sum_{b} L_b(V_b) \leq L_T \right\} \tag{4}$$

If we assume that the JPEG2000 decoder can efficiently correct the data then the constrained optimization can be expressed as,

$$f(V_b) = - \sum_{j=1}^{N'_c-1} \left(\sum_{k=1}^{j} d_k \right) \left(\prod_{m=1}^{j} \left[1 - P(r_m, \frac{l_m}{r_m}) \right] \right) P(r_{j+1}, \frac{l_{j+1}}{r_{j+1}})$$
$$- \left(\sum_{k=1}^{N'_c} d_k \right) \left(\prod_{m=1}^{N'_c} \left[1 - P(r_m, \frac{l_m}{r_m}) \right] \right) + \lambda \sum_{n=1}^{N'_c} \frac{l_n}{r_n} \tag{5}$$

where r_i is the rate of ith code pass, d_i is the associated distortion reduction of l_i bytes, $P(r_i, \frac{l_i}{r_i})$ is the probability that error has occurred using ith code pass and N'_c is the number of code in a certain V_b.

Exhaustive search method can be used to obtain an optimal V_b. This method searches all possible V_b code-blocks which is equivalent to searching overall search space, that is, $\sum_{i=1}^{N_c} R^i$. It can be observed that exhaustive search method is memory wise inefficient. To address this limitation, constrained search technique can be used. To this end, Equation 5 is reformulated as,

$$f(V_b) = \sum_{i=1}^{N'_c} \left[\left\{ \prod_{j=1}^{i} \left(1 - P(r_j, \frac{l_j}{r_j}) \right) \right\} (-d_j) + \lambda \frac{l_i}{r_i} \right] \qquad (6)$$

Solving Equation 6 results in optimum rate which can be expressed as,

$$r^*_p = \begin{cases} \underset{r_{k+2} \in \Re(k+2)}{\operatorname{argmin}} J_{k+1}(r_{k+1}), & \text{when } p = k+2 \\ \underset{r_p \in \Re(p)}{\operatorname{argmin}} J_{p-1}(r^*_{p-1}), & \text{when } p = k+2 \end{cases} \qquad (7)$$

where J_k is the cost function at stage k. Further details on this method can be found in (Wu et al., 2005).

3. Video

Video contains spatial redundancy as well as temporal redundancy due to moving images. Similar to image data, for efficient transmission or storage, all redundancy should be removed. However, to make video transmissions immune to transmission errors due to noisy channel, channel coding is used. This section provides a brief overview of video compression methods and transmission of video over a wireless channel.

3.1 Source coding of videos

Video is a sequence of frames/pictures being played at certain rate, for example, 15 or 30 frames per second. Video compression methods exploit spatial and temporal redundancy in the video data. Most video compression techniques are lossy and operate on the premise that much of the data present before compression is not necessary for achieving good perceptual quality. For example, DVDs use MPEG-2 video coding standard that can achieve compression ratio of 15 to 30, while still producing a picture quality which is generally considered high-quality for standard-definition video. Video compression is a trade off between disk space, video quality, and the cost of hardware required to decompress the video in a reasonable time. However, if the video is over compressed in a lossy manner, visible (and sometimes distracting) artifacts can appear. Fig. 5 shows a general video encoder.

3.2 MPEG video basics

The Moving Picture Expert Group (MPEG), worked to generate the specifications under the International Organization for Standardization (ISO). The MPEG video actually consists of three finalized standards, MPEG-1, MPEG-2 and the most recent MPEG-4. The MPEG-1 & -2 standards are similar in basic concepts. They both are based on motion compensated

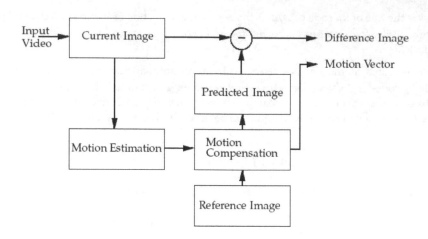

Fig. 5. General video encoder Drozdek (2002).

block-based transform coding techniques, while MPEG-4 deviates from these more traditional approaches in its usage of software image construct descriptors, for target bit-rates in the very low range (< 64Kb/sec).

3.2.1 MPEG video layers

MPEG video is broken up into a hierarchy of layers to combat errors, random search and editing, and synchronization. From the top level, the first layer is known as the video sequence layer, and it is any self-contained bit stream, for example a coded movie or an advertisement. The second layer is the Group of Pictures (GOP), which is composed of 1 or more groups (GOPs) of intra (*I*) frames and non-intra (*P* or *B*) frames. Of course, the third layer is the picture layer itself, and the next layer beneath it is called the slice layer. Each slice is a contiguous sequence of raster ordered *macroblocks*, most often on a row basis in typical video applications, but not limited to this by the specification. Each slice consists of macroblocks, which are 16x16 arrays of luminance pixels, or picture data elements, with 8*times*8 arrays of associated chrominance pixels. The macroblocks can be further divided into distinct 8*times*8 blocks, for further processing such as transform coding. Each of these layers has its own unique 32 bit start code defined in the syntax to consist of 23 zero bits followed by a 1, then followed by 8 bits for the actual start code. These start codes have no limitation on number of zero bits preceding them.

3.2.2 Intra frame coding techniques

The term *intra frame coding* refers to the fact that various lossless and lossy compression techniques are performed relative to information that is contained only within the current frame, and not relative to any other frame in the video sequence. In other words, no temporal processing is performed outside of the current frame. The basic processing blocks used for I-frame coding are the video filter, DCT, DCT coefficient quantizer, and run-length amplitude/variable length coder.

3.2.3 P/B frame coding techniques

The I-frame coding techniques are limited to processing the video signal on a spatial basis, relative only to information within only the I-frame only. Considerable amout of compression efficiency is obtained by exploiting inherent temporal redundancies. Temporal processing to exploit this redundancy uses a technique known as motion compensation. Details of prediction (P) and bidirectional (B) frame coding techniques are discussed next.

1. **P Frame Encoding**: Starting with I-frame, the encoder can forward predict a future frame. This is commonly referred to as a P frame, and it may also be predicted from other P frames, although only in a forward time manner. Consider, for example, a GOPs consisting of 5 frames. In this case, the frame ordering can be expressed as I, P, P, P, P, I, P, P, P, P, I, ... Each P frame in this sequence is predicted from the frame immediately preceding it, whether it is an I frame or a P frame.

2. **B Frame Encoding**: B frames are commonly referred to as bi-directional interpolated prediction frames. These frames can use forward/backward interpolated prediction. As an example of the usage of I, P, and B frames, consider a GOPs consisting of 8 frames, for example, I, B, P, B, P, B, P, B, I, B, P, B, P, B, P, B, I, ... As I frames are coded spatially only and the P frames are encoded using forward prediction based on previous I and P frames. The B frames, on the other hand, are coded based on a forward prediction from a previous I or P frame, as well as a backward prediction from a succeeding I or P frame. Consider, for example, sequence of GOPs consisting of 8 frames, the first B frame is predicted from the first I frame and first P frame, the second B frame is predicted from the second and third P frames, and the third B frame is predicted from the third P frame and the first I frame of the next group of pictures, and so on. It can be observed from the above example that backward prediction requires that the future frames that are to be used for backward prediction be encoded and transmitted first, out of order. The main advantage of the usage of B frames is coding efficiency. In most cases, B frames results in less bits being coded overall. Quality can also be improved in the case of moving objects that reveal hidden areas within a video sequence. Backward prediction in this case allows the encoder to make more intelligent decisions on how to encode the video within these areas. Since B frames are not used to predict future frames, errors generated will not be propagated further within the sequence.

3.2.4 Motion estimation

The temporal prediction technique used in MPEG video is known as *motion estimation*. The basic premise of motion estimation is that in most cases, consecutive video frames will be similar except for changes induced by objects moving within the frames. In the trivial case of zero motion between frames, it is easy for the encoder to efficiently predict the current frame as a duplicate of the previous frame. When this is done, the only information necessary to transmit to the decoder becomes the syntactic overhead necessary to reconstruct the picture from the original reference frame. When there is motion in the images, the situation is not as simple. To solve motion estimation problem, a comprehensive 2D spatial search is performed for each luminance macroblock. Motion estimation is not applied directly to chrominance in MPEG video, as it is assumed that the color motion can be adequately represented with the same motion information as the luminance. The MPEG standard does not define how this search should be performed.

3.2.5 Coding of residual errors

The residual error frame is generated by subtracting predicted frame from its reference frame. The residual error is coded using processing steps similar to I frame encoding. However, DCT cofficent quantization method is different. A constant matrix (of value 16) for each of the 64 locations is set as default quantization matrix for non-intra frames. The non-intra quantization step function contain dead zone around zeros to eliminate any single DCT coefficent to maximize the run length amplitude efficiency. The variable length code and the differential value are calculated for the residual block inforamtion to measure the motion vector based on their statistical likelihood of occurrence.

3.3 Channel coding of videos

The channel coding is an essential component in reliable transmission of video data over a wireless channel. This section provides a brief overview of commonly used channel coding methods used for video transmission over a wireless channel. Since video contains huge amount of data, for optimum use of resources, joint source-channel coding strategy is generally used.

Dyck and Miller (Dyck & Miller, 1999) have proposed rate allocation schemes for source and channel codes, designing of channel codes for specific source codes, and power allocation for modulated symbols, etc. Fig. 6 shows joint source-channel coding framework as proposed in (Dyck & Miller, 1999).

Fig. 6. Encoder decoder model presented in (Dyck & Miller, 1999).

In the JSCC block, the source encoder operates on an input vector X which belongs to n-dimensional space $\Re^n$ and is used to generate quantization index $I \in \Im$, where $\Im$ is the index set such that $\Im = \{1, 2, ..., N\}$. The channel maps I to J such that $J \in \Im$.

The JSCC decoder estimates $\hat{X}$ from J. The optimal mapping of X to J that minimize the average distortion between source and destination is obtained by using Vector Quantization (VQ). The expected distortion for transmission of videos over wireless link is given as

$$E(D) = \sum_{i=1}^{N} \sum_{x \in \chi_r \,:\, x \in \Re_r} \sum_{j=1}^{N} P(j|i)d(x, y_i) \tag{8}$$

where $P(\cdot|\cdot)$ is the channel transition probability, $d(\cdot, \cdot)$ is the dissimilarity metric between two vectors (in case of Minimum Mean Square Estimator (MMSE) the $d(x, y) = \|x - y\|^2$), N is the number of decoder indices, χ and R are the source and encoder realization respectively. The optimal encoding rule to minimize Equation 8 is given as (Kumazawa et al., 1984),

$$y_i = \frac{\sum_{i=1}^{N} \sum_{x \in \chi_r \,:\, x \in \Re_i} P(j|i)E[X|X \in \Re_i]}{\sum_{i=1}^{N} \sum_{x \in \chi_r \,:\, x \in \Re_i} P(j|i)} \qquad (9)$$

$$= E[X|j]$$

where

$$R_i = \sum_{j=1}^{N} P(j|i)d(x, y_i) \le \sum_{j=1}^{N} P(j|k)d(x, y_i), \quad \forall\, k. \qquad (10)$$

In the decoding process after assignment of appropriate index to the source symbol is decoded using either MAP or conditional Mean Square Estimation (MSE) method.

In case of MAP decoding, decoder estimates the transmitted sequence and use them to estimate the original transmitted symbols. The basic method for MAP decoder is to select the symbol that maximizes the a posteriori probability, i.e, $P[i|j]$. Since it is assumed that the channel is memory less, it can be written as $\hat{i} = \underset{i}{\mathrm{argmax}} P[i|j]$.

In case of conditional MSE decoding, the decoder decodes source symbols using conditional MSE. The joint source channel coding for conditional MSE is considered by (Miller & Park, 1998). The expected distortion can be written in the form

$$E[D(X, y)|J] = \frac{\sum_i \left(\sum_{t=1}^{T} E[d(X_t, y_t)|I = i] \right) P[J = j|I = i]P[I = i]}{\sum_i P[J = j|I = i]P[I = i]}. \qquad (11)$$

To find y by minimizing distortion, many algorithms are available (Baum et al., 1970)., for example

$$\hat{D} = \sum_{t=1}^{T} \sum_{l=1}^{T} \|y(l) - y_t\|^2 P[I_t = i|J = j]. \qquad (12)$$

Based on the expected distortion given in Equation 12, the optimal decoder with minimum expected distortion, is given as

$$y_t = \sum_{k=1}^{N} y(k)P[I_t|J = j], \quad \forall\, t \qquad (13)$$

where y_t is the decoder estimate which minimizes the distortion such that it becomes the optimal channel vector quantization decoder. In Equation 13, the a posteriori probabilities $P[I_t|J = j]$ are computed either by BCJR algorithm (Bahl et al., 1974) by forward and backward recursive equation, or by Hidden Markov Model (HMM) (Baum et al., 1970).

In mobile communications, the channel behaves as a Rayleigh fading channel due to mobility and variable path delays. Under Rayleigh fading conditions, the channel can be more noisy, therefore, robust methods are required for such applications. The methods for decoding are discussed by considering vector quantization only. However, for more effective transmission, we need to introduce channel coding along with source coding (Man et al., 1997).

Kwon et al., (Kwon & kyoon Kim, 2002) have proposed an adaptive scheme for code rate selection in the video communication. This adaptive technique is useful for transmission over noisy channel in terms of its computational efficiency. The transmission side contains video encoder followed by a channel encoder and a rate controller, which adaptively learns the channel condition and allocates the rate accordingly. In this work, the distortion at any time t can be expressed as,

$$D(t) = D_s(R_s(t)) + D_c(R_c(t)) \qquad (14)$$

where $D_s(R_s(t))$ is the distortion caused by the source and $D_c(R_c(t))$ is the distortion caused by the channel. These two distortions are assumed to be uncorrelated. The $R_s(t)$ is the source coding rate, and $R_c(t)$ is the channel coding rate. Generally, statistical characterization of both distortions are assumed to be known. To minimize the distortion via selecting a code rate, the channel is assumed to be independent and exhibits bursty nature. The adaptive scheme is based on average Peak Signal to Noise Ratio (PSNR). The adaptive scheme encodes at an optimal rate r^* which provides the maximum average PSNR, that is,

$$r^* = \arg \max_{r^*} avgPSNR(r^*, P_s, L_B) \qquad (15)$$

where P_s is the symbol error probability and L_B is the average burst error length. The approach of finding the maximum of average PSNR for the given r, P_s and L_B can be a time consuming process. However, for a given r, P_s, L_B and the average residual error probability P_R^{avg}, the optimum code rate can be found as,

$$r^* = \operatorname*{argmin}_{r}[P_R(r, P_s, L_B) - P_R^{avg}] \qquad (16)$$

Yingjun (Yingjun et al., 2001) have also proposed an adaptive scheme based on adaptive segmentation for video transmission over a wireless channel. It is known that the P frame has both spatial and temporal redundancy, hence, its error resistance is more than I frame, which only has spatial redundancy. The proposed scheme only focuses on error resistance of I frame. By protecting the I frame, this scheme provide good visual quality. This transmission scheme is shown in Fig. 7.

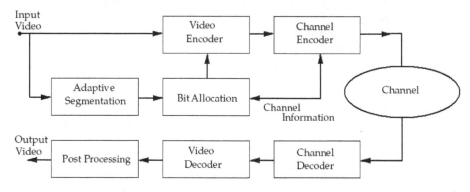

Fig. 7. Video transmission model (Yingjun et al., 2001).

In the transmission system, the video frames are divided into segments at macro level, the rate distortion analysis is performed which provides the basis of finding optimal bit allocation scheme (Lu et al., 1998). The bit allocation is a tradeoff between quantization level and the channel coding rate. In the next step, the resulted segmentation is coded and transmitted over a wireless channel and at the receiver, the inverse process is performed in reverse order to recover the transmitted video. In order to conceal the error, post processing block is added. The proposed joint source channel design based on Hotelling transformation and the rate distortion function is given as,

$$T_{rd} = C_V(V_{rd} - m_V) \qquad (17)$$

where C_V is the variance and m_V is the mean of rate distortion vector V_{rd}. The component of transformed version of rate distortion vector T_{rd} is observed to have zero value. Hence the vector dimension is reduced significantly by this transformation. In addition, the transformed version helps to find an optimal bit allocation mechanism. The segmentation is performed in adaptive fashion. In the adaptive scheme, first the threshold T is decided for control segmented regions number. Then D_{rd} is rate distortion function which can be expressed as,

$$D_{rd}(i,j) = \|U_{rd,i} - U_{rd,j}\|. \qquad (18)$$

In addition to adaptive learning algorithms, an iterative algorithm has also been proposed by Nasruminallah (Nasruminallah & Hanzo, 2011). The system model considered for iterative source channel coding is given in Fig. 8.

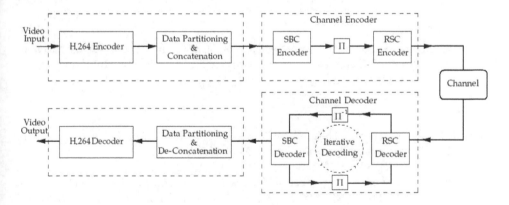

Fig. 8. System model in (Nasruminallah & Hanzo, 2011).

A more realistic formulation of H.264/AVC instead of conventional mathematical modeling for video source encoding is presented in (Nasruminallah & Hanzo, 2011). The video is encoded with H.264/AVC, followed by a data partitioning block, which de-multiplexes the data and concatenates it to generate a bit stream. This bit stream is then fed to the channel encoder which first passes it through the Short Block Codes (SBC). These encoded bits are then interleaved and fed to the Recursive Systematic Convolutional (RSC) encoder also known as serial concatenation, with inner scheme as RSC and outer scheme as SBC. The symbols at the output of RSC encoder are modulated (not shown in Fig. 8) and then transmitted over the channel. The channel corrupts the modulated signals with the assumption that the channel is narrow band and temporally correlated with Rayleigh fading. The signal at the receiver end is demodulated and the corrupted version of the source symbols are fed to the RSC decoder, which shares the data with the SBC decoder to start the iterative process. The channel decoder uses standard iterative decoding process (Berrou & Glavieux, 1996), i.e., with the exchange of extrinsic information between the two decoders, for message decoding. The overall process can be summarized as the soft information is at the input of RSC decoder which processes it to extract the Log-Likelihood Ratios (LLR) estimates. These estimates are de-interleaved and fed to the SBC decoder. This process repeats until the decoding converges to some reasonable estimate. Kliewer (Kliewer et al., 2006) have proposed the condition to ensure convergence of the iterative decoding. The encoding of SBC encoder for rate $\frac{K}{K+1}$ such as $\frac{2}{3}, \frac{3}{4}, \frac{4}{5}$, etc., can be achieved by placing the redundant bit at any position in a codeword by taking the Exclusive-OR (XOR) of the source bits as,

$$r = [b(1) \oplus b(2) \oplus b(3) \oplus ... \oplus b(K)] \tag{19}$$

where $\oplus$ denotes XOR operation.

This bit can be placed at any $K + 1$ position in the codeword. Furthermore, to attain a more powerful code, the SBC encoder produces information rate $\frac{K}{N}$ where $N = m \times K$. The first $((m - 1) \times K)$-tuples are produced by repeating the information block of size K and the last set is produced as,

$$r(p) = [b(1) \oplus b(2) \oplus b(3) \oplus ...(b(p) = 0) \oplus ... \oplus b(K)] \tag{20}$$

where p can take values between $[1, 2, ...K]$.

Nasruminallah has demonstrated the effectiveness of SBC and RSC methods based on different code rates for SBC and rate $\frac{1}{4}$ for RSC with constituent code $g_1 = [1011], g_2 = [1101], g_3 = [1101], g_4 = [1111]$.

4. References

Ayanoglu, E. & Gray, R. (1987). The design of joint source and channel trellis waveform coders, *IEEE Transactions on Information Theory* 33(6): 855–865.

Bahl, L., Cocke, J., Jelinek, F., & Raviv, J. (1974). Optimal decoding of linear codes for minimizing symbol error rate, *IEEE Transactions on Information Theory* 20(2): 284–287.

Baum, L. E., Petrie, T., Soules, G. & Weiss, N. (1970). A maximization technique occurring in the statistical analysis of probabilistic functions of Markov chains, *Annals Mathematics Statistics* 41(1): 164–171.

Berrou, C. & Glavieux, A. (1996). Near optimum error correcting coding and decoding: turbo-codes, *IEEE Transactions on Communication* 44(10): 1261–1271.

Cai, J. & Chen, C. W. (2000). Robust joint source-channel coding for image transmission over wireless channels, *IEEE Transactions on Circuits and Systems for Video Technology* 10(6): 962–966.

Cover, T. M. & Thomas, J. A. (1991). *Elements of Information Theory*, John Wiley and Sons Inc.

Cover, T. M. & Thomas, J. A. (2006). *Elements of Information Theory*, John Wiley and Sons Inc.

Drozdek, A. (2002). *Elements of Data Compression*, Bill Stenquist.

Dyck, R. E. V. & Miller, D. J. (1999). Transport of wireless video using separate, concatenated, and joint source-channel coding, *Proceedings of IEEE* 87(10): 1734–1750.

Farvardin, N. & Vaishampayan, V. (1987). Optimal quantizer design for noisy channels: An approach to combined source - channel coding, *IEEE Transactions on Information Theory* 33(6): 827–838.

Goodman, D., Moulsley, T.J. & Holmdel, N. (1988). Using simulated annealing to design digital transmission codes for analogue sources, *IEEE Electronics Letters* 24(10): 617–619.

Gray, R. M. & Ornstein, D. S. (1976). Sliding-block joint source/noisy-channel coding theorems, *IEEE Transactions on Information Theory* 22(6): 682–690.

Kliewer, J., Goertz, N. & Mertins, A. (2006). Iterative source-channel decoding with Markov random field source models, *IEEE Transactions on Signal Processing* 54(1): 3688–3701.

Kumazawa, H., Kasahara, M. & Namekawa, T. (1984). A construction of vector quantizers for noisy channels, *Electronics and Communications in Japan* 67(4): 39–47.

Kwon, J. C. & Kim, J. K. (2002). Adaptive code rate decision of joint source-channel coding for wireless video, *IEEE Electronics Letters* 38(25): 1752–1754.

Lu, J., Liou, M. L., Letaief, K. B. & Chuang, J. C. I (1998). Mobile image transmission using combined source and channel coding with low complexity concealment signal processing, *IEEE Signal Processing and Image Communication* 86(5): 974–997.

Man, H., Kossentini, F. & Smith, M. J. (1997). Robust EZW image coding for noisy channels, *IEEE Signal Processing Letters* 4(1): 227–229.

Miller, D. J. & Park, M. (1998). A sequence-based, approximate MMSE decoder for source coding over noisy channels using discrete hidden Markov models, *IEEE Transactions on Communication* 46(1): 222–231.

Modestino, J., Daut, D. & Vickers, A. (1981). Combined source-channel coding of images using the block cosine transform, *IEEE Transactions on Communication* 29(9): 1261–1274.

Modestino, J. W. & Daut, D. G. (1979). Combined source-channel coding of images, *IEEE Transactions on Communication* 27(11): 1644–1659.

Nasruminallah & Hanzo, L. (2011). Joint source-channel iterative decoding of arithmetic codes, *IEEE Communications Surveys and Tutorials* 1(99): 1–27.

Sabir, M. F., Sheikh, H. R., Heath, R. W. & Bovik, A. C. (2006). Joint source-channel distortion model for JPEG compressed images, *IEEE Transactions on Communication* 15(6): 1349–1364.

Sayood, K., Gibson, J. D. & Liu, F. (1988). Implementation issues in map joint source/channel coding, *Twenty-Second Asilomar Conference on Signals, Systems and Computers* 1(1): 102–106.

Shannon, C. E. (1948). A mathematical theory of communication, *Bell System Technical Journal* 27(1): 379–423, 623–656.

Wu, Z., Bilgin, A. & Marcellin, M. W. (2005). Joint source/channel coding for image transmission with JPEG2000 over memoryless channels, *IEEE Transactions on Image Processing* 14(8): 389–400.

Wyrwas, R. & Farrell, P. (1989). Joint source-channel coding for raster document transmission over mobile radio, *IEEE Proceedings Communications, Speech and Vision* 136(6): 375–380.

Yingjun, S., Jianhua, L., Wang, J., Letaier, K. B. & Gu, J. (2001). Adaptive segmentation based
    joint source-channel coding for wireless video transmission, *IEEE VTS 53rd Vehicular
    Technology Conference VTC* 3(1): 1752–1754.

Ziv, J. & Lempel, A. (1978). Compression of individual sequences by variable rate coding,
    IEEE Transactions on Information Theory 24(1): 530–536.

Part 3

Measuring User Experience

6

Current Challenges and Opportunities in VoIP over Wireless Networks

Ala' F. Khalifeh[1] and Khalid A. Darabkh[2]
[1]German Jordan University
[2]The University of Jordan
Jordan

1. Introduction

The tremendous emergence of different wireless technologies has created many opportunities for extending many Internet applications and services to the wireless domain, and has envisioned many new ones. When we refer to wireless networks, people thoughts go directly to the Wireless Fidelity (WiFi) technology. However, WiFi networks are one type of the wireless networks that have been used for several years on a small scale areas and buildings such as schools, offices, companies, restaurants, and airports. The other types of wireless networks that cover larger geographical areas are the third and fourth Generation wireless networks, abbreviated as 3G, 4G networks, respectively, which basically use the mobile infrastructure. Some examples of these networks are High Speed Packet Access (HSPA), Worldwide Interoperability for Microwave Access (WiMax), and Long Term Evolution (LTE). In this book chapter, when we refer to the wireless network, we refer to both types of networks unless we specify one of them.

In the future, people are expected to rely more on wireless networks. This is due to the fact that these networks are easy to deploy and manage, support mobility, and provide fast Internet service, especially with the latest HSPA+ and LTE technologies which can provide relatively high speed up to 30 Mbps. As such, many Internet applications and services are used by people over the wireless domain, which may impose more challenges that did not appear in the wired networks. This is due to the natural of the wireless networks that is more prone to interferences and noises that are generated by the transmission media and atmosphere. In other words, transmitting data over wireless networks result in more packet losses than the wired networks, which will in turn cause more retransmission attempts in case of Transmission Control Protocol (TCP) based applications and traffic, such as Hypertext Transfer Protocol (HTTP) traffic and more packet loss and performance degradation in case of User Datagram Protocol (UDP) based applications and traffic such as multimedia traffic. As such, transmitting over wireless networks needs more mechanisms and methods to detect and possibly correct these network impairments that did not exist under the wired environment.

Transmitting voice over the Internet protocol or what is widely used as Voice over Internet Protocol (VoIP) is one of the promising applications that proved its popularity in the past decade and started to be used by people over the wireless networks, especially with the advent of the smart mobile phones that are capable of supporting many VoIP protocols such as the Session Initiation Protocol (SIP), which opens the horizon to the developers and programmers to write mobile applications (apps) that can conduct VoIP calls over the mobile phones. These apps gain popularity by mobile users since they not only save them a lot of money especially when conducting international calls, but also provide them the mobility and freedom they used to have using their mobile phones. However, in order to eliminate the need of typical mobile phones and provide a good substitution for the typical phones, VoIP services have to be equipped with mechanisms and algorithms to guarantee some Quality of Service (QoS) assurance especially when it comes to packet losses which is the most annoying network impairment factor to the VoIP users. VoIP users are aware that a superior toll quality service cannot be achieved over the Internet, due to the well known fact that the Internet is not well suited to provide real-time services, and also to the fact that users pay much less money to the VoIP calls, when compared to the expensive circuit switched phone calls, so they can tolerate some quality degradation. However, they still expect an acceptable quality that does the job and will not end up wasting their time and money.

Many VoIP vendors have realized the future trend toward the wireless and mobile environments and started developing customized VoIP apps that can be installed on the smart mobile phones. Skype is a very well-known example of a successful and widely used VoIP application that is used by millions of people over the entire world. Skype has recently issued a mobile app that allows users to conduct VoIP calls over their mobile phones. However, the developed app does not take into account all the aspects and challenges imposed by the wireless domain. Therefore, the call performance of the mobile app was much lower than the wired app. This fact was validated by [1] who has done a performance profiling study for Skype over different wireless networks and environments.

In this book chapter, we aim to highlight some of the challenges introduced by different wireless technologies, and how they affected the performance of some Internet applications that migrated directly to the wireless domain without taking into account the differences between the wired and the wireless networks. VoIP will be the main application of interest in this book chapter. However, similar algorithms and schemes can be developed for other applications such as audio and video streaming over wireless networks.

The structure of the chapter is divided as follows: Section 2 will provide a quick overview about VoIP service in general followed by a more detailed description about the typical wireless network infrastructure used for carrying VoIP calls. Section 3 will introduce some of the common used VoIP mobile applications available in the market and will focus on the main challenges introduced by the wireless media and how they affect VoIP performance. It will also provide a performance evaluation profiling for one VoIP application over the wireless network. Section 4 will shed the light on some of the state-of-the-art solutions and frameworks proposed in the literature and how they addressed some of the afro mentioned challenges, Finally, Section 5 will conclude the chapter.

2. VoIP network infrastructure

We first open this section by defining what is meant by VoIP and the basic building blocks for providing such a service. As shown by figure 1, carrying voice over the IP network or

VoIP is achieved by first converting the voice signal into the digital domain and this can be done using Analog to Digital Converters (ADC), which are embedded into the computer sound card or installed inside the mobile phone audio signal processing unit. Once the voice is converted into the digital format, it can be packetized into IP packets that are ready to be transmitted utilizing the UDP transpose protocol. UDP is preferred over TCP due to the fact that UDP is much faster, simpler, and does not impose acknowledging the reception of each packet, which saves a lot of time and makes it more appropriate for real-time applications such as VoIP. Once the VoIP packets are transmitted over the transmission media, some packets may get lost, and at the receiver side, the received packets are de-packitized into a stream of ones and zeros. After that, the binary stream is fed to the Digital to Analog Converter (DAC) unit which converts the digital bit stream back to the analog format and play it back.

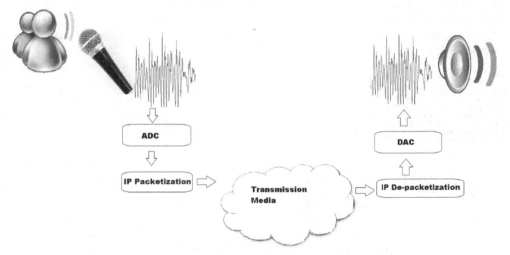

Fig. 1. VoIP packetization and transmission

Now, in order to transmit the sequence of packets over the Internet, some networking protocols and services have to be deployed. Figure 2 depicts the network architecture for a VoIP enabled network, including both wired and wireless VoIP terminals, utilizing WiFi wireless network infrastructure. For simplicity, we assume that the Session Initiating Protocol (SIP) is the protocol used for signaling purposes and call set up. Considering the fact that the main focus of this section is to familiarize the reader with the major components and the architecture of the VoIP network, we refer the reader to look at [1, 2] for more hardware and software details.

The following scenario shows how a VoIP call over wireless network is conducted. Let us suppose that user A in Domain 1 would like to call user B in Domain 2. When user A accesses the wireless network using his VoIP enabled mobile phone, the Quality of Service Access Point (QoSAP) uses Call Admission Control (CAC) algorithm to determine whether or not the wireless network can safely admit the new VoIP call. Different access points may deploy different CAC algorithms, but the common factor for all these different algorithms is to accept/reject calls based on the wireless network capacity. If the call is admitted, user A will send a call setup request to the VoIP softswitch (SIP INVITE message) shown in figure

3. The called softswitch (Proxy server in case SIP protocol is used or Gatekeeper in case H.323 protocol is used) [3] will perform some operations; such as authorization, authentication, and accounting. After that, the softswitch will lookup the IP address of the destination domain (Domain 2). Notice that in some networks, address lookup can be done in the local Domain Name Server (DNS) of the network. Once the destination IP address is determined; the VoIP gateway checks the link status by using an appropriate CAC mechanism. End-to-End Measurement-Based Admission Control is one of the widely used admission control mechanisms in VoIP gateways [4]. The VoIP gateway gauges the quality of the network path by sending probes to the destination IP address, which is usually the IP address of the destination gateway or the destination softswitch, and measures the end-to-end delay, packet loss, and jitter delay of these probed packets to determine the quality of the network path [4], which will be reported to the softswitch. The VoIP gateway uses these information to determine whether the call can be admitted or not. If the call is not admitted, the connection is rejected and a busy signal will be sent to the VoIP terminal. The process is repeated till the call is successfully established.

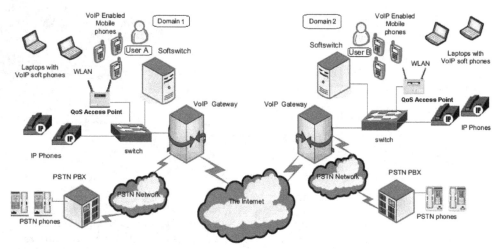

Fig. 2. Network architecture for VoIP over wireless networks [12]

> INVITE SIP: USER A @ Domanin1.com SIP/ 2.0
> Via:SIP/2.0/UDP
> From: sip: USER A @ Domain1.com
> To: sip: USER B@ Domain2.com

Fig. 3. SIP invite message format [12]

Notice that the above scenario assumed the usage of QAP that deployed some CAC algorithm to accept or reject phone calls. In addition, another CAC algorithm is deployed at the networking level to determine the quality of the end-to-end Internet connection and whether it meets the minimum VoIP quality requirements. In other words, one should take into account that neither the QAP nor the CAC algorithm may exist in case of wireless VoIP, which may add extra challenges for providing an acceptable VoIP service.

Figure 4 shows another possible scenario in which a 3G/4G wireless Internet connection is used. In this case, the challenge of deploying VoIP is even more due to the fact that the wireless link covers larger distance ranges to hundreds of meters when compared to the wireless LAN.

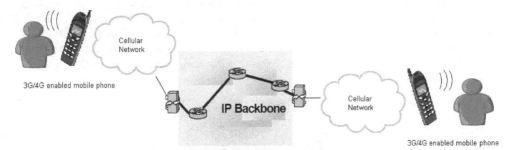

Fig. 4. 3G/4G wireless VoIP call path

3. Current VoIP applications, performance profiling, and challenges

Many VoIP vendors and developers realized the tremendous emergence of different wireless technologies and also the widespread adoption of smartphones. In fact, according to the Disruptive Analysis research firm [5] which expects that the number of VoIP-over-3G users will be around 250 million by the end of 2012. Accordingly, many of them start developing mobile applications that are capable of conducting VoIP call utilizing the wireless Internet connection supported by the mobile phones. In this section, we will explore some of the most famous VoIP mobile applications and their supported features. We will then focus on one of these applications, Skype particularly, and investigate its performance over different wireless networks.

3.1 VoIP applications

In what follows, we briefly describe some of the current widely used VoIP applications specifically customized for mobile phones and terminals. As an example, we will provide a brief description of the following applications: Truphone, Fring, and Skype.

3.1.1 Truphone

Truephone is considered as one of the pioneers in developing mobile apps that is capable of conducting VoIP over the mobile's wireless internet connectivity [6]. The company even provides its customers a VoIP number that can be reached from the Internet, which maybe useful especially when there is no or weak network coverage from the mobile provider. In addition, calling this VoIP number will be free of charge for the people who call from/to the Internet. Furthermore, they have developed a new service called Call Through, in which Truphone customers can still conduct a low cost VoIP calls even if they do not have a WiFi or 3G Internet connection on their mobile phones. This works by first conducting a local mobile call to a Truphone access number, which conduct a VoIP call to the final destination. In this way, the user will be charged for the local mobile phone call and the cheap VoIP international call.

3.1.2 Fring

Another well-established company that offers several services such as video, voice calling, and instant chat messaging all utilizing the Internet connectivity of the mobile phone [7]. As shown in figure 5, the application provides the users an interface similar to the typical mobile interface, which makes it both easy and attractive to the normal users. Furthermore, Fring users can enjoy other services that are not available in the normal mobile phones such as video conferencing, communicating with the Internet users using instant and text messages, and calling Skype users.

Fig. 5. A screenshot of the Fring VoIP application on smartphones

3.1.3 Skype

With over 600 million users, Skype with no doubt is the biggest and largest VoIP service provider that shapes and leads the industry in this field [8]. As any other provider, Skype decided to provide its services over mobile phones by developing a mobile app for the current smartphones. However, as will be shown in the next section, the performance of Skype over the wireless network is much lower than the wired network, and that is due to the fact that most of the current developed applications do not take into account the characteristics of the wireless channel and devices. As such, migrating the application designed for the wired network needs to take into account the additional challenges and difficulties introduced by the wireless channel.

3.2 Performance profiling of skype over wireless networks

To demonstrate the fact that the current VoIP applications designed for the wired environment need to be further developed and enhanced such that it does not degrade under the wireless environment, we will briefly describe the research work of [1] which experimentally shows that the performance of Skype degrades dramatically under different wireless environments. In what follows, we explain to the extent level the conducted experiments used in the performance evaluation, the performance evaluation results, as well a summary of what are the necessary enhancements for improving the quality of voice after being transmitted over mobile environments.

3.2.1 Scenario setup

All experiments are conducted utilizing Experimental Testbed for Research Enabling Mobility Enhancements (EXTREME) [9], which is developed for testing network algorithms and technologies of the Centre Tecnològic de Telecommunications de Catalunya (CTTC) in Barcelona, where the Wireless Local Area Network (WLAN) infrastructure is supported and its configuration is made with Asymmetric Digital Subscriber Line (ADSL) of rate 1 Mbps and 300 Kbps for uplink and downlink, respectively. Moreover, the production network operator of Orange mobile is directly interconnected with it via loosely coupled mechanism. Skype clients are used as either PC (Pentium IV with 512 MB RAM memories) or mobile terminal (SPV M5000 or Otek 9000) nodes. The SPV M5000 uses a processor of Intel Bulverde 520 MHz with 64 MB cache memory. The Access point used in WLAN uses Atheros-based cards integrated with Madwifi driver [10]. The scenario setup used is depicted in figure 6.

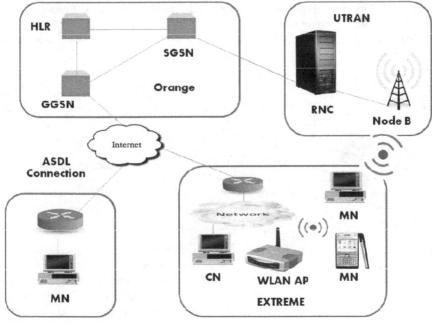

Fig. 6. Scenario setup [1]

3.2.2 VoIP quality measurement and evaluation

To measure the voice quality, the Perceptual Evaluation of Speech Quality (PESQ) algorithm, which is described by the ITU-T recommendation P.862, is used [11]. In this algorithm, a comparison is made between the degraded analog audio signal, which is the signal transmitted over the communication channel, with the analog audio reference (original) signal. Consequently, the call quality is evaluated using the Mean Opinion Score (MOS) performance metric which represents the average quality score considering a wide set of subjects. The range of MOS usually varies between -0.5 to denote for poor perceived voice quality and 4.5 to describe the best possible obtained voice quality.

About experiments setup, there are two clients (Client 1 and Client 2) considered, as shown in figure 7, where the VoIP session is established between them. Furthermore, there are also two PCs, PC 1 and PC 2 connected with Client 1 and Client 2, respectively. Client 1 represents a PC-based node while Client 2 indicates either a PC-based node or SPV M5000 Personal Digital Assistant (PDA). In all experiments, the adopted network of Client 1 connection is LAN while this is not the case for Client 2 connection that depends on the scenario being under test. During the voice session between Client 1 and Client 2, a WAV file which shows a spoken English text without noise is recorded by PC 2 using the *wavrec* application and consequently reproduced by PC 1 using the *wavplay* application. Therefore, two audio cables are required in all tests. The first one connects the microphone jack of Client 1 with earphone jack of PC 1 and the vice versa for the other one considering PC 2 and Client 2. The process of recording at PC 2 and reproducing at PC 1 occur simultaneously using Network Time Protocol (NTP) and due to end-to-end delay, it requires a minimum duration of 20 seconds including silence at the beginning and the end of WAV file. Also, it is automated using a script that is also responsible for estimating the PESQ score between the resulting WAV files. On the other hand, the WAV file is sampled at 8 KHz sampling rate and encoded with 16 bits per sample.

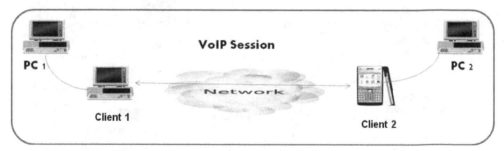

Fig. 7. Voice quality experiments setup [1]

It is reported that the voice quality is affected mainly by four different parameters [1]: The audio volume of reproducing device, CPU load, end-to-end delay, packet loss, as well as audio cables. For the first parameter, different tests provide different PSEQ scores through mainly calibrating the volume level. Hence, it is of interest to repeat the tests focusing on volume calibration for maximizing the PESQ scores. Considering the second parameter, it is proven that the CPU load is the major factor that degrades the performance of perceived voice when Skype client is a mobile terminal and this factor is dependent on the applications running on the mobile terminal. During experimentation, the Pocket Hack Master application is used to check the CPU load of SPV M5000 PDA. For end-to-end-delay, which is not involved in PESQ evaluation, the measurements that are taken into consideration are those which have end-to-end delays below 150 ms where the interactivity is guaranteed leading to complete concentration on the audio signal quality. For the last parameter, it is proven through a set of experiments that different PSEQ results are obtained when audio cables get varied and this is due to the following: material, process of digital-to-analog conversion, analog audio transmission, and analog-to-digital conversion.

It is interesting to discuss some of the obtained results of the conducted experiments for evaluating the perceived voice quality of the Skype calls. Table 1 shows the MOS scores when considering the scenario where the Skype client is a PC-based node. The MOS scores are presented for different network environments, namely, ADSL, LAN, and WLAN. It is observed from this table that the achieved MOS scores in all networks are above 3.6 which reflect acceptable perceived voice quality. It is also shown that the differences between MOS scores in all networks are small and this is expected since the throughput of a Skype call is much less than the available bandwidth in all networks' connections.

Network Environment	Uplink Traffic	Downlink Traffic
ADSL	3.989	3.935
LAN	3.838	3.838
WLAN	3.631	3.631

Table 1. MOS scores when running Skype client as PC-based nodes

Table 2 is done to provide MOS scores for different networks' interfaces WLAN and Universal Mobile Telecommunications System (UMTS); one of the mostly widely used 3G wireless technology in Europe, when a Skype client is a mobile terminal (SPV M500 PDA). As mentioned earlier that the CPU load has a great impact on the quality of Skype calls. Therefore, Table 2 provides MOS scores for CPU load ranges from 66% to 81% in WLAN and UMTS connections, respectively. Results show the all obtained MOS scores are not promising since they fall below 3.6. Hence, the voice quality is poor (unacceptable) compared with the results discussed in Table 1. It is interesting to see that during the traffic from PDA to PC, the MOS score is about 3.39 while it is, in the reverse traffic, about 2.85. Actually, this is due to the effect of many factors, including terminal hardware, operating system, and the running Skype version. One more observation can be extracted that the MOS score in the reverse traffic of UMTS interface is higher than that of direct traffic and this is due to the way the operating system interact with UMTS cards.

Also it is important to mention that according to the results of Tables 1 and 2, one can notice that the voice quality for the wired network utilizing ADSL and LAN networks was better than the wireless counterparts (WLAN and UMTS). Furthermore, the voice quality for the WLAN was much better than the UMTS case. One reason for that since calls over this network will traverse larger distance in the wireless channel which makes it more prone to interferences and errors, while the signal will traverse smaller distance in the wireless channel when the WLAN is used.

Network Environment	Uplink Traffic	Downlink Traffic
WLAN	3.390	2.850
UMTS	2.636	2.873

Table 2. MOS scores when running Skype client as a SPV M5000 PDA

Table 3 presents MOS scores for the same networks' interfaces used in Table 2 but with more increase in the CPU load of both connections, as a range from 83% to 90%. When comparing this table with Table 2 and considering WLAN, The MOS scores are decreased to 2.496 and 2.477 for uplink and down link traffic, respectively. These scores are also decreased, when using UMTS connection, to 2.617 and 2.66 for uplink and downlink traffic, respectively. This is due to not only the hardware resources, but also the terminal processing which lead to getting poor perceived voice quality. Furthermore, it is noticed that the MOS scores for UMTS connection exceed those obtained for WLAN connection. This can be justified through the better optimization made in processing of SPV M5000 terminal when using UTMS.

Network Environment	Uplink Traffic	Downlink Traffic
WLAN	2.496	2.477
UMTS	2.617	2.660

Table 3. MOS scores when running Skype client as a SPV M5000 PDA (with increase in CPU load)

3.2.3 Concluding remarks and recommendations

As a summary, a comprehensive study is made to evaluate the Skype calls, using PSEQ method, over fixed and mobile network connections, namely, LAN, WLAN, ADSL, and UMTS. Many factors may affect severely the performance of Skype calls if it is not investigated and designed properly, including audio volume, CPU load when PDA used as a mobile terminal, end-to-end delay, as well as audio cables. Another important factor comes from the fact that the current Skype application used for the wireless environment does not take into account the additional channel impairments such as bit errors due to wireless channel interference which in turn will increase the packet loss. Indeed, this additional challenge did not exist in the wired environment, so it should be also taken into account when designing a high-quality VoIP application. Results show when using a Skype client as a PC-based node that the quality of perceived voice is much better than the one obtained when using that client as a mobile terminal. Therefore, current VoIP applications that run on fixed networks need to be enhanced and optimized more so that their performance over wireless networks is not degraded.

3.3 VoIP over wireless challenges

In what follow, we describe the main challenges associated with wireless transmission and how they affect the transmission quality. Namely, we will focus on bit errors introduced by other interfering signals, packet loss due to buffers overflow of the intermediate nodes, and finally, we describe the importance of having efficient and effective CAC algorithms and how the current algorithms can be further enhanced to improve the network utilization and voice quality.

3.3.1 Bit errors due to interference

A Radio Frequency (RF) transmitted over the open space maybe interfered by any other RF signals within the same frequency range, which may cause bit errors to the original signal, which in turn corrupts the transmitted packets. Furthermore, it is important to demonstrate what do we mean by bit errors, which means simply that some bits flip from zero to one or vice versa. In other words, the receiver still receives the entire transmitted sequence of bits but not exactly like the same transmitted status. It is also important to emphasize that bit errors do mainly exist in the wireless media and not in the wired one due to the natural of the wireless media which makes the transmitted signal more prone to any other interfering signals, while in the wired media, the signal is protected from these interfering signals by the wired media. In case of wireless transmission, interference may occur from any other electronic devices that may emit noise such as microwave ovens, cordless phones, and the legacy wireless LAN devices.

Interfering signals are not permanent and may exist in certain periods of times. This can be modeled as a two-state Markov Chain model that is shown in figure 8. In this model, the wireless channel is represented into two states; good and bad. In good channel conditions, there is a big probability to receive the bits without any errors, while the bits are more likely to be received in error while being in the bad state. Moreover, the channel conditions alternate between the good and bad states with probabilities P1, P2, respectively, and will remain in the good or bad states with probabilities 1-P1, 1-P2, respectively.

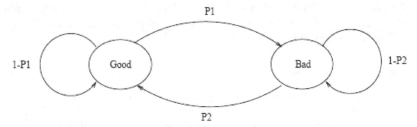

Fig. 8. A two state Markov model for the wireless channel

3.3.2 Packet loss due to congestion

Transmitting voice packets over wireless eventually will involve communicating with the wired network. As shown in figure 4, this backhaul network may introduce packet losses due to the buffers' congestion of the intermediate routers and nodes. It is also important here to distinguish between the natural of bit errors introduced by the wireless network and the packet loss introduced by the wired network. As described earlier, bit errors will simply flip some of the bits, so the stream of bits is completely received but not necessary in the same sent structure. For example, if the sent bit stream was 1010101010, the received stream maybe like this: 1010101111. Notice that some bits (bit number 8 and 10 in this example) flipped from 0 to 1. While in packet loss, the entire packet is lost and dropped due to the fact that the intermediate routers' buffers may not have enough space to accommodate any new arriving packets. Consequently, at the receiving end, we may not have the same number of the transmitted packets.

3.3.3 Call admission control

One of the most important factors that affect voice call quality is the number of calls admitted to the wireless network. Wireless network has certain bandwidth and capacity and if the number of admitted voice calls exceeds its capacity, calls start to degrade in quality and users will not be satisfied. As such, CAC algorithms are often introduced to limit the number of admitted voice calls according to the wireless network capacity and bandwidth. Furthermore, CAC algorithms are also implemented in the wired backhaul network, more precisely in the VoIP gateway, which is responsible to establish an SIP connection to the destination node. CAC in this stage works by probing the VoIP call path, i.e. sending probe packets to the destination VoIP gateway, and measures the parameters that affect the transmission quality such as the packet loss, end-to-end delay, delay variation (jitter), and other network parameters that directly affect voice quality which will be used in the admission process. The author of [12] explored the fact that in wireless WiFi VoIP, there are two separate CAC algorithms running; one in the wireless network, which is responsible for admitting voice calls over the wireless domain, and the other one in the wired network that admit/reject the call based on the QoS status of the network path that the voice call is expected to follow. As we can notice, both CAC algorithms run independently and without any coordination with each other which may lead to a low network utilizing. This may occur due to fact that calls maybe accepted by the wireless domain but eventually maybe rejected by the VoIP gateway due to the fact that the network paths of these calls maybe congested. As such, the author of [12] showed that better network utilization and better VoIP performance can be achieved if both CAC algorithms coordinate with each other, which will be positively reflected on the voice quality of the admitted calls. The proposed solution will be further described in the next section.

4. Opportunistic solutions

Most of the VoIP proposed systems and applications do not take into account the new challenges of the wireless network, so they just customize the interfaces and the design of their applications to make it work with different wireless mobile platforms and devices, or make minor changes in the implemented algorithms and structures. However, as depicted in the previous section, simple design and platform upgrades of the applications specifically designed to computers, laptops, mobiles, and handheld applications may not be sufficiently efficient to meet the expectations of the mobile phone users who expect a comparable VoIP quality to the typical mobile phone voice quality. Otherwise, these applications will not be appealing and will not constitute a valid and strong alternative to their typical mobile phone voice service. In this section, we describe the state-of-the-art solutions and algorithms proposed to compact bit errors and packet loss introduced by the wireless channel that can be integrated into the current VoIP mobile applications, and also how CAC algorithms can be further improved to achieve higher network utilization and better voice quality.

4.1 Solutions to bit errors and packet loss

When VoIP developers and companies started to provide VoIP services and solutions over the wired network, they were mainly concerned about protecting voice packets against packet loss introduced by the transmission media. As such, several mechanisms and methods were introduced to recover and combat these lost packets. Figure 9 shows two widely used mechanisms in many wired VoIP applications. We call the first scheme as the Packet-Level Forward Error Correction scheme (PL-FEC), where the second scheme is named as the Media-Dependent Error Correction scheme (MD-EC). Moreover, we are assuming that in both packetization schemes, each packet contains only one voice frame. However, this assumption is accepted despite its high packetization overhead especially for real-time applications such as VoIP, in which end-to-end delay is very essential and need to be greatly minimized. Thus, putting one voice frame on each packet will reduce the end-to-end delay and the play-out time. In what follows, we will provide a brief description of each scheme and then we will discuss new proposed schemes and methods especially designed for the wireless network, which in turn provide better transmission quality and performance than the legacy wired applications.

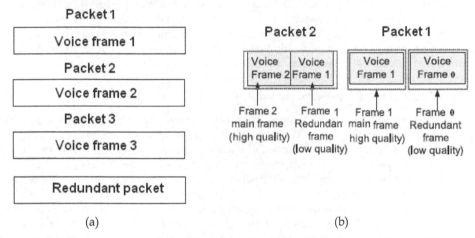

(a)   (b)

Fig. 9. Shows two error correction schemes used to protect against packet loss. (a) The Packet-level Forward Error Correction scheme, and (b) The Media-Dependent Error Correction scheme

4.1.1 Packet- level error correction scheme

The basic idea of this scheme is to group a small number of packets and do some operations on them to generate a redundant packet, then if any packet out of this group of packets is lost, then this packet can be recovered using the other received packets. Figure 9 (a) shows an example of this scheme, here a group of 3 packets are grouped together (packets 1,2,3), a redundant packet is composed by performing a bit-wise XOR-ing operation with the other packets, as such, losing any packet from the four packets can be easily compensated at the receiver side by XOR-ing the received packets. The main advantage of this scheme that it is simple and easy to implement. However, it is not very efficient, as the transmission overhead is high (in this case, the transmission overhead is 25%), and it works if only one packet out of the n-transmitted packets is lost. Also, the receiver has to wait till it receives the n-transmitted packets, which may increase the end-to-end delay.

4.1.2 Media-dependent error correction scheme

The second mechanism widely used to mitigate packet loss is depicted in Fig 9 (b). In this scheme, each voice frame is encoded into high and low quality encoding rates. An example of a high quality encoded rate will be to encode the voice frame using 13 Kbps encoding rate, while the encoding rate of 5.3 Kbps can be used for the low quality encoded voice frames. Once the voice frames are encoded, the high quality encoded frame is packetized in one packet, and the lower quality version is packetized in the packet immediately after it. Now, if the packet containing the high quality frame is lost, and the packet containing the low quality is received, then the receiver uses the low quality packet to conceal the lost high quality voice packet. If both the low and high quality packets are received, the receiver uses the high quality packet, if both packets are lost, the receiver uses other received packets (normally the one after or before it) to conceal the lost packet. For example, Figure 9(b) shows an example of this packetization scheme, packet 1 contains two voice frames, one high quality voice frame (voice frame 1), and the a low quality frame (voice frame 0), the low quality version of voice frame 1 is packetized in a different packet (packet 2), so if packet 1 is lost and packet 2 is received, then the low quality version of voice frame 1 will be used to substitute the lost high quality voice frame.

4.1.3 PL-FEC and MD-EC for wireless VoIP

After discussing the two most widely used error correction schemes for wired VoIP applications, we now discuss the deficiencies of these mechanisms in case of having bit errors introduced by the wireless channel. The main weakness point here that in case of bit errors, the entire packet will be corrupted and dropped even if one bit was in error, even worse, if bit errors were distributed among several packets, all packets will be redeemed lost and none of the above packet level error correction schemes will work. The only solution to mitigate bit errors is to use error correcting codes that can be applied on the bit-stream. These error correction schemes work by dividing the bit stream into a group of symbols of a predetermined size, where the symbol of size (s) is simply a group of s bits, then certain polynomial operation can be applied to generate some redundant symbols that can be used in detecting and correcting random bit errors. One widely used error correction code is Reed Solomon codes [14]. In this book chapter, we will describe how using these techniques can greatly improve the performance of wireless VoIP transmission. However, describing how error correction and detection codes work is beyond the book chapter scope and we encourage the reader refer to other resources such as [13,14] for further information.

4.1.4 A hybrid media error correction scheme for wireless VoIP

In this subsection, we describe our novel approach in solving the problem of transmitting voice packets over wireless channel susceptible to both types of errors; bit errors and packet loss. Knowing that we greatly encourage the reader to refer to [15] for more details and description.

Figure 10 shows our proposed approach for protecting packets against both types of errors. As shown in the figure, the proposed scheme utilizes the Media-Dependent Error Correction scheme described in the previous subsection for providing protection against packet loss. For example, each voice frame is encoded using two different encoding schemes, one for high quality and another one for low quality version of the audio frame. The low quality encoded version is considered as a redundant copy of the high quality frame, and it is used to substitute the high quality frame if it is lost. Now, in order to protect packets against bit errors, we have proposed to use error correction and detection codes such as the Reed-Solomon codes on the packet level, so each packet is divided into a group of symbols, and a polynomial function is used to generate redundant symbols that can be set by the algorithm, which controls the error correcting capabilities of this packet such that the higher the redundant symbols, the larger number of errors can be corrected using this error correction scheme. In figure 10, these redundant symbols are described using the symbol RS CC, which stands for Reed Solomon Channel Code. However, the higher the redundant symbols, the higher the transmission overhead, so it is at the end a trade-off between the error correcting capabilities and the introduced overhead. So in this scheme, if bit errors happened, then using the Reed-Solomon codes, these errors can be corrected instead of just dropping the entire packet. In our proposed approach [15], we even take into account applying unequal error correction symbols to each packet according to the perceptual importance of each packet. In other words, voice packets are different on their perceptual importance, some of them may contain higher and larger energy than other silent or unvoiced packets, as such, loosing these packets may greatly affect the quality of the entire voice call, while losing less importance voice packets may have lower impact on perceiving voice calls. Moreover, the location of the voice frame determines its perceptual importance, for example, voice frames that are located in the transition portions from voiced to unvoiced and vice versa are more important than non-transition frames. As such, more protection (means higher number of redundant symbols) should be applied to these important packets. We highly recommend the reader to refer to our work for more details on how we determine which packet is more important and how we distribute the redundant symbols among different packets such that the expected received quality of the group of packets is maximized.

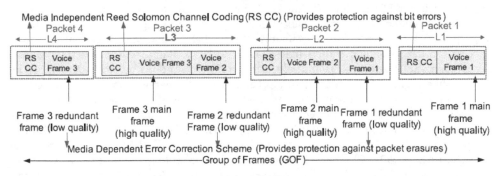

Fig. 10. Hybrid Media Error Correction scheme [15]

Furthermore, we would like to mention why this scheme is named as a hybrid scheme. This is due to the fact that it uses two different types of error corrections schemes, the one used for detecting bit errors, which is considered as a media-independent error correction scheme, while the other one which is used for correcting packet loss which uses a media-dependent low quality copies of the original voice frames. It is also worth mentioning that the proposed scheme utilizes the power of using Multiple Input Multiple Output (MIMO) antennas which has the effect of further reducing bit errors introduced by the wireless channel, and gives more protection to the transmitted bit stream.

Finally, figure 11 shows a performance evaluation results of the proposed Hybrid Media-Error Correction scheme (HM-EC) and compares it to other schemes that are designed mainly for the wired transmission media and can only provide error correction capabilities against packet loss. The experiment setup was as follows. First, the speech signal is divided into a group of voice frames (GOF), each GOF is analyzed and processed separately. Then, each voice frame is encoded using the Speex encoder [16] into low and high bit rates, then the high encoded frames are packetized into one packet and the Reed Solomon error correction scheme is applied to each packet. The number of redundant symbols used for each voice frame is determined based on solving an optimization problem fully described in the paper, which takes into account multiple parameters such as the wireless channel quality, the packet loss, and the perceptual importance of each voice frame. Then, the low quality frames are packetized with the subsequent packet along with the higher quality version of the next frame, and Reed Solomon Channel Coding symbols are applied to the entire packet. To simulate bit errors and packet loss introduced by the wireless channel, two different independent models for the wireless channel were used, the first one is the Gilbert-Eliot model used to simulate bit errors, while the second one is the Gilbert model used to simulate packet loss. More details about the specifications and the mathematical details of the wireless channel model are available at [17].

Once bit and packet errors are simulated at the transmitted stream, the received stream is decoded using the Speex decoder, then error concealment is applied to conceal the lost and non-correctable packets, and then the received voice packets are played out. However, in order to evaluate the quality of the received voice sequence, the received packets were saved into a WAV file and compared with the reference transmitted voice signal using two different metrics, the first one is the Log Spectral Amplitude Distortion (LSAD), defined in [15], where lower LSAD values mean better voice quality, and the second metric is the Perceptual Evaluation of Speech Quality algorithm [12], where higher score indicates better voice quality. In the performance evaluation figures below, one can notice that the x-axis represents different values of the wireless Signal to Noise Ratio in the Good state (SNR_G) measured in dB. Lower values indicate bad wireless conditions channel and higher bit errors, while higher SNR_G values indicate better wireless channel conditions and less bit errors. In the conducted experiments, we varied the packet loss ratios and the bit errors into different rates, and in order to verify the effectiveness of our approach, we compare the performance of our approach with two other approaches. The first one is called the Optimal Unequal Protection scheme (OUP), and the other one is called Optimal Piggy-backing Error Correction scheme (OPEC). The OUP scheme relies on protecting the most perceptual voice packets by utilizing the packet level error correction scheme described earlier. This scheme is a modified version of the work proposed by [18]. In this scheme, the expected distortion for losing each voice packet is calculated, and the ones with highest distortion among the other packets in the Group of Frame (GOF) are protected using the packet level forward error correcting scheme. The number of redundant packets per GOF depends on the allocated transmission budget. While the OPEC utilizes the adaptive piggy-backing error protection policy used in many VoIP applications such as the Robust Audio Tool (RAT) [19]. In this scheme, the sender protects the most important voice packets by providing a low quality version of these voice packets piggy-backed with the following packet, so if the original voice packet get lost and the low quality packet was received, then the receiver uses the low quality version to conceal the lost packet. The sender determines the most important packets by calculating the expected distortion of losing each packet within the group of frames, and then depending on the transmission budget, it chooses the packets with the highest distortion and marks them as the most important perceptual packets.

As can be seen from figure 11, the performance of HM-EC which is aware of the wireless channel impairments and can provide protection to both types of channel errors; bit errors (utilizing the Reed Solomon error correction scheme), and packet loss utilizing the MD-EC scheme, has lower distortion and higher PESQ values for different SNR$_G$ values, and outperforms its counterparts (OUP, and OPEC) who can provide protection to packet loss only and not well suited for the wireless transmission media.

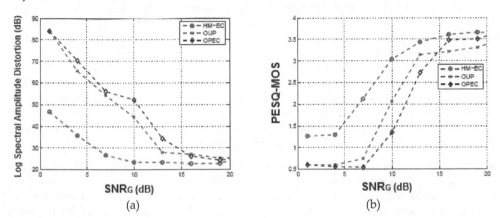

(a)   (b)

Fig. 11. Performance evaluation results of (a) LSAD as a function of SNR$_G$, and (b) PESQ-MOS as a function of SNR$_G$. The dg145 speech clip [23] is used to simulate a VoIP call with a transmission budget of BT = 8,056 Kbytes utilizing 2 X 2 MIMO link, the average packet loss rate is set to 10% [15]

4.1.5 Optimal rate adaptation for VoIP over wireless

Another approach proposed in the literature that provides efficient protection for voice packets against bit error and packet loss is based on utilizing variable rate voice encoders that can encode the voice frames using different encoding rates. The main idea here is to divide the transmission budget (the amount of bytes the sender is willing to spend to transmit the VoIP call), into two portions, the source code portion; the bytes used to encoded voice packets, and the channel coding budget; the bytes used to provide error protection such as the Reed-Solomon error correction codes. The main challenge here is to determine the best splitting ratio of the budget between the source and channel budgets. This problem is know in the literature as the joint source-channel coding, and it is an optimization problem in which increasing the source coding budget in one hand, improves the voice quality and reduces the coding distortion. On the other hand, the channel coding budget decreases, which in turn reduces the error correcting capabilities. So it is a trade-off between voice quality and error correcting capabilities. This problem was tackled and a proposed solution was suggested in [20]. In what follows, we briefly describe the proposed solution but we highly encourage the reader to refer to the paper for more details.

Figure 12 shows how this scheme works. First, voice frames are divided into group of frames (M) named as a Talk Spurt (TS), these voice frames are analyzed and processed to determine what is the optimal encoding rate (R_1, R_2,...,R_O) for each voice frame (F_1, F_2,...,F_M). The decision to chose which encoding rate should be assigned to each voice frame takes into consideration many parameters and issues such as: the perceptual importance of each voice frame, the wireless channel conditions, and the network packet loss rates. All of these factors are quantified and inserted into a mathematical objective function that aims at maximizing the expected quality of the received voice packets. The optimization problem is solved and the optimal encoding rates of each voice frames are determined. Notice that once the encoding rates are determined, the amount of channel coding symbols that can be allocated to each frame is also determined. This fact becomes clearer if we look at figure 12 (b), which depicts the packetization process. First, the symbols S_{xy}, and C_{zh} refer to the source coding and channel coding symbols, respectively. Each column represents a channel coding block of size (L), so as we can see, the number of source coding symbols (S_{xy}) and channel coding symbols (C_{zh}) for each voice frame should be equal to L. For example, the first column represents the source and channel coding symbols that belongs to the first voice frame, so the subscripts x, and z in the variables S_{xy}, and C_{zh} refer to the frame number, where the subscripts y, and h refer to the number of source and channel symbols allocated to each frame, respectively. For example, in this figure frame 1 was allocated three source coding symbols (S_{11}, S_{12}, S_{13}), and three channel coding symbols (C_{11}, C_{12}, C_{13}).

As we can notice, the higher the encoding rate of each voice frame, the larger the number of source coding symbols S_{xy}, which results in a better voice quality and lower encoding distortion. However, the number of channel coding symbols C_{zh} will be lower for that frame, since the sum of S_{xy} and C_{zh} is equal to L, which in turn, will reduce the error correcting capabilities of that frame. So it is a trade-off between the voice encoding quality and the error correcting capabilities of each frame.

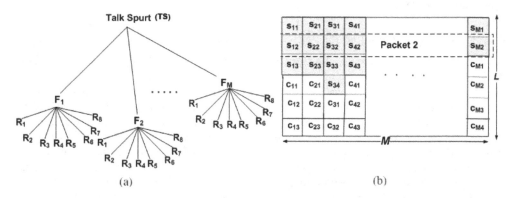

(a)   (b)

Fig. 12. (a) Shows how the frames that belong to a certain Talk Spurt (TS) are encoded differently using on of the possible encoding rates ($R_1, R_2,...,R_O$) supported by the Speex encoder, (b) shows how each voice frame is aligned vertically, such that packets are formed horizontally such that each packet contains one symbol from each voice frame [20]

Now once the optimal source and channel encoding rates are determined for each voice frame, the symbols are aligned into a two-dimensional grid of symbols as shown on figure 12 (b), where the encoded voice frames with their channel coding symbols are aligned vertically, and packets are formulated horizontally, i.e. the packet is formulated by taking one symbol from each voice frame. Notice that we suggested using the Reed-Solomon channel coding scheme, which is capable of detecting and correcting symbol errors and erasures.

It is important here to mention how this scheme is capable of protecting packets against both types of errors (bits error and packet erasure). First, one can notice that the way the packets are formulated will help in mitigating packet loss, as can be seen, each packet is formulated by taking one symbol from each voice frame (from each column), as such, losing one packet will result in losing one symbol from each voice frame, which can be corrected using the channel coding symbols allocated to each voice frame. Also, the same applies for bit errors, these errors can be corrected utilizing the channel coding symbols as well.

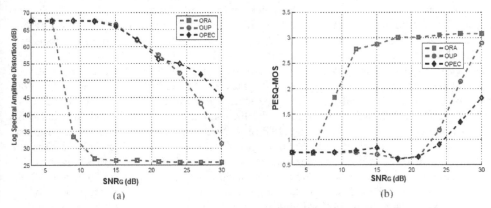

(a)   (b)

Fig. 13. Performance evaluation of ORA algorithm, using the dg129 speech clip [23] to simulate a VoIP call, utilizing 1x1 MIMO link configuration, with a transmission budget of BT = 5,6 Kbytes, and a 10% average packet erasure rate[20]

We conclude this subsection by showing the performance evaluation results of the optimal rate adaptation scheme under tandem wireless channel that is prone to bit errors and packet erasure. The same experiment setup used in the previous subsection is used here. Notice that again that ORA scheme has much better performance than the OUP and the OPEC schemes, especially at low SNR$_G$ values in which the wireless channel is in bad condition. Once more, this scheme shows the importance of having error correction and protection scheme especially designed for the wireless channel, and also shows that other schemes especially designed for the wired network are not necessary efficient under noisy wireless channels.

4.2 End-to-end aware CAC algorithm

In this subsection, we will describe our proposed scheme published in [12], and show how it can improve the network performance and utilization, which in turn results in a better VoIP quality service and an increase in the number of successful VoIP calls conducted within specific period of time and within a specific network.

Probing the expected path of the VoIP call over the wired network is one technique widely used in many CAC algorithms at the VoIP gateways. In this technique, the end-to-end link status is used in determining whether the call can be admitted or not. However, as mentioned earlier, in wireless VoIP service, we will have two stages for CAC, one at the wireless channel level, in which the wireless access point will check if the wireless link capacity can accept one more call without affecting the quality of the existing ones, and one at the wired level, that will check if the end-to-end path can meet the minimum VoIP QoS requirements. Currently, both algorithms do not interact with each other. We have proposed to exchange information between the two CAC algorithms and to use this information in the decision of the first CAC algorithm that takes place at the wireless domain. More particularly, we proposed to report the end-to-end link status information of each call discovered by the VoIP gateway to the Quality of Service Access Point too, so it can be used as a policy in the call admission process implemented in the wireless domain. According to this new setup, the QAP algorithm, will also check the link status of this call, reported by the VoIP gateway and use it to decide if the call should be admitted or not. If the information reported about the end-to-end path link of this call indicates that the destination path is congested and this call can not be admitted, the QAP rejects the call and does not register it in the Hybrid Coordination Controlled Channel Access (HCCA) polling list [21], consequently, the wireless resources will not be wasted in admitting unsuccessful VoIP call that will be ultimately rejected by the VoIP gateway. At the beginning, neither the VoIP gateway nor the QAP has entries in their link status table, so the QAP will admit at all calls, and the VoIP gateway will start building the link status table for these calls, so once this table is populated, it will be sent to the QAP to be used for the new incoming calls. The link information for the destination networks is stored in a lookup table that contains the destination addresses, and their paths statuses. So once the VoIP call is received by the QAP, its destination address is checked using that table, and the call is admitted only if its end-to-end path conditions are satisfactory. Caching concept is also used in our proposed scheme, so the link statuses information for the destination networks are kept in the cache memory for a certain time-out period, the VoIP gateway keeps updating the status of the destination networks attempted so far. After certain time-out period, the link status information related to a certain network destination is removed from the table, if no one accessed that network. Figure 14 depicts how our policy can be integrated with the QAP call admission algorithm.

To further show the benefits and the justifications of implementing this policy, let us look at a scenario in which the caller is trying to establish a VoIP call to a congested network. As discussed above, after the caller's terminal device establishes a connection with the access point, and registers itself as one of the admitted stations in the polling list, the caller will contact the VoIP gateway, and go through billing, authentication, authorization, destination IP address look up stages, and finally check whether the call can be admitted or not. In this case, the call is rejected and a busy signal is sent back to the caller terminal, which will try again to establish a connection and go through the previous process, until the destination link becomes less congested, so the call can be admitted, or until the caller gives up and stops from setting up the call. As we can notice that during the failed call setup attempts, the caller terminal utilized the wireless channel, and registers itself in the polling list for the whole period of time used in attempting to conduct the call. This time might be significant for the following reasons:

1. Contacting the VoIP gateway might take some time due to the fact that in real networks, it is usually hosted in the Internet Service Provider (ISP) network, not in the local wireless network.

2. Some time will be wasted for doing authentication and other functions mentioned earlier, which is considered useless as far as the call will be rejected, needless to say that these operations will consume some of the valuable VoIP gateway processing power and time.

3. The VoIP gateway might be loaded or its links might be congested, which might increase the process and access time and increase the delay in responding to the issued requests.

4. Usually, once the VoIP is rejected by the VoIP gateway, the caller station will still be registered in the QAP polling list, so the caller will keep trying many times to establish a call, and according to the network congestion statistics, the successive trials most likely will fail, since usually the congestion in networks lasts for a period of time [22]. While according to our policy, rejecting the call from the first time will give the opportunity to other stations to access the network, which might conduct VoIP calls with different destination networks that do not have congestion, thus improving the utilization of the wireless network, and increasing the number of successful VoIP calls.

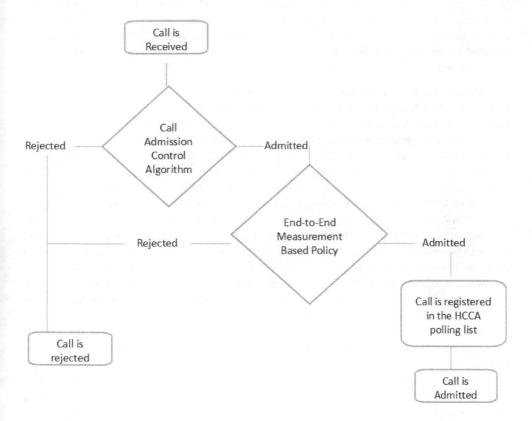

Fig. 14. Integrating the suggested policy with the typical QAP Call Admission algorithms [12]

5. Conclusion

VoIP over wireless is a promising and a challenging service that started to flourish between mobile and wireless users. Cost effectiveness and also the additional available services that VoIP can deliver are two driving forces that greatly motivate the Internet service providers and solution developers to develop new software and systems that are capable of delivering a competitive VoIP quality over the mobile network. Another great advantage that wireless VoIP can offer to its users is mobility. The mobile user will be able to use his own VoIP wireless number wherever he goes, in other words; the user will keep the same number even though the user may travel abroad or change the location. Different from the mobile phone, in this case, the user does not need to contact his mobile service provider to enable the expensive rooming service, all what is needed is to secure an Internet connection to the mobile phone. Also, recently, many mobile operators look at wireless VoIP service as a backup service for their customers when they do not have good mobile coverage at their homes for example or even in certain spots where there is not enough coverage from the mobile towers, so in this case, if the customer have an Internet connection, the user's mobile phone can connect to a device called femtocell [22], which will establish a connection with the mobile phone and conduct a VoIP call between the mobile phone and the mobile call center, where the call will be normally conducted as a normal mobile call to the final destination, on other words, wireless VoIP maybe used as an intermediate stage in many scenarios and solutions.

In conclusion, there are plethora of applications and opportunities for this service in the current and near future. As such, there is a need to develop new systems and applications to take into account the differences between the network impairments faced by the wired network, and the additional challenges faced by the wireless domain. In this chapter, we discussed some of these challenges, mainly bit errors introduced by the tandem wireless channel due to interference from other wireless devices, congestion and packet loss introduced by the intermediate nodes of the network, and the designing of an efficient Call Admission Control algorithm that takes into account the wired and wireless network status when admitting/rejecting VoIP calls. Another limitation briefly discussed in this book chapter is the relatively limited CPU power capabilities of the mobile devices and terminals, so the deployed algorithms and applications should take that into account. Furthermore, we have discussed some of the proposed solutions in the literature that can greatly improve the performance of wireless VoIP, namely we discussed two main approaches; the first one is called the Hybrid Media- Error-Correction scheme [15] and the second one is the Optimal Rate Adaptation scheme [20]. Finally, we discussed a proposed extension to the current Call Admission Control schemes used in the wireless domain. Our extension allow the wireless access point to interact with the VoIP gateway, which will eventually determine whether the VoIP call can be conducted or not, which is normally decided based on the expected end-to-end link status quality of each attempted VoIP call. We proposed to pass the link status information of the VoIP calls to the wireless access point and use it in admitting or rejecting VoIP calls over the wireless domain, which in turn will save a lot of bandwidth, improve the VoIP performance and increase the number of conducted VoIP calls in the wireless domain.

6. References

[1] M. Cardenete-Suriol, J. Mangues-Bafalluy, A. Maso, M. Gorricho," Characterization and Comparison of Skype Behaviour in Wired and Wireless Network Scenarios", IEEE Global Telecommunications Conference, 2007.

[2] F. Ohrtman. Voice over 802.11. Artech house, 2004

[3] J. Kurose and K. Ross. Computer Networking: A Top-Down Approach Featuring the Internet. Addison-Wesley, third edition, 2004.

[4] http://www.cisco.com/univercd/cc/td/doc/cisintwk/intsolns/voipsol/cac.pdf

[5] http://www.disruptive-analysis.com

[6] http://www.truphone.com

[7] Fring website http://www.fring.com

[8] Skype website http://www.skype.com

[9] M. Portoles-Comeras, M. Requena-Esteso, J. Mangues-Bafalluy, and M. Cardenete-Suriol, "EXTREME: Combining The Ease of Management of Multi-User Experimental Facilities and The Flexibility of Proof of Concept Testbeds," Proceedings of IEEE TridentCom, 2006.

[10] The Madwifi project http://sourceforge.net/projects/madwifi/

[11] ITU-T, "Perceptual evaluation of speech quality (PESQ)," ITU-T Recommendation P.862, February 2001.

[12] A. Khalifeh, "An End-to-End Measurement Based Call Admission Control Policy for VoIP", IEEE Wireless Communications and Networking Conference (WCNC), 2008.

[13] Stephen B. Wicker, Vijay K. Bhargava , Reed-Solomon Codes and Their Applications , IEEE press 1994.

[14] Wesley Peterson, E J. Weldon, Error Correction Coding: Mathematical Methods and Algorithms. MIT press, 1972

[15] A.Khalifeh, H. Yousefi'zadeh,"A Hybrid Media Scheme for Wireless VoIP", IEEE Data Compression Conference (DCC), 2010.

[16] Speex website http://www.speex.org

[17] A. Khalifeh, H. Yousefi'zadeh, "An An Optimal UEP Scheme of Audio Transmission over MIMO Wireless Links", IEEE Wireless Communications & Networking Conference (WCNC), 2008.

[18] M. Chen and M. Murthi. "Optimized Unequal Error Protection for Voice over IP". In Proc. IEEE ICASP, 2004.

[19] Robust Audio Tool (RAT) website http://www-mice.cs.ucl.ac.uk/multimedia/software/rat/index.html

[20] A. Khalifeh, H. Yousefi'zadeh, "Optimal Rate Adaptation for VoIP Over Wireless Tandem Links", IEEE MILCOM, 2010.

[21] S. Mangold, C. Sunghyun, G.R. Hiertz, O. Klein, and B. Walke, "Analysis of IEEE 802.11e for QoS support in wireless LANs", In Proc. IEEE Wireless Communication, pages 40–50 Vol. 10, Dec. 2003.

[22] A.Markopoulou, F.Tobagi, and M.Karam, "Loss and Delay Measurements of Internet Backbones", Elsevier Computer Communications, (Special Issue on Measurements and Monitoring of IP networks), pages 1590–1604 Vol.29, 2006.

[23] ITU P.862 Perceptual Evaluation of Speech Quality (PESQ) conformance tests files, Pseries.

[24] A. Khalifeh, H. Yousefi'zadeh,"Audio Transmission over Error-Prone Wireless Links", IEEE Trans. on Multimedia, 2010.

7

Designing and Evaluating Mobile Multimedia User Experiences in Public Urban Places: Making Sense of the Field

Jan Seeburger, Marcus Foth and Dian Tjondronegoro

Queensland University of Technology

Australia

1. Introduction

The majority of the world's population now lives in cities (United Nations, 2008) resulting in an urban densification requiring people to live in closer proximity and share urban infrastructure such as streets, public transport, and parks within cities. However, "physical closeness does not mean social closeness" (Wellman, 2001, p. 234). Whereas it is a common practice to greet and chat with people you cross paths with in smaller villages, urban life is mainly anonymous and does not automatically come with a sense of community per se. Wellman (2001, p. 228) defines community "as networks of interpersonal ties that provide sociability, support, information, a sense of belonging and social identity."

While on the move or during leisure time, urban dwellers use their interactive information communication technology (ICT) devices to connect to their spatially distributed community while in an anonymous space. Putnam (1995) argues that available technology privatises and individualises the leisure time of urban dwellers. Furthermore, ICT is sometimes used to build a "cocoon" while in public to avoid direct contact with collocated people (Mainwaring et al., 2005; Bassoli et al., 2007; Crawford, 2008). Instead of using ICT devices to seclude oneself from the surrounding urban environment and the collocated people within, such devices could also be utilised to engage urban dwellers more with the urban environment and the urban dwellers within.

Urban sociologists found that "what attracts people most, it would appear, is other people" (Whyte, 1980, p. 19) and "people and human activity are the greatest object of attention and interest" (Gehl, 1987, p. 31). On the other hand, sociologist Erving Goffman describes the concept of civil inattention, acknowledging strangers' presence while in public but not interacting with them (Goffman, 1966). With this in mind, it appears that there is a contradiction between how people are using ICT in urban public places and for what reasons and how people use public urban places and how they behave and react to other collocated people. On the other hand there is an opportunity to employ ICT to create and influence experiences of people collocated in public urban places.

The widespread use of location aware mobile devices equipped with Internet access is creating networked localities, a digital layer of geo-coded information on top of the physical world (Gordon & de Souza e Silva, 2011). Foursquare.com is an example of a location based social network (LBSN) that enables urban dwellers to virtually check-in into places at which they are physically present in an urban space. Users compete over 'mayorships' of places with Foursquare friends as well as strangers and can share recommendations about the space.

The research field of Urban Informatics is interested in these kinds of digital urban multimedia augmentations and how such augmentations, mediated through technology, can create or influence the UX of public urban places. "Urban informatics is the study, design, and practice of urban experiences across different urban contexts that are created by new opportunities of real-time, ubiquitous technology and the augmentation that mediates the physical and digital layers of people networks and urban infrastructures" (Foth et al., 2011, p. 4). One possibility to augment the urban space is to enable citizens to digitally interact with spaces and urban dwellers collocated in the past, present, and future. "Adding a digital layer to the existing physical and social layers could facilitate new forms of interaction that reshape urban life" (Kjeldskov & Paay, 2006, p. 60).

This methodological chapter investigates how the design of UX through such digital place-based mobile multimedia augmentations can be guided and evaluated. First, we describe three different applications that aim to create and influence the urban UX through mobile mediated interactions. Based on a review of literature, we describe how our integrated framework for designing and evaluating urban informatics experiences has been constructed. We conclude the chapter with a reflective discussion on the proposed framework.

2. Subject of study

During a three-year study, three software applications have been developed aiming to create and influence the experience of collocated people in urban public places through digital place-based mobile multimedia augmentations and anonymous mobile mediated interactions between collocated urban dwellers who congregate in the past, present, or future.

Fig. 1. Capital Music

Capital Music (Seeburger et al., 2010) is a mobile application designed for iOS, enabling collocated people to listen to their music as usual but also sharing a patchwork of the coverart of the songs currently played in the vicinity. Users can anonymously exchange messages based on viewing other people's song choices. Figure 1 visualises the user interface of Capital Music.

Fig. 2. Sapporo World Window

Sapporo World Window (Seeburger & Choi, 2011) is an interactive social media mash-up deployed in a newly built urban public underground space in Sapporo, Japan. The project utilises ten public screens and mobile phones of urban dwellers. Sapporo World Window enables users to share their favourite locations with locals and visitors through integrating various social media contents into a coherent screen presentation. Figure 2 visualises one screen of the Sapporo World Window system with the respective mobile website providing additional information to the promoted location.

The PlaceTagz project investigates how physical artefacts in public urban places can be utilised and combined with mobile phone technologies to facilitate interactions. PlaceTagz are QR codes printed on stickers linking to a digital message board enabling collocated users to interact with each other over time resulting in a place-based digital memory. PlaceTagz are deployed through removable stickers placed on the walls of public toilet as a digital alternative to toilet graffiti. Figure 3 visualises PlaceTagz and a respective mobile website after scanning the QR code as well as PlaceTagz attached to various public urban spaces.

Fig. 3. PlaceTagz

All three projects add a digital layer to the physical urban environment, enabling collocated people to anonymously interact with each other and the specific information they share. These projects are in response to the question 'how can ICT be applied to create and influence the UX in public urban places?'. The study requires a methodology that assesses how the UX is influenced by these applications and their specific interaction qualities.

3. Review of the user experience literature

HCI research largely focussed on usability studies to evaluate activities such as task completion time and ease of use of software applications designed to fulfil given work tasks. The term "experience" is widely used to describe various aspects of HCI that go beyond the usability of work-related products and especially used when focusing on the UX concerning interactive consumer products. Garrett (2003) states that UX is not about how products tackle a problem to achieve a solution they were made for but rather, UX is about how products behave when people actually use and interact with them. While the ISO FDIS 9241-210:2009 norm on ergonomics of human system interaction defines UX as "a person's perceptions and responses that result from the use or anticipated use of a product, system or service," recently published studies in UX research highlight the lack of a common definition for UX, e.g. Law et al. (2009), Bargas-Avila & Hornbæk (2011), and Battarbee & Koskinen (2005).

Alben (1996, p. 12) defines experience as "all the aspects of how people use an interactive product: the way it feels in their hands, how well they understand how it works, how they feel about it while they're using it, how well it serves their purposes, and how well it fits into the entire context in which they are using it." Alben (1996) states six characteristics, which directly influence the quality of experience, and two characteristics, which indirectly influence the quality of experience through the product designers. Direct characteristics are needs, learnability and usability, appropriation, aesthetics, mutability, and manageability. Indirect characteristics are the understanding of users and an effective design process.

Hassenzahl & Tractinsky (2006) argue that UX research should go beyond the instrumental and address surprise, diversion, or intimacy. UX should consider emotions in terms of joy, fun, and pride as well as the experiential, which means that a product is used in a specific situation resulting in the experience. "UX is about technology that fulfils more than just instrumental needs in a way that acknowledges its use as a subjective, situated, complex and dynamic encounter. UX is a consequence of a user's internal state (predispositions, expectations, needs, motivation, mood, etc.), the characteristics of the designed system (e.g. complexity, purpose, usability, functionality, etc.) and the context (or the environment) within which interaction occurs (e.g. organizational/social setting, meaningfulness of the activity, voluntariness of use, etc.)" (Hassenzahl & Tractinsky, 2006, p. 95).

McCarthy & Wright (2004) developed a framework to analyse experience with technology. The framework consists of four threads: (1) Compositional: "How do the elements of an experience fit together to form a coherent whole?" – e.g. narrative structure, action possibility, consequences and explanations of actions. (2) Sensual: "What does the design and texture and the overall atmosphere make us feel?" – e.g. look and feel of an application. (3) Emotional: "What emotions color the experience for us?" – e.g. fun, excitement, and frustration. (4) Spatio-Temporal: "What effects do place and time have on our experience?" – e.g. time speed up or slow, space may open or close down. Furthermore, it consists of six interrelated sense-making processes: (1) Anticipating: "We never come to technology unprejudiced." (2) Connecting: "We make a judgement in an instant and without much thought." (3) Interpreting: "We work out what's going on and how we feel about it." (4) Reflecting: "We examine and evaluate what is happening in an interaction." (5) Appropriating: "We work out how a new experience fits with other experiences we have had and with our sense of self." (6) Recounting: "We enjoy story telling and make sense of experience in stories." The framework is designed for interactive products. However, this research is interested in influencing the UX of public urban places through digital place-based augmentations and mobile mediated interactions and therefore the emotional and spatio-temporal threads of the framework are especially interesting: how does technology change the experience of places and can technology open up public places and connect the urban dwellers within them to make the space more accessible in a digital way?

Forlizzi & Ford (2000, p. 420) state that "a singular experience is made up of an infinite amount of smaller experiences, relating to contexts, people, and products." They created a framework to understand what influences experiences and dimensions of experiences. Prior experiences of users, their values, emotions and feelings all influence their experience. A product influences the experience through its usability, quality, aesthetics and so on. Additionally, some products are personal items that have specific meanings to particular users such as a specific golf ball that was used for a hole-in-one shot. The user-product interaction takes place in context influenced by social and cultural factors what requires the designers to "understand the users, products, contexts, and nature of interactions that may happen" (Forlizzi & Ford, 2000, p. 420). The authors describe four dimensions of an experience: (1) sub-conscious experiences that are fluent and automatic experiences such as using the coffee machine, (2) cognitive experiences that require users attention and problem solving skills such as interacting with an unfamiliar software, (3) narrative experiences that force people to think and formalise what they are doing and experiencing, and (4) storytelling experiences that are created through sharing experiences. Forlizzi & Battarbee (2004) describe three types of user-product interactions: (1) fluent interactions enabling automated interactions such as riding a bike, (2) cognitive interactions requiring problem solving skills, and (3) expressive interactions creating a relationship with a product. Additionally Forlizzi & Battarbee (2004) differentiate between three types of experiences: (1) experience, a constant stream of information while interacting with the world, (2) an experience, an interaction with the world which can be named, and (3) co-experience, which "reveals how the experiences an individual has and the interpretations that are made of them are influenced by the physical or virtual presence of others" (Forlizzi & Battarbee, 2004, p. 263). Battarbee & Koskinen (2005) criticise that current UX research mostly focuses on the individual and does not consider experiences that are created together. The term co-experience is used "to describe experiences with products in terms of how the meanings of individual experiences emerge and change as they become part of social interaction" (Battarbee & Koskinen, 2005, p. 7).

The definitions show that emotional attributes such as enjoyment, contextual attributes such as place and environment, as well as the social setting have to be taken into account when conducting HCI research. Furthermore, existing definitions discuss products, services, or interfaces. However, this research is interested in designing and influencing the UX in public urban places through digital place-based mobile multimedia augmentations and mobile mediated interactions. In a broader sense, this research creates applications that mediate the UX by augmenting the urban space rather than creating a UX isolated on the mobile device. This urban UX is influenced by people who are collocated in the past, present, or future interacting with each other in an anonymous way mediated through their mobile device resulting in the creation of a digital layer on top of the geographical space. "People create, elaborate, and evaluate experiences together with other people, and products may be involved as the subject, object or means of these interactions" (Battarbee & Koskinen, 2005, p. 15).

The literature review highlights that various attempts have been made to define and scope diverse types of UX. Additionally, having in mind that a variety of variables before, during, and after application usage can influence a user's experience is further contributing to the challenge of systematically studying them. This methodological chapter integrates the various attempts of previous research into a unified framework providing guidelines for researchers to design and evaluate the UX of digital place-based mobile multimedia augmentations and mobile mediated interactions.

4. Framework construction

Given the lack of a common definition of UX and how to design or evaluate them, we integrated the findings from the literature review in order to create our own framework to guide the design and evaluation of Urban Informatics interventions enabling mobile mediated interactions.

The Urban Informatics definition highlights three influential factors to study, design, and practice the urban experience: real time ubiquitous technologies, people networks, and urban contexts and infrastructures (Foth et al., 2011). Place and location are playing a central role in Urban Informatics research and are the focal point of investigation. The aim is to create and influence the urban UX through technological interventions used in public urban places. Rather then focusing on the technological intervention itself, we are interested in how the combination of people, place, and technology can form new UX in an integrated way. Therefore the framework utilises the people, place, and technology notions of urban informatics as a starting point of investigation. Some of the existing UX definitions use similar categories whereas in our approach we specifically use the term place as context of interaction:

- User's internal state, characteristics of the designed system, context within the interaction occurs (Hassenzahl & Tractinsky, 2006)
- Contexts, people, products (Forlizzi & Ford, 2000)
- People and technology (McNamara & Kirakowski, 2006)
- People, products, context (Alben, 1996)

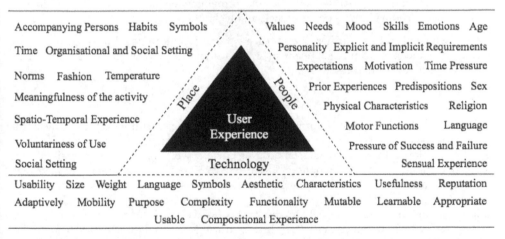

Fig. 4. Aggregated elements of UX (Forlizzi & Ford, 2000; Hassenzahl & Tractinsky, 2006; Alben, 1996; McCarthy & Wright, 2004; Arhippainen & Tähti, 2003) recategorised under the people, place, and technology categories

The place category investigates the possibilities of digital layers and augmentations of the particular space. Is the deployed application suitable for a specific public urban place and do the interaction possibilities align to current norms and practices of that space? What possibilities for digital augmentations and mobile mediate interactions does the place offer? How do other collocated people and the used technology influence the perception of place? Gordon and de Souza e Silva (2011) state that experiences of urban spaces always have been mediated through technologies such as buildings, cars and streets but new ubiquitous and location aware technologies add additional possibilities to influence this experience. The technology section is about the characteristics, functionality, and usability of the deployed urban informatics interventions. The people section focuses on how people feel about the technology used in a specific space. Does the application enable sociality, support positive emotions, and what kinds of feelings are triggered?

The various elements of UX mentioned in literature have been collected and recategorised under the people, place, and technology notions of Urban Informatics. This approach is visualised in Figure 4 and shows a wide variety of elements within each category. Figure 4 also illustrates that the existing UX frameworks emphasise the user and the technology. Place or context of use is not always considered in the existing literature. However, in having a technological intervention in a public urban place with the aim to create and influence an experience, people are the object of interest while place is the focal point of investigation whereas technology is the mediator of the experience.

The elements visualised in Figure 4 are very broad in nature. An Urban Informatics intervention will most likely not require all of them to be considered during a study. For example, having a mobile application as the technological subject of study, the researcher will not be able to influence or be interested in investigating how the size or weight of the mobile device resonates with the UX. Therefore, the next step in the construction of the framework is the elimination of elements irrelevant for our study. Table 1, Table 2, and Table 3 in the following subsections list the remaining elements after the elimination process, categorised within the people, place, and technology notions.

The following subsections further discuss each category in more detail through proposing investigative questions for each element within the category while suggesting some methodological tools and frameworks for study.

4.1 Place

A starting point for an Urban Informatics study should begin with its context of use, the place following an observation of how people use the space. An ethnographic approach can help "to develop a thorough understanding of current work practises as a basis for the design of computer support" (Simonsen & Kensing, 1997, p. 82). Furthermore, ethnography aims "to see activities as social actions embedded within a socially organised domain and accomplished in and through the day-to-day activities of participants" (Hughes, King, Rodden & Andersen, 1995, p. 58). In the context of Urban Informatics research, work practice refers to how people use ICT devices during day-to-day activities. Day-to-day activities refer in this research to the time people spend at urban public places of their city.

It is important to identify what kinds of activities take place in the analysed space and of what kind of nature the activities are. For example, are people just using the place to traverse through the city or as a third place to meet friends or strangers between home and work? Are people mostly alone or accompanied by people and during what time(s) is the place mostly used? Table 1 lists the relevant elements in the place category providing guidelines to use while observing the space. The elements and questions stated in Table 1 should be considered to inform the design and purpose of the application. After application development, the elements mentioned in the framework design by McCarthy & Wright (2004) should be considered to investigate the spatio-temporal influence of the experience of people in the public urban place.

Answering the questions stated in Table 1 will help to design applications supporting mobile mediated interactions suitable to a specific public urban place. Urban Informatics intervention should align to current social practices and behaviour of people in public urban places rather than creating new ones (Pedersen & Valgårda, 2004). Therefore, studying the place and the applications' context of use are vital factors in influencing the UX. The overall aim of answering the questions while studying the place is, what kind of data can be collected by urban dwellers and utilised in an Urban Informatics intervention.

Element	Description
Meaningfulness of the activities in the place	Are the activities in the place in the nature of business, pleasure, idling, or other settings?
Organisational/ social setting	What kinds of activities are accomplished in the organisational and/or social setting?
Fashion	What is 'in fashion' according to the place?
Habits	What are the habits in the place?
Norms	What are the norms in the place?
Time of mobile mediated interaction	When does the interaction between urban dwellers occur? Are they synchronous, asynchronous, or both
Place of mobile mediated interaction	Where does the interaction take place? What kind of place is it? What are the entry barriers? (if any)
Accompanying persons	Do other persons usually accompany people or are people rather by themselves?

Table 1. Elements in the place category

4.2 Technology

After analysing the place and its elements as listed in Table 1 the technology section provides guidelines for developing an application deployed in the analysed space. Table 2 lists the elements in the technology section.

First of all, the results of the ethnographic observations need to be analysed. The results should inform system development, which utilise the available data and location information as well as available ICT devices used in the place. For the Capital Music application, we observed public transport users and selected music listeners' song choices and their mp3-players and mobile phones for an Urban Informatics intervention.

Element	Description
Purpose	What is the purpose of the application? Why should someone use it?
Functionality	Is the functionality sufficient to fit its purpose?
Complexity	Is the software complex enough to fulfil its task without hindering usability?
Usability	Is the software easy to use?
Aesthetics	Is the designed technology visually pleasing? Does the design support usability?
Acceptance	Does the application suit the place and support current social practices?

Table 2. Elements in the technology category

To ensure that the purpose, functionality, characteristics, and complexity of the proposed application align with the needs of the users, they have to be involved during the development process. A user-centred design methodology will ensure that the mobile application meets the needs of the users (Kangas & Kinnunen, 2005). For example we evaluated the concept of sharing of song choices through a paper-based study reported in Seeburger et al. (2010).

During and after application development, usability studies have to be conducted. Thereby Tractinsky (1997, p. 121) found that "perceptions of interface aesthetic are closely related to apparent usability and thus increase the likelihood that aesthetics may considerably affect system acceptability." This implies that the visual design of the studied intervention has to be sufficient enough to not hinder usability. Lavie & Tractinsky (2004) developed a measurement instrument for evaluating perceived aesthetics of computer interfaces. They subdivided aesthetics into "classical aesthetics," emphasizing clear and ordered designs as well as "expressive aesthetics," emphasizing designers' creativity and originality to break common design rules.

The acceptance element in Table 2 has been derived from the usefulness element mentioned in Arhippainen & Tähti (2003). Traditional research on technology acceptance models includes perceived usefulness and ease of use of an information system as predictors of how likely a system will be used. Perceived usefulness has been defined as "the degree to which a person believes that using a particular system would enhance his or her job performance" (Davis, 1989, p. 320). As this research is focusing on hedonic information systems rather then utilitarian systems, "perceived usefulness loses its dominant predictive value in favor of ease of use and enjoyment" (van der Heijden, 2004, p. 695). We added acceptance instead of usefulness to the technology category for this framework consisting of perceived usefulness, ease of use, and enjoyment. Validated items are researched to investigate these variables (van der Heijden, 2004).

4.3 People

"When users are confronted with a product, a process is triggered: First, an apparent product character is constructed. It is a user's personal reconstruction of the designer's intended product character. Second, the fit of the apparent character and the current situation will lead to consequences, such as a judgement about the momentary appealingness of the product, and emotional or behavioural consequences." (Hassenzahl, 2005, p. 33)

Following the observation and analysis of the place and involvement of the user during the design process of the software application, people have to be further considered to generate insights into the quality of the experience created through using the designed application.

A survey on current UX research by Bargas-Avila & Hornbæk (2011) states that the most researched dimensions of UX are emotions and affect, enjoyment, and aesthetics (aesthetics in this framework has been re-categorized into the technology category). Additionally the authors state that new dimensions such as enchantment, engagement, tangible magic, aesthetics of interaction, and relevance has been proposed to research (Bargas-Avila & Hornbæk, 2011).

Element	Description
Requirements	What are the technological requirements people must master to use the technology?
Motivation	What motivates people to use the technology? What need does it fulfil?
Prior Experiences	How do prior experiences influence technology usage?
Feelings	How do people feel about using the technology?
Affect	How does the technology affect the user?
Emotions	What kinds of emotions are created through using the technology?
Enjoyment	Do people enjoy using the technology?
Likeability	Do people like the technology?
Social Interaction	How does the technology support sociability? What kind of social interaction takes place?

Table 3. Elements in the people category

This framework proposes a three-fold process to investigate how people experience the technology. First, the application has to be made available in the designated space and be used by real users. The software application itself can be used as a data collection tool, logging data about software usage and interaction. This kind of data logging enables conclusions, for example, how often, for how long, and to what extent has the application be used. Second, as UX is subjective, semi-structured interviews with users is a promising approach to collect qualitative data about how users feel about the application. Thereby, we propose to ask application and place specific questions about how using the developed system influences, changes, and possibly enhances the experience. After the semi-structured interview, a paper-based survey for collecting basic demographic data as well as getting insight into various elements of the UX using the validated items should be applied.

To measure emotions, Huisman and Van Hout (2008) selected eight emotion terms such as joy and sadness, desire and disgust, fascination and boredom, and satisfaction and dissatisfaction to evaluate interactive digital systems. These eight emotion terms are also related to different concepts such as aesthetics or usability. The AttrakDiff (Hassenzahl, 2008) questionnaire provides insights into the pragmatic (effectiveness, efficiency) and hedonistic (e.g. stimulation, identification) qualities of an interactive product. Hassenzahl (2008, p. 322) argues that "[u]sing a product with a particular product character in a particular situation will lead to consequences, such as emotions (e.g., satisfaction, pleasure), explicit evaluations (i.e. judgements of appeal, beauty, goodness), or overt behavior (approach, avoidance)." Watson et al. (1988) developed and validated two mood scales with 10 items to measure positive affect (interested, distressed, exited, upset, strong, guilty, scared, hostile, enthusiastic, proud) and negative affect (irritable, alert, ashamed, inspired, nervous, determined, attentive, jittery, active, afraid) of peoples' mood. Watson & Clark (1994) extended the positive affect and negative affect scale and added fear, hostility, guilt, and, sadness as basic negative emotion scales, joviality, self-assurance, and attentiveness as basic positive emotion scales as well as shyness, fatigue, serenity, and surprise as other affective states.

Table 3 lists the elements in the people category and the main questions behind each element. We also added social interaction to the framework as this framework is designed to

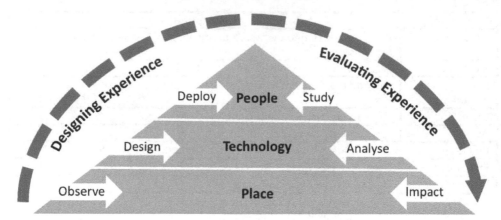

Fig. 5. User experience framework overview

evaluate systems enabling mobile mediated interactions. Battarbee & Koskinen (2005, p.15) state that "user experiences are created together and are thus different from the user experiences people have alone" and suggest to analyse the interactions which occur between users. The three software applications described in this chapter enable mobile mediated interactions with collocated people who congregate in the past, present, or future. Having interactions in real-time with collocated people rather then over-time with people who have been or will be at the same place might further impact the UX in various ways. Additionally, analysing the interactions is especially important in the field of mobile mediated interactions between collocated people in urban public places as the experience of using such an application is heavily dependent on other application users. For example, a user utilising an application enabling information sharing with collocated people such as Capital Music, the user will have a significantly different experience through using the system if they open the application and no one else is in their surroundings rather than when plenty of users are available with which to interact. Conversely, scanning a PlaceTag with a mobile phone and being the first one to leave a message provides a different UX then finding a stream of messages and joining an existing conversation.

Figure 5 summarises the UX framework for designing experiences and investigating the quality or impact of the experience presented in this chapter. As described in this section, the framework proposes to start with an observation of the place following the utilisation of the gathered knowledge to design a technology suitable for the place. All three applications described in this chapter were used as place-based design interventions and were deployed and made available to users in the designated space followed by in situ user studies and observations. Additionally, logging mechanisms were added to the applications in order to get insights into the co-created experiences of collocated users. Through following the steps described in this section researchers are able to study and explore the quality of the created experience.

5. Discussion

The chapter proposed steps and guidelines in terms of what kind of research activities should be undertaken in the software design, development, and evaluation phase. However, we do not propose that each single question stated in the people, place, and technology categories have to be strictly followed. Designers have to consider which steps are necessary and valuable for their particular investigation.

The PlaceTagz project, which is deployed in public toilets, does not necessarily require an observation of the place and an analysis of the activities within the space, as usage is obvious. Additionally, usability studies are not necessary as the underlying system uses the commonly known and extensively used Wordpress weblog system. The Sapporo World Window project, which does not necessarily require user interaction with the system itself to be useful and appealing to onlookers, does not necessarily require an in-depth analysis of the meaningfulness of the activities within the space as content is mainly presented to by-passers. Additionally the acceptance element – how does the application fit into the place and support current social practices – in the place category is not highly relevant as urban screens and displays are more and more commonly used in urban spaces. The Capital Music project, designed for public transport, does not require rich aesthetics studies as the visual component of the application mainly focuses on the album artworks of the songs currently played in users' vicinity.

Additionally, the methods used in the people section can vary from case to case. In general, all applications enabling mobile mediated interactions in public urban places should be evaluated in the real world environment they have been designed for. However, this can be crucial for some Urban Informatics applications.

For Example Capital Music relies on multiple users using the application at the same time in the same space and preferably should not know each other. Enforcing such conditions in a lab environment might not result in realistic results. One way to gather reliable data from users in such conditions could be the utilisation of the Experience Sampling Method (Consolvo & Walker, 2003), adding self-reporting mechanisms into the deployed application. Additionally the Wizard of Oz (WoZ) method (Höysniemi & Read, 2005) could be utilised whereas the researcher is simulating other application users in a lab environment. This approach has the benefit that participants are available for semi-structured interviews after application usage. Furthermore, using an early prototype in combination with a WoZ study can closely simulate a contextual evaluation (Reilly et al., 2005).

Sapporo World Window on the other hand is deployed in a busy urban space. Time-lapse observations of the public urban space (Whyte, 1980) in combination with log files of screen interaction and follow-up structured interviews or questionnaires can help to get an deeper understanding of the impact of the created UX, for example in Brynskov et al. (2009).

As already mentioned above, the PlaceTagz study, which is deployed in public toilets, does not allow observations or interviews due to the nature of the place. People using the place and the technology are difficult to access without making them feel uncomfortable. On the other hand each PlaceTag collects text-based messages left by users, varying in context and content. Furthermore, during the data collection period some users left their email address in the form provided for writing comments. Conducting a content analysis in combination with interviewing people who left their contact details can give further insights into the quality of the created experience.

6. Conclusion

This chapter presented our framework for creating and evaluating UX under the umbrella of Urban Informatics. We are aware that much theoretical research has been done in researching UX. However, given the lack of a common definition, elements, scope, and methods for creating and evaluating them, we reviewed the relevant literature in UX and recategorised them into the people, place, and technology notions of Urban Informatics.

This chapter has focused on a methodological approach for the study of UX in urban public spaces. It is written as a response to the inconsistent use and the intangibility of the term 'user experience' and the resulting questions such as what is part of an experience, how to design, influence and how to assess a UX. Having three applications aligned and tailored along this framework we hope to inspire other researchers to practically study, design, and evaluate UX in such an interconnected approach of people, place, and technology.

7. Acknowledgment

This research was carried out as part of the activities of, and funded by, the Smart Services Cooperative Research Centre (CRC) through the Australian Government's CRC Programme (Department of Innovation, Industry, Science and Research).

8. References

Alben, L. (1996). Quality of experience: defining the criteria for effective interaction design. *interactions, 3*(3), 11-15.

Arhippainen, L., & Tähti, M. (2003). *Empirical Evaluation of User Experience in Two Adaptive Mobile Application Prototypes.* Paper presented at the Mobile and Ubiquitous Multimedia - MUM.

Bargas-Avila, J. A., & Hornbæk, K. (2011). *Old Wine in New Bottles or Novel Challenges? A Critical Analysis of Empirical Studies of User Experience.* Paper presented at the CHI 2011.

Bassoli, A., Brewer, J., Martin, K., Dourish, P., & Mainwaring, S. (2007). Underground Aesthetics: Rethinking Urban Computing. *Pervasive Computing, IEEE, 6*(3), 39-45.

Battarbee, K., & Koskinen, I. (2005). Co-experience: user experience as interaction. *International Journal of CoCreation in Design and the Arts, 1*(1), 5-18.

Brynskov, M., Dalsgaard, P., Ebsen, T., Fritsch, J., Halskov, K., & Nielsen, R. (2009). Staging Urban Interactions with Media Façades. In T. Gross, J. Gulliksen, P. Kotzé, L. Oestreicher, P. Palanque, R. Prates & M. Winckler (Eds.), *Human-Computer Interaction – INTERACT 2009* (Vol. 5726, pp. 154-167): Springer Berlin / Heidelberg.

Consolvo, S., & Walker, M. (2003). Using the Experience Sampling Method to Evaluate Ubicomp Applications. *IEEE Pervasive Computing, 2*(2), 24-31.

Crawford, A. (2008). Taking Social Software to the Streets: Mobile Cocooning and the (An-)Erotic City. *Journal of Urban Technology, 15*(3), 79-97.

Davis, F. D. (1989). Perceived usefulness, perceived ease of use, and user acceptance of information technology. *MIS Quarterly, 13*(3), 319-340.

Forlizzi, J., & Ford, S. (2000). *The building blocks of experience: an early framework for interaction designers.* Paper presented at the Proceedings of the 3rd conference on Designing interactive systems: processes, practices, methods, and techniques.

Forlizzi, J., & Battarbee, K. (2004). *Understanding Experience in Interactive Systems*. Paper presented at the Designing Interactive Systems (DIS).

Foth, M., Choi, J. H.-j., & Satchell, C. (2011). *Urban informatics*. Paper presented at the ACM Conference on Computer Supported Cooperative Work (CSCW 2011).

Garrett, J. J. (2003). *The Elements of User Experience: User-Centered Design for the Web*. New York: American Institute of Graphic Arts.

Gehl, J. (1987). *Life Between Buildings*. New York: Van Nostrand Reinhold Company.

Goffman, E. (1966). *Behavior in Public Places*. New York: The Free Press.

Gordon, E., & de Souza e Silva, A. (2011). *Net Locality: Why Location Matters in a Networked World*: Wiley-Blackwell.

Hassenzahl, M. (2005). The Thing and I: Understanding the Relationship Between User and Product. In M. Blythe, K. Overbeeke, A. Monk & P. Wright (Eds.), *Funology: From Usability to Enjoyment* (pp. 31-42): Springer Netherlands.

Hassenzahl, M., & Tractinsky, N. (2006). User experience - a research agenda. *Behaviour & Information Technology, 25*(2), 91-97.

Hassenzahl, M. (2008). The interplay of beauty, goodness, and usability in interactive products. *Hum.-Comput. Interact., 19*(4), 319-349.

van der Heijden, H. (2004). User Acceptance of Hedonic Information Systems. *MIS Quarterly, 28*(4), 695-704.

Höysniemi, J., & Read, J. (2005). *Wizard of Oz Studies with Children - Ethical dilemmas and experiences from the field*. Paper presented at the IDC 2005.

Hughes, J., King, V., Rodden, T., & Andersen, H. (1995). The role of ethnography in interactive systems design. *interactions, 2*(2), 56-65.

Huisman, G., & Van Hout, M. (2008). *The development of a graphical emotion measurement instrument using caricatured expressions: the LEMtool*. Paper presented at the Workshop Proceedings Emotion in HCI - Designing for People.

Kangas, E., & Kinnunen, T. (2005). Applying user-centered design to mobile application development. *Communications of the ACM, 48*(7), 55-59.

Kjeldskov, J., & Paay, J. (2006). Public Pervasive Computing: Making the Invisible Visible. *Computer, 39*, 60-65.

Lavie, T., & Tractinsky, N. (2004). Assessing dimensions of perceived visual aesthetics of web sites. *International Journal of Human-Computer Studies, 60*(3), 269-298.

Law, E. L.-C., Roto, V., Hassenzahl, M., Vermeeren, A. P. O. S., & Kort, J. (2009). *Understanding, scoping and defining user experience: a survey approach*. Paper presented at the 27th international conference on Human factors in computing systems.

Mainwaring, S. D., Anderson, K., & Chang, M. F. (2005). *Living for the global city: Mobile kits, urban interfaces, and ubicomp*. Paper presented at the UbiComp 2005: Ubiquitous Computing

McCarthy, J., & Wright, P. (2004). Technology as experience. *interactions, 11*(5), 42-43.

McNamara, N., & Kirakowski, J. (2006). Functionality, usability, and user experience: three areas of concern. *interactions, 13*(6), 26-28.

Pedersen, J., & Valgårda, A. (2004). *Viability of Urban Social Technologies*. Paper presented at the UbiComp in the Urban Frontier 2004

Putnam, R. D. (1995). Bowling Alone: America's Declining Social Capital. *Journal of Democracy, 6*(1), 65-78.

Reilly, D., Dearman, D., Welsman-Dinelle, M., & Inkpen, K. (2005). Evaluating Early Prototypes in Context: Trade-offs, Challenges, and Successes. *IEEE Pervasive Computing*, 4(4), 42-50.

Seeburger, J., Foth, M., & Tjondronegoro, D. W. (2010). Capital music : personal expression with a public display of song choice. Paper presented at the 6th Nordic Conference on Human-Computer Interaction.

Seeburger, J., & Choi, J. (2011). Creative Engagement through Public Urban Screens. Paper presented at the Digital Cities 7 in conjunction with Communities & Technologies (C&T).

Simonsen, J., & Kensing, F. (1997). Using ethnography in contextual design. *Communications of the ACM*, 40(7), 82-88.

Tractinsky, N. (1997). *Aesthetics and apparent usability: empirically assessing cultural and methodological issues*. Paper presented at the Proceedings of the SIGCHI conference on Human factors in computing systems.

United Nations. (2008). World Urbanization Prospects: The 2007 Revision. New York, NY: Department of Economic and Social Affairs, United Nations Secretariat.

Watson, D., Clark, L. A., & Tellegen, A. (1988). Development and validation of brief measures of positive and negative affect: The PANAS scales. *Journal of Personality and Social Psychology*, 54(6), 1063-1070.

Watson, D., & Clark, L. A. (1994). The PANAS-X Manual for the Positive and Negative Affect Schedule - Expanded Form. from http://www.psychology.uiowa .edu/faculty/Clark/PANAS-X.pdf

Wellman, B. (2001). Physical place and cyberplace: the rise of personalized networking. International Journal of Urban and Regional Research, 25; Part 2, 227-252

Whyte, W. H. (1980). *The Social Life of Small Urban Spaces*. Washington: The Conservation Foundation.

Permissions

The contributors of this book come from diverse backgrounds, making this book a truly international effort. This book will bring forth new frontiers with its revolutionizing research information and detailed analysis of the nascent developments around the world.

We would like to thank Associate Professor Dian Tjondronegoro, for lending his expertise to make the book truly unique. He has played a crucial role in the development of this book. Without his invaluable contribution this book wouldn't have been possible. He has made vital efforts to compile up to date information on the varied aspects of this subject to make this book a valuable addition to the collection of many professionals and students.

This book was conceptualized with the vision of imparting up-to-date information and advanced data in this field. To ensure the same, a matchless editorial board was set up. Every individual on the board went through rigorous rounds of assessment to prove their worth. After which they invested a large part of their time researching and compiling the most relevant data for our readers. Conferences and sessions were held from time to time between the editorial board and the contributing authors to present the data in the most comprehensible form. The editorial team has worked tirelessly to provide valuable and valid information to help people across the globe.

Every chapter published in this book has been scrutinized by our experts. Their significance has been extensively debated. The topics covered herein carry significant findings which will fuel the growth of the discipline. They may even be implemented as practical applications or may be referred to as a beginning point for another development. Chapters in this book were first published by InTech; hereby published with permission under the Creative Commons Attribution License or equivalent.

The editorial board has been involved in producing this book since its inception. They have spent rigorous hours researching and exploring the diverse topics which have resulted in the successful publishing of this book. They have passed on their knowledge of decades through this book. To expedite this challenging task, the publisher supported the team at every step. A small team of assistant editors was also appointed to further simplify the editing procedure and attain best results for the readers.

Our editorial team has been hand-picked from every corner of the world. Their multi-ethnicity adds dynamic inputs to the discussions which result in innovative outcomes. These outcomes are then further discussed with the researchers and contributors who give their valuable feedback and opinion regarding the same. The feedback is then collaborated with the researches and they are edited in a comprehensive manner to aid the understanding of the subject.

Apart from the editorial board, the designing team has also invested a significant amount of their time in understanding the subject and creating the most relevant covers. They scrutinized every image to scout for the most suitable representation of the subject and create an appropriate cover for the book.

The publishing team has been involved in this book since its early stages. They were actively engaged in every process, be it collecting the data, connecting with the contributors or procuring relevant information. The team has been an ardent support to the editorial, designing and production team. Their endless efforts to recruit the best for this project, has resulted in the accomplishment of this book. They are a veteran in the field of academics and their pool of knowledge is as vast as their experience in printing. Their expertise and guidance has proved useful at every step. Their uncompromising quality standards have made this book an exceptional effort. Their encouragement from time to time has been an inspiration for everyone.

The publisher and the editorial board hope that this book will prove to be a valuable piece of knowledge for researchers, students, practitioners and scholars across the globe.

List of Contributors

Vlado Menkovski and Antonio Liotta
Eindhoven University of Technology, The Netherlands

Wei Song, Dian Tjondronegoro and Michael Docherty
Queensland University of Technology, Australia

Denis do Rosário, Kássio Machado, Antônio Abelém, Dionne Monteiro, Eduardo Cerqueira, Paulo Bezerra, Adalberto Melo, Billy Pinheiro, Thiago Coqueiro, Antônio Abelém, Agostinho Castro and Eduardo Cerqueira
Federal University of Pará (UFPA), Brazil

Hammad Dilpazir and Hasan Mahmood
Department of Electronics, Quaid-i-Azam University, Islamabad, Pakistan

Tariq Shah
Department of Mathematics, Quaid-i-Azam University, Islamabad, Pakistan

Hafiz Malik
Department of Electrical and Computer Engineering, University of Michigan - Dearborn, Dearborn, MI, USA

Ala' F. Khalifeh
German Jordan University, Jordan

Khalid A. Darabkh
The University of Jordan, Jordan

Jan Seeburger, Marcus Foth and Dian Tjondronegoro
Queensland University of Technology, Australia

Printed in the USA
CPSIA information can be obtained
at www.ICGtesting.com
JSHW011343221024
72173JS00003B/196

9 781632 403506